AUTOBIOGRAPHY

of

A FUGITIVE NEGRO

AUTOBIOGRAPHY

of

A FUGITIVE NEGRO

HIS *ANTI-SLAVERY LABORS*

in

THE UNITED STATES, CANADA, & ENGLAND

By

SAMUEL RINGGOLD WARD

EBONY CLASSICS

———

Johnson Publishing Company Inc.
Chicago, 1970

Publisher's Note

The Ebony Classics series has been designed for clarity and elegance in the hope of reaching a public outside the research libraries. The text has been entirely reset in a combination of Bodoni typefaces which echo the original editions, but are easier to read. Corrections of typographical errors and inconsistencies of style are the only amendments that have been made.

Other titles currently available in this series are:

> *Black and White* by Timothy Thomas Fortune
> *The Narrative of Sojourner Truth*
> *The Underground Railroad* by William Still
> *My Bondage and My Freedom* by Frederick Douglass
> *Men of Mark* by William J. Simmons

From the edition published in 1855 by John Snow of London

Reprinted 1970 by Johnson Publishing Company, Inc.
Foreword by Vincent Harding copyright © 1970

Library of Congress Catalog Card No. 77-102980
SBN No. 87485-032-0
Printed in the United States of America
by the Rand McNally Company
$4.95

FOREWORD TO THE 1970 EDITION

It is amazing how little we really know about Samuel Ringgold Ward, and it is no less striking that so much of what we do know is at once enigmatic and elusive. At the height of his relatively brief career in the United States, Canada, and the British Isles, the imposing, coal-black figure of Samuel Ward was constantly to be seen on the lecture platforms of the 19th century reformist organizations. Indeed, he was considered second only to Frederick Douglass as an Abolitionist orator. Yet no full speech of his can now be found, and the remaining fragments evoke no significant echoes of the grandeur his contemporaries ascribed to him.

He was a rather orthodox Christian minister and was considered a leader of Black people, but neither of his two short-lived pastorates was in a black congregation. He joined the ranks of the Liberty Party at its founding, filled with all of its best righteous fervor for the destruction of slavery and the salvation of America. Then when the scourging of the nation had temporarily ended and slavery was pronounced officially dead, few persons knew whether Ward himself was dead or alive. For he had left his native land at the onset of the terrible 1850's and had closed his life on the island of Jamaica on some still undetermined date, dying that peculiar kind of imploded alien death in which Black Americans have become so skilled.

Perhaps the greatest enigma of all is that we should have such an unclear vision of Ward as this edition of his *Autobiography of a Fugitive Negro* marks its 115th anniversary of publication. For the truth is that the *Autobiography* is one of the central sources of our puzzlement—beginning with the fact that it is neither an autobiography in the truest sense of the word, nor a "Slave Narrative" as it has so often been described.

Originally published in London in 1855, the most clearly autobiographical section of this work is to be found in its first twenty-five pages. There

we learn that Ward was born in 1817, the same year and in the same state (Maryland) as Frederick Douglass, following Douglass' birth by only eight months. The flight of his parents, with him in arms, came some three years later, so there is only the briefest story in the escape genre that fills so many of the Narratives with drama. Indeed, most things relating directly to his own life are told in a very cursory way. His childhood and youth in New Jersey and New York, his blood relationship to Henry Highland Garnet, his schooling, teaching, pastorates in the Congregational Church in western New York State, lecturing for the American Anti-Slavery Party and for the Liberty Party—all these slip by with almost frustrating speed. His marriage rates only a sentence and his wife is hardly described at all. He mentions briefly some study of medicine and of law during the late 1830's and early 1840's, but this too is only in passing. Perhaps to go into detail on those matters would have necessitated his saying more of the children who died in infancy and childhood.

Whatever his reasons, Ward compresses his 34 years of life in this country into a very brief span. He tells of his decision to leave the United States for Canada in 1851, partly as a result of the general oppressiveness of the Fugitive Slave Law of 1850, partly because of his own participation in the rescue of William Henry, the principal in the famous "Jerry" case in Syracuse (where Ward was then living) in 1851.

Even though the major segment of the *Autobiography* is devoted to Ward's years in Canada and the British Isles as a lecturer for the Canadian Anti-Slavery Society, it is still not essentially autobiography. For instance we learn that he leaves his family in Canada in 1853 to travel to England, but we are never told if his family ever comes across during his two years there. Ward offers a rather extensive account of his travels and contacts in England, Scotland, Wales and Ireland, but there is only the most passing of references to the decision which led him to choose to spend the rest of his life in Jamaica. Indeed, it is only from other sources that we learn that by the time Ward's book was published in London late in 1855, he was on his way to Jamaica.

If Samuel Ward's *Autobiography* offers us very little in the way of direct details concerning his personal life, it is nevertheless filled with commentaries which are of significant value. His constant references to the "ever-present, ever-crushing Negro-hate" of New York and the other northern cities during nineteenth century antebellum days are important documentation for studies of the black experience above the Mason Dixon line. Related to that experience are Ward's constant words of condemnation concerning the racism and prejudice displayed throughout the organizations which made up the crucial reformist movements of the nineteenth century—the so-called "Benevolent Empire." From the largest, the American Board of Commissioners for Foreign Missions, to the Temperance and Peace Societies, Ward testified from experience of their constant inability to reform their own prejudices towards Black people.

His description of Black communities in Canada during the first years of the 1850's is perhaps one of our most valuable contemporary accounts of those exiles from America. Also helpful is his account of the many ways in which the British people, their government and their economic leaders continued to give significant support to the American slave trade after slavery had been outlawed in the British colonies. His cataloging of the Anti-slavery lecture itinerary in the British Isles and the hundreds of persons he met supplies some additional idea of what the overseas experience meant to black American men. Indeed, in Ward's case it seemed to have meant more than to almost any of the other travellers.

And this is the other aspect of what the *Autobiography* tells. Weak on details of Samuel Ward's life, it is strong as a documentation of many of his attitudes—especially in regard to the upper class white world. His work reflects a constantly elitist view, with its ever-present references to "the superior classes" and those persons of "the best origin" who—in Ward's mind—are clearly friends of Black people and much less prejudiced than other whites. Then when he speaks of his experiences in England, no page is complete without at least several comments on how "honored" he was to be received into the presence of whatever member of the nobility (or other prestigious personage) he happened to be remembering at that point. It becomes almost fawning at times, and one is disturbed though not surprised to realize that it was 1855 in Africa too when Ward wrote from England:

The British colonies are both the agency by which and the medium through which, the gospel can, ought, *must* be given to the heathen world.

All this comprises one of the most troubling aspects of the *Autobiography*. It is expressed in many ways, and raises questions about the militant image we have of Ward. The utter obeisance to nobility and British culture goes hand in hand with such a statement as

Though I recollect nothing of slavery, I am every day showing something of my slave origin. It is among my thoughts, my superstitions, my narrow views, my awkwardness of manners. Ah, the infernal impress is upon me, and I fear

I shall transmit it to my children, and they to theirs! How deeply seated, how far reaching, a curse it is.

Such admiration for the upper class culture of the white world is reconcilable with his rejoicing in the fact that "the Negroes who are bondsmen are being rapidly improved, by . . . the increasing admixture of Anglo-Saxon blood."

So, by the time Ward had been through a life of personal tragedies, deprivations and economic disasters and had talked his way through the world of British respectability, he was ready to say, "Black men must seek wealth." Indeed he claimed he was convinced that

he who does most to promote his own and his neighbor's weal in this regard, does most to promote the interests of the race.

Perhaps it is in this context that some of the many questions left unanswered by the *Autobiography* are at least clarified. Was this doctrine of wealth (and his personal need for economic security) the major driving force behind Ward's decision to accept a gift of land in Jamaica and settle there? Was it this emphasis which made it possible for him to ignore the call that came from Frederick Douglass in 1855, the call to return to the American "battleground"?

Ward makes no direct reference to this call from Douglass in his volume. (Indeed, there is in the *Autobiography* no reference at all to the many debates between the two men over such issues as the constitutionality of slavery, or to their personal relationship.) Nevertheless, it was also in 1855 that he penned what almost appears to have been his epitaph—so far as active struggle was concerned. He wrote,

I beg to say, that after smattering away, or teaching, law, medicine, divinity, and public lecturing, I am neither lawyer, doctor, teacher, divine, nor lecturer; and at the age of eight-and-thirty I am glad to hasten back to what my father first taught me, and from what I never should have departed—the tilling of the soil, the use of the hoe.

Were those words sheer rationalization or did they indeed give witness to a man's apprehending a new vision of his life? If it was a new light, a search for integrity by new paths, how did the English experience affect the coming of that new vision?

None of these questions is answered in this volume. Rather, Samuel Ringgold Ward, one of the most effective campaigners against slavery, drops out of sight into the hills of Jamaica at the height of his manhood powers. Later Frederick Douglass would say,

In depth of thought, fluency of speech, readiness of wit, logical exactness, and general intelligence, Samuel R. Ward has left no successor among the colored men amongst us . . .

Nevertheless, there is not even a clear record of when Samuel Ward died in Jamaica. It was either 1865 or 1866, still short of his fiftieth year. His last known work was a pamphlet, *Reflections on the Gordon Rebellion,* but even here the enigma plagues us. For no copies of the document have been found, and we are not sure which side Ward took in his reflections on the life and execution of the Black radical political leader, George Gordon of Jamaica. It would be important to know.

There is much more about Samuel Ringgold Ward that it is important to know. The story of his relationship to the Liberty Party, the full account of his life among two white congregations, a relating of his own family life, the story of his intellectual development—all these need to be known. He appears to have been a brilliant young Black man whose life was filled with personal tragedies, breaks in the pattern of existence, which he constantly met surrounded by white companions and co-workers. We need to know how this affected his sense of solidarity with the Black communities of America and Canada, how it influenced his rather disparaging remarks about the nature of the slave experience, about the lack of a history of African civilization. And what of Jamaica in this context? Was it a final going home, or simply the setting up of a black-masked white domain?

There is not yet the biography that Ward deserves. Indeed, there is none at all at this moment. His *Autobiography* points the way to the sources in Canada, England, Jamaica and here. For his sake as well as for ours, we need to know Samuel Ringgold Ward.

VINCENT HARDING

Martin Luther King, Jr. Memorial Center
Atlanta, Georgia
November, 1969

To Her Grace

THE DUCHESS OF SUTHERLAND

MADAM:

      The frank and generous sympathy evinced by your Grace in behalf of American slaves has been recognized by all classes, and is gratefully cherished by the Negro's heart.

A kind Providence placed me for a season within the circle of your influence, and made me largely share its beneficent action, in the occasional intercourse of Nobles and Ladies of high rank, who sympathize in your sentiments. I am devoutly thankful to God, the Creator of the Negro, for this gleam of his sunshine, though it should prove but a brief token of his favour; and desire that my oppressed kindred may yet show themselves not unworthy of their cause being advocated by the noblest of all lands, and sustained and promoted by the wise and virtuous of every region.

I cannot address your Grace as an equal; though the generous nobility of your heart would require that I should use no expression inconsistent with the dignity of a man, the creation of God's infinite wisdom and goodness. I cannot give flattering titles, or employ the language of adulation: I should offend your Grace if I did so, and prove myself unworthy of that good opinion which I earnestly covet.

To you, Madam, I am indebted for many instances of spontaneous kindness, and to your influence I owe frequent opportunities of representing the claims of my oppressed race. I should not have felt emboldened to attempt the authorship of this Volume, had it not been for a conviction, sustained by unmistakable tokens, that in all classes, from the prince to the peasant, there is a chord of sympathy which vibrates to the appeals of my suffering people.

Before your Grace can see these lines, I shall be again traversing the great Atlantic. Will you, Madam, pardon this utterance of the deep-felt sentiment of a grateful heart, which can only find indulgence and relief in the humble dedication of this Volume to you, as my honoured patron-ess, and the generous friend of the Negro people in all lands?

I am not versed in the language of courts or the etiquette of the peer-age; but my heart is warm with gratitude, and my pen can but faintly express the sense of obligations I shall long cherish toward your noble House and the illustrious members of your Grace's family, from whom I have received many undeserved kindnesses.

I have the honour to be, Madam,
Your Grace's most obedient and grateful Servant,
SAMUEL RINGGOLD WARD

LONDON, 31st October, 1855

AUTHOR'S PREFACE

The idea of writing some account of my travels was first suggested to me by a gentleman who has not a little to do with the bringing out of this work. The Rev. Dr. Campbell also encouraged the suggestion. I then thought that a series of letters in a newspaper would answer the purpose. Circumstances over which I had no control placed it beyond my power to accomplish the design in that form of publication.

A few months ago I was requested to spend an evening with some ardent friends of the Negro race, by the arrangement of Mrs. Massie, at her house, Upper Clapton. Her zeal and constancy in behalf of the American Slave are well known on both sides of the Atlantic. Nor is there, I believe, a more earnest friend of my kindred race than is her husband. With him I have repeatedly taken counsel on the best modes of serving our cause. Late in August last, Dr. Massie urged on me the propriety of preparing a volume which might remain as a parting memorial of my visit to England, and serve to embody and perpetuate the opinions and arguments I had often employed to promote the work of emancipation. Peter Carstairs, Esq., of Madras, being present, cordially and frankly encouraged the project; and other friends, in whose judgment I had confidence, expressed their warmest approval. My publisher has generously given every facility for rendering the proposal practicable. To him I owe my warmest obligations for the promptitude and elegance with which the Volume has been prepared.

I do not think the gentlemen who advised it were quite correct in anticipating that so much would be acceptable, in a Book from me. I should have gone about it with much better courage if I had not felt some fears on this point. However, amidst many apprehensions of imperfection, I place it before the reader, begging him to allow me a word by way of apology. I was obliged to write in the midst of most perplexing, most embarrassing, private business, and had not a solitary book or paper to refer to, for a fact or passage; my brain alone had to supply all I wished to compose or compile. Time, too, was very limited. Under these circumstances, that I should have committed some slight inaccuracies, will not appear very strange, though I trust they are not very great or material. I beg the reader generously to forgive the faults he detects, and to believe that my chief motive in writing is the promotion of that cause in whose service I live. I hope that this Book will not be looked upon as a specimen of what a well educated Negro could do, nor as a fair representation of what Negro talent can produce—knowing that, with better materials, more time, and in more favourable circumstances, even *I* could have done much better; and knowing also, that my superiors among my own people would have written far more acceptably.

It will be seen that I have freely made remarks upon other things than slavery, and compared my own with those of other peoples. I did the former as a Man, the latter as a Negro. As a Negro, I live and therefore write for my people; as a Man, I freely speak my mind upon whatever concerns me and my fellow men. If any one be disappointed or offended at that, I shall regret it; all the more, as it is impossible for me to say that, in like circumstances, I should not do *just the same* again.

The reader will not find the dry details of a journal, nor any of my speeches or sermons. I preferred to weave into the Work the themes upon which I have spoken, rather than the speeches themselves. The Work is not a literary one, for it is not written by a literary man; it is no more than its humble title indicates—the Autobiography of a Fugitive Negro. In what sense I am a fugitive, will appear on perusal of my personal and family history.

S. R. W.

Radley's Hotel,
31st October, 1855.

CONTENTS

AUTOBIOGRAPHY

ANTI-SLAVERY LABOURS
PART I—UNITED STATES

AUTOBIOGRAPHY

CHAPTER I

Family History

———

I was born on the 17th October, 1817, in that part of the State of Maryland, U.S., commonly called the Eastern Shore. I regret that I can give no accurate account of the precise location of my birthplace. I may as well state now the reason of my ignorance of this matter. My parents were slaves. I was born a slave. They escaped, and took their then only child with them. I was not then old enough to know anything about my native place; and as I grew up, in the State of New Jersey, where my parents lived till I was nine years old, and in the State of New York subsequently, where we lived for many years, my parents were always in danger of being arrested and re-enslaved. To avoid this, they took every possible caution: among their measures of caution was the keeping of the children quite ignorant of their birthplace, and of their condition, whether free or slave, when born; because children might, by the dropping of a single word, lead to the betrayal of their parents. My brother, however, was born in New Jersey; and my parents, supposing (as is the general presumption) that to be born in a free State is to be born free, readily allowed us to tell where my brother was born; but *my* birthplace I was neither permitted to tell nor to know. Hence, while the secresy and mystery thrown about the matter led me, most naturally, to suspect that I was born a slave, I never received direct evidence of it, from either of my parents, until I was four-and-twenty years of age; and then my mother informed my wife, in my absence. Generous reader, will you therefore kindly forgive my inability to say exactly where I was born; what gentle stream arose near the humble cottage where I first breathed—how that stream sparkled in the sunlight, as it meandered through green meadows and forests of stately oaks, till it gave its increased self as a contribution to the Chesapeake Bay—if I do not tell you the name of my native town and county, and some interesting details of their geographical, agricultural, geological, and revolutionary history —if I am silent as to just how many miles I was born from Baltimore the metropolis, or Annapolis the capital, of my native State? Fain would I satisfy you in all this; but I cannot, from sheer ignorance. I was born a slave—where? Wherever it was, it was where I dare not be seen or known, lest those who held my parents and ancestors in slavery should make a claim, hereditary or legal, in some form, to the ownership of my body and soul.

My father, from what I can gather, was descended from an African prince. I ask no particular attention to this, as it comes to me simply from tradition—such tradition as poor slaves may maintain. Like the sources of the Nile, my ancestry, I am free to admit, is rather difficult of tracing. My father was a pure-blooded Negro, perfectly black, with wooly hair; but, as is frequently true of the purest Negroes, of small, handsome features. He was about 5 feet 10 inches in height, of good figure, cheerful disposition, bland manners, slow in deciding, firm when once decided, generous and unselfish to a fault; and one of the most consistent, simple-hearted, straightforward Christians, I ever knew. What I have grouped together here concerning him you would see in your first acquaintance with him, and you would see the same throughout his entire life. Had he been educated, free, and admitted to the social privileges in early life for which nature fitted him, and for which even slavery could not, did not, altogether *unfit* him, my poor crushed, outraged people would never have had nor needed a better representation of themselves—a better specimen of the black gentleman. Yes: among the heaviest of my maledictions against slavery is that which it deserves for keeping my poor father—and many like him—in the midnight and dungeon of the grossest ignorance. Cowardly system as it is, it does not dare to allow the slave access to the commonest sources of light and learning.

After his escape, my father learned to read, so that he could enjoy the priceless privilege of searching the Scriptures. Supporting himself by his trade as a house painter, or whatever else offered (as he was a man of untiring industry), he lived in Cumberland County, New Jersey, from 1820 until 1826; in New York city from that year until 1838; and in the city of Newark, New Jersey, from 1838 until May 1851, when he died, at the age of 68.

In April I was summoned to his bedside, where I found him the victim of paralysis. After spending some few days with him, and leaving him very much better, I went to Pennsylvania on business, and returned in about ten days, when he appeared still very comfortable; I then, for a few days, left him. My mother and I knew that another attack was to be feared—another, we knew too well, would prove fatal; but when it would occur was of course beyond our knowledge; but we hoped for the best. My father and I talked very freely of his death. He had always maintained that a Christian ought to have his preparation for his departure made, and completed in Christ, before death, so as when death should come he should have nothing to do BUT TO DIE. "That," said my father, "is enough to do at once: let repenting, believing, everything else, be sought at a proper time; let dying alone be done at the dying time." In my last conversation with him he not only maintained, but he *felt*, the same. Then, he seemed as if he might live a twelve-month; but eight-and-forty hours from that time, as I sat in the Rev. A. G. Beeman's pulpit, in New Haven, after the opening services, while singing the hymn which immediately preceded the sermon, a telegraphic despatch was handed me, announcing my father's death. I begged

Mr. Beeman to preach; his own feelings were such, that he could not, and I was obliged to make the effort. No effort ever cost me so much. Have I trespassed upon your time too much by these details? Forgive the fondness of the filial, the bereaved, the fatherless.

My mother was a widow at the time of her marriage with my father, and was ten years his senior. I know little or nothing of her early life: I think she was not a mother by her first marriage. To my father she bore three children, all boys, of whom I am the second. Tradition is my only authority for my maternal ancestry: that authority saith, that on the paternal side my mother descended from Africa. Her mother, however, was a woman of light complexion; her grandmother, a mulattress; her great-grandmother, the daughter of an Irishman, named Martin, one of the largest slaveholders in Maryland—a man whose slaves were so numerous, that he did not know the number of them. My mother was of dark complexion, but straight silklike hair; she was a person of large frame, as tall as my father, of quick discernment, ready decision, great firmness, strong will, ardent temperament, and of deep, devoted, religious character. Though a woman, she was not of so pleasing a countenance as my father, and I am thought strongly to resemble her. Like my father, she was converted in early life, and was a member of the Methodist denomination (though a lover of all Christian denominations) until her death. This event, one of the most afflictive of my life, occurred on the first day of September, 1853, at New York. Since my father's demise I had not seen her for nearly a year; when, being about to sail for England, at the risk of being apprehended by the United States' authorities for a breach of their execrable republican Fugitive Slave Law, I sought my mother, found her, and told her I was about to sail at three p.m., that day (April 20th, 1853), for England. With a calmness and composure which she could always command when emergencies required it, she simply said, in a quiet tone, "To England, my son!" embraced

me, commended me to God, and suffered me to depart without
a murmur. It was our last meeting. May it be our last parting!
For the kind sympathy shown me, upon my reception of the melancholy news of my mother's decease, by many English friends,
I shall ever be grateful: the recollection of that event, and the
kindness of which it was the occasion, will dwell together in my
heart while reason and memory shall endure.

In the midst of that peculiarly bereaved feeling inseparable
from realizing the thought that one is both fatherless and mother-
less, it was a sort of melancholy satisfaction to know that my dear
parents were gone beyond the reach of slavery and the Fugitive
Law. Endangered as their liberty always was, in the *free* Northern
States of New York and New Jersey—doubly so after the law of
1851—I could but feel a great deal of anxiety concerning them.
I knew that there was no living claimant of my parents' bodies
and souls; I knew, too, that neither of them would tamely submit
to re-enslavement: but I also knew that it was quite possible there
should be creditors, or heirs at law; and that there is no State in
the American Union wherein there were not free and independent
democratic republicans, and *soi-disant* Christians, "ready, aye
ready" to aid in overpowering and capturing a runaway, *for pay*.
But when God was pleased to take my father in 1851, and my
mother in 1853, I felt relief from my greatest earthly anxiety.
Slavery had denied them education, property, caste, rights, liberty; but it could not deny them the application of Christ's blood,
nor an admittance to the rest prepared for the righteous. They
could not be buried in the same part of a common graveyard,
with whites, in their native country; but they can rise at the sound
of the first trump, in the day of resurrection. Yes, reader: we
who are slaveborn derive a comfort and solace from the death of
those dearest to us, if they have the sad misfortune to be BLACKS
and AMERICANS, that you know not. God forbid that you or yours
should ever have occasion to know it!

My eldest brother died before my birth: my youngest brother,

Isaiah Harper Ward, was born April 5th, 1822, in Cumberland
County, New Jersey; and died at New York, April 16th, 1838, in
the triumphs of faith. He was a lad partaking largely of my father's qualities, resembling him exceedingly. Being the youngest
of the family, we all sought to fit him for usefulness, and to shield
him from the thousand snares and the ten thousand forms of
cruelty and injustice which the unspeakably cruel prejudice of
the whites visits upon the head and the heart of every black
young man, in New York. To that end, we secured to him the
advantages of the Free School, for coloured youth, in that city—
advantages which, I am happy to say, were neither lost upon him
nor unappreciated by him. Upon leaving school he commenced
learning the trade of a printer, in the office of Mr. Henry R.
Piercy, of New York—a gentleman who, braving the prejudices
of his craft and of the community, took the lad upon the same
terms as those upon which he took white lads: a fact all the more
creditable to Mr. Piercy, as it was in the very teeth of the abom-
inably debased public sentiment of that city (and of the whole
country, in fact) on this subject. But ere Isaiah had finished his
trade, he suddenly took a severe cold, which resulted in pneu-
monia, and—in death.

I expressed a doubt, in a preceding page, as to the legal validity of my brother's freedom. True, he was born in the nominally
Free State of New Jersey; true, the inhabitants born in Free
States are *generally* free. But according to slave law, "the child
follows the condition of the mother, during life." My mother
being born of a slave woman, and not being legally freed, those
who had a legal claim to her had also a legal claim to her offspring, wherever born, of whatever paternity. Besides, at that
time New Jersey had not entirely ceased to be a Slave State.
Had my mother been legally freed before his birth, then my
brother would have been born free, because born of a free woman.
As it was, we were all liable at any time to be captured, enslaved,
and re-enslaved—first, because we had been robbed of our lib-

erty; then, because our ancestors had been robbed in like manner; and, thirdly and conclusively, in law, because we were black Americans.

I confess I never felt any personal fear of being retaken— primarily because, as I said before, I knew of no legal claimants; but chiefly because I knew it would be extremely difficult to identify me. I was less than three years old when brought away: to identify me as a man would be no easy matter. Certainly, slaveholders and their more wicked Northern parasites are not very particularly scrupulous about such matters; but still, I never had much fear. My private opinion is, that he who would have enslaved me would have "caught a Tartar": for my peace principles never extended so far as to *either seek or accept peace at the expense of liberty*—if, indeed, a state of slavery can by any possibility be a state of peace.

I beg to conclude this chapter on my family history by adding, that my father had a cousin, in New Jersey, who had escaped from slavery. In the spring of 1826 he was cutting down a tree, which accidentally fell upon him, breaking both thighs. While suffering from this accident his master came and took him back into Maryland. He continued *lame* a very great while, without any *apparent* signs of amendment, until one fine morning he was gone! They never took him again.

Two of my father's nephews, who had escaped to New York, were taken back in the most summary manner, in 1828. I never saw a family thrown into such deep distress by the death of any two of its members, as were our family by the re-enslavement of these two young men. Seven-and-twenty years have past, but we have none of us heard a word concerning them, since their consignment to the living death, the temporal hell, of American slavery.

Some kind persons who may read these pages will accuse me of bitterness towards Americans generally, and slaveholders particularly: indeed, there are many *professed* abolitionists, on both sides of the Atlantic, who have no idea that a black man should feel towards and speak of his tormenters as a white man would concerning his. But suppose the blacks had treated *your* family in the manner the Americans have treated *mine*, for five generations: how would you write about these blacks, and their system of bondage? You would agree with me, that the 109th Psalm, from the 5th to the 21st verses inclusive, was written almost purposely for them.

———

CHAPTER II

Personal History

I have narrated when and where I was born, as far as I know. It seems that when young I was a very weakly child, whose life for the first two years and a half appeared suspended upon the most fragile fibre of the most delicate cord. It is not probable that any organic or constitutional disease was afflicting me, but a general debility, the more remarkable as both my parents were robust, healthy persons. Happily for me, my mother was permitted to "hire her time," as it is called in the South—*i.e.*, she was permitted to do what she pleased, and go where she pleased, provided she paid to the estate a certain sum annually. This she found ample means of doing, by her energy, ingenuity, and economy. My mother was a good financier. (O that her mantle had fallen on me!) She paid the yearly hire, and pocketed a *surplus*, wherewith she did much to add to the comforts of her husband and her sickly child. So long and so hopeless was my illness, that the parties owning us feared I could not be reared for the market —the only use for which according to their enlightened ideas, a young negro could possibly be born or reared; their only hope was in my mother's tenderness. Yes: the tenderness of a mother, in that *intensely* FREE country, is a matter of trade, and my poor mother's tender regard for her offspring had its value in dollars and cents.

When I was about two years old (so my mother told my wife), my father, for some trifling mistake or fault, was stabbed in the fleshy part of his arm, with a penknife: the wound was the entire length of the knife blade. On another occasion he received a severe flogging, which left his back in so wretched a state that my mother was obliged to take peculiar precaution against mortification. This sort of treatment of her husband not being relished by my mother, who felt about the maltreatment of her husband as any Christian woman ought to feel, she put forth her sentiments, in pretty strong language. This was insolent. Insolence in a negress could not be endured—it would breed more and greater mischief of a like kind; then what would become of wholesome discipline? Besides, if so trifling a thing as the *mere marriage relation* were to interfere with the supreme proprietor's right of a master over his slave, next we should hear that slavery must give way before marriage! Moreover, if a negress may be allowed free speech, touching the flogging of a negro, simply because that negro happened to be her husband, how long would it be before some such claim would be urged in behalf of some other member of a negro family, in unpleasant circumstances? Would this be endurable, in a republican civilized community, A.D. 1819? By no means. It would sap the very foundation of slavery—it would be like "letting out of water": for let the principle be once established that the negress Anne Ward may speak as she pleases about the flagellation of her husband, the Negro William Ward, as a matter of right, and like some alarming and death-dealing infection it would spread from plantation to plantation, until property in husbands and wives would not be worth the having. No, no: marriage must succumb to slavery, slavery must reign supreme over every right and every institution, however venerable or sacred; *ergo*, this free-speaking Anne Ward must be made to feel the greater rigours of the domestic institution. Should she be flogged? that was questionable. She never had been whipped, except, perhaps, by her parents; she was now three-and-thirty years old—rather late for the commencement of training; she weighed 184 lbs. avoirdupoise; she was strong enough to whip an ordinary-sized man; she had as much strength of *will* as of mind; and what did not diminish the awkwardness of the case was, she gave most unmistakable evidences of "rather tall resistance," in case of an attack. Well, then, it were not wise to risk this; but one most convenient course was left to them, and that course they could take with perfect safety to themselves, without yielding one hair's breadth of the rights and powers of slavery, but establishing them—they could sell her, and sell her they would: she was their property, and like any other stock she *could* be sold, and like any other unruly stock she *should* be brought to the market.

However, this sickly boy, if practicable, must be raised for the auction mart. Now, to sell his mother *immediately*, depriving him of her tender care, might endanger his life, and, what was all-important in his life, his saleability. Were it not better to risk a little from the freedom of this woman's tongue, than to jeopardize the sale of this *article?* Who knows but, judging from the pedigree, it may prove to be a prime lot—rising six feet in length, and weighing two hundred and twenty pounds, more or less, some day? To ask these questions was to answer them; there was no resisting the force of such valuable and logical considerations. Therefore the sale was delayed; the young animal was to run awhile longer with his—(I accommodate myself to the ideas and facts of slavery, and use a corresponding nomenclature)—dam. Thus my illness prevented the separation of my father and my mother from each other, and from their only child. How God sometimes makes the affliction of His poor, and the very wickedness of their oppressors, the means of blessing them! But how slender the thread that bound my poor parents together! the convalescence of their child, or his death, would in all seeming probability snap it asunder. What depths of anxiety must my mother have endured! How must the reality of his condition have weighed down the fond heart of my father, concerning their child! Could they pray for his continued illness? No; they were parents. Could they petition God for his health? Then they must soon be parted for ever from each other and from him, were that prayer answered. Ye whose children are born free, because you were so born, know but little of what this enslaved pair endured, for weeks and months, at the time to which I allude.

At length a crisis began to appear: the boy grew better. God's blessing upon a mother's tender nursing prevailed over habitual weakness and sickness. The child slept better; he had less fever; his appetite returned; he began to walk without tottering, and seemed to give signs of the cheerfulness he inherited from his father, and the strength of frame (and, to tell truth, of will also) imparted by his mother. Were not the owners right in their "calculations"? Had they not decided and acted wisely, in a business point of view? The dismal prospect before them, connected with the returning health of their child, damped the joy which my parents, in other circumstances, and in a more desirable country, would have felt in seeing their child's improved state. But the more certain these poor slaves became that their child would soon be well, the nearer approached the time of my mother's sale. Motherlike, she pondered all manner of schemes and plans to postpone that dreaded day. She could close her child's eyes in death, she could follow her husband to the grave, if God should so order; but to be sold from them to the far-off State of Georgia, the State to which Maryland members of Churches sold their nominal fellow Christians—sometimes their own children, and other poor relations—*that* was more than she could bear. Submission to the will of God was one thing, she was prepared for that, but submission to the machinations of Satan was quite another thing; neither her womanhood nor her theology could be reconciled to the latter. Sometimes pacing the floor half the night with her child in her arms—sometimes kneeling for hours in secret prayer to God for deliverance—sometimes in long earnest consultation with my father as to what must be done in this dreaded emergency—my mother passed days, nights, and weeks of anguish which wellnigh drove her to desperation. But a thought flashed upon her mind: she indulged in it. It was full of danger; it demanded high resolution, great courage, unfailing energy, strong determination; it might fail. But it was only a thought, at most only an indulged thought, perhaps the fruit of her very excited state, and it was not yet a plan; but, for the life of her, she could not shake it off. She kept saying to herself, "supposing I should"——Should what? She scarcely dare say to herself, what. But that thought became familiar, and welcome, and more welcome; it began to take another, a more definite form. Yes; almost ere she knew, it had incorporated itself with her will, and become a resolution, a determination. "William," said she to my father, "we must take this child and run away." She said it with energy; my father felt it. He hesitated; he was not a mother. She was decided; and when decided, *she was decided* with all consequences, conditions, and contingencies accepted. As is the case in other families where the wife leads, my father followed my mother in her decision, and accompanied her in—I almost said, her *hegira*.

CHAPTER III

The Fugitives from Slavery

What was the precise sensation produced by the departure of my parents, in the minds of their owners—how they bore it, how submissively they spoke of it, how thoughtfully they followed us with their best wishes, and so forth, I have no means of knowing: information on these questionable topics was never conveyed to us in any definite, systematic form. Be this as it may, on a certain evening, without previous notice, my mother took her child in her arms, and stealthily, with palpitating heart, but unfaltering step and undaunted courage, passed the door, the outer gate, the adjoining court, crossed the field, and soon after, followed by my father, left the place of their former abode, bidding it adieu for ever. I know not their route; but in those days the track of the fugitive was neither so accurately scented nor so hotly pursued by human sagacity, or the scent of kindred bloodhounds, as now, nor was slave-catching so complete and regular a system as it is now. Occasionally a slave escaped, but seldom in such numbers as to make it needful either to watch them very closely when at home, or to trace them systematically when gone. Indeed, our slave-catching professional may thank the slaves for the means by which they earn their dishonourable subsistence; for if the latter had never reduced running away to system, the former had never been needed, and therefore never employed at their present wretched occupation, as a system. " 'Tis an ill wind that blows nobody good."

At the time of my parents' escape it was not always necessary to go to Canada; they therefore did as the few who then escaped mostly did—aim for a Free State, and settle among Quakers. This honoured sect, unlike any other in the world, in this respect, was regarded as the slave's friend. This peculiarity of their religion they not only *held*, but so *practised* that it impressed itself on the ready mind of the poor victim of American tyranny. To reach a Free State, and to live among Quakers, were among the highest ideas of these fugitives; accordingly, obtaining the best directions they could, they set out for Cumberland County, in the State of New Jersey, where they had learned slavery did not exist— Quakers lived in numbers, who would afford the escaped any and every protection consistent with their peculiar tenets—and where a number of blacks lived, who in cases of emergency could and would make common cause with and for each other. Then these attractions of Cumberland were sufficient to determine their course.

I do not think the journey could have been a very long one: but it must be travelled on foot, in some peril, and with small, scanty means, next to nothing; and with the burden (though they felt it not) of a child, nearly three years old, both too young and too weakly to perform his own part of the journey. One child they had laid in the grave; now their only one must be rescued from a fate worse than ten thousand deaths. Upon this rescue depended their continued enjoyment of each other's society. The many past evils inseparable from a life of slavery, their recently threatened separation, and the dangers of this *exodus*, served to heighten that enjoyment, and doubly to endear each to the other; and the thought that they might at length be successful, and as free husband and wife bring up their child in the nurture and admonition of the Lord, according to the best of their ability, stimulated them to fresh courage and renewed endurance. Step by step, day after day, and night after night, with their infant charge passed alternately from the arms of the one to those of the other; they wended

on their way, driven by slavery, drawn and stimulated by the hope
of freedom, and all the while trusting in and committing themselves to Him who is God of the oppressed. I can just remember
one or two incidents of the journey; they now stand before me,
associated with my earliest recollections of maternal tenderness
and paternal care: and it seems to me, now that they are both
gathered with the dead, that I would rather forget any facts of
my childhood than those connected with that, to me, in more
respects than one, all-important journey.

Struggling against many obstacles, and by God's help sur-
mounting them, they made good progress until they had got a little
more than midway their journey, when they were overtaken and
ordered back by a young man on horseback, who, it seems, lived
in the neighborhood of my father's master. The youth had a whip,
and some other insignia of slaveholding authority; and knowing
that these slaves had been accustomed from childhood to obey the
commanding voice of the white man, young or old, he foolishly
fancied that my parents would give up the pursuit of freedom for
themselves and their child at *his bidding. They thought otherwise;*
and when he dismounted, for the purpose of enforcing authority
and compelling obedience by the use of the whip, he received so
severe a flogging at the hands of my parents as sent him home
nearly a cripple. He conveyed word as to our flight, but prudently
said he received his hurts by his horse plunging, and throwing
him suddenly against a large tree. Through this young man our
owners got at the bottom of their loss. There was the loss of the
price of my mother, the loss of my present and propective self,
and, what they had had no reason before to suspect, the loss of
my father! Some say it was the commencement of a series of ad-
versities from which neither the estate nor the owners ever afterwards recovered. I confess to sufficient selfishness never to have
shed a tear, either upon hearing this or in subsequent reflections
upon it.

After this nothing serious befell our party, and they safely

arrived at Greenwich, Cumberland County, early in the year
1820. They found, as they had been told, that at Springtown, and
Bridgetown, and other places, there were numerous coloured
people; that the Quakers in that region were truly, practically
friendly, "not loving in word and tongue," but in deed and truth;
and that there were no slaveholders in that part of the State, and
when slave-catchers came prowling about the Quakers threw all
manner of *peaceful* obstacles in their way, while the Negroes
made it a little too *hot* for their comfort.

We lived several years at Waldron's Landing, in the neighbourhood of the Reeves, Woods, Bacons, and Lippineutts, who were
among my father's very best friends, and whose children were
among my schoolfellows. However, in the spring and summer of
1826, so numerous and alarming were the depredations of kid-
napping and slave-catching in the neighbourhood, that my parents, after keeping the house armed night after night, determined
to remove to a place of greater distance and greater safety. Being
accommodated with horses and a waggon by kind friends, they
set out with my brother in their arms for New York City, where
they arrived on the 3rd day of August, 1826, and lodged the first
night with relations, the parents of the Rev. H. H. Garnett, now
of Westmoreland, Jamaica. Here we found some 20,000 coloured
people. The State had just emancipated all its slaves—viz., on the
fourth day of the preceding month—and it was deemed safer to
live in such a city than in a more open country place, such as we
had just left. Subsequent events, such as the ease with which my
two relatives were taken back in 1828—the truckling of the mercantile and the political classes to the slave system—the large
amount of slaveholding property owned by residents of New
York—and, worst, basest, most diabolical of all, the cringing,
canting, hypocritical friendship and subserviency of the religious
classes to slavery—have entirely dissipated that idea.

I look upon Greenwich, New Jersey, the place of my earliest
recollections, very much as most persons remember their native

place. There I followed my dear father up and down his garden, with fond childish delight; the plants, shrubs, flowers, &c., I looked upon as of his creation. There he first taught me some valuable lessons—the use of the hoe, to spell in three syllables, and to read the first chapter of John's Gospel, and my figures; then, having exhausted his literary stock upon me, he sent me to school. There I first read the Bible to my beloved mother, and read in her countenance (what I then could not read in the book) what that Bible was to her. Were my native country *free*, I could part with any possession to become the owner of that, to me, most sacred spot of earth, my father's old garden. Had I clung to the use of the hoe, instead of aspiring to a love of books, I might by this time have been somebody, and the reader of this volume would not have been solicited by this means to consider the lot of the oppressed American Negro.

CHAPTER IV

Struggles Against the Prejudice of Colour

I grew up in the city of New York as do the children of poor parents in large cities too frequently. I was placed at a public school in Mulberry Street, taught by Mr. C. C. Andrew, and subsequently by Mr. Adams, a Quaker gentleman, from both of whom I received great kindness. Dr. A. Libolt, my last preceptor in that school, placed me under lasting obligations. Poverty compelled me to work, but inclination led me to study; hence I was enabled, in spite of poverty, to make some progress in necessary learning. Added to poverty, however, in the case of a black lad in that city, is the ever-present, ever-crushing Negro-hate, which hedges up his path, discourages his efforts, damps his ardour, blasts his hopes, and embitters his spirits.

Some white persons wonder at and condemn the tone in which some of us blacks speak of our oppressors. Such persons talk as if they knew but little of human nature, and less of Negro character, else they would wonder rather that, what with slavery and Negro-hate, the mass of us are not either depressed into idiocy or excited into demons. What class of whites, except the Quakers, ever spoke of *their* oppressors or wrongdoers as mildly as we do? This peculiarly American spirit (which Englishmen easily enough imbibe, after they have resided a few days in the United States) was ever at my elbow. As a servant, it denied me a seat at the table with my white fellow servants; in the sports of childhood and youth, it was ever disparagingly reminding me of my colour and origin; along the streets it ever pursued, ever ridiculed, ever abused me. If I sought redress, the very complexion I wore was pointed out as the best reason for my seeking it in vain; if I desired to turn to account a little learning, in the way of earning a living by it, the idea of employing a black clerk was preposterous—too absurd to be seriously entertained. I never knew but one coloured clerk in a mercantile house. Mr. W. L. Jeffers was lowest clerk in a house well known in Broad Street, New York; but he never was advanced a single grade, while numerous white lads have since passed up by him, and over him, to be members of the firm. Poor Jeffers, till the day of his death, was but one remove above the porter. So, if I sought a trade, white apprentices would leave if I were admitted; and when I went to the house of God, as it was called, I found all the Negro-hating usages and sentiments of general society there encouraged and embodied in the Negro pew, and in the disallowing Negroes to commune until *all the whites,* however poor, low, and degraded, had done. I know of more than one coloured person driven to the total denial of all religion, by the religious barbarism of white New Yorkers and other Northern champions of the slaveholder.

However, at the age of sixteen I found a friend in George Atkinson Ward, Esq., from whom I received encouragement to persevere, in spite of Negro-hate. In 1833 I became a clerk of Thomas L. Jennings, Esq., one of the most worthy of the coloured race; subsequently my brother and I served David Ruggles, Esq., then of New York, late of Northampton, Massachusetts, now no more.

In 1833 it pleased God to answer the prayers of my parents, in my conversion. My attention being turned to the ministry, I was advised and recommended by the late Rev. G. Hogarth, of Brooklyn, to the teachership of a school for coloured children, established by the munificence of the late Peter Remsen, Esq., of New Town, N.Y. The most distinctive thing I can say of myself, in this my first attempt at the profession of a pedagogue, is that I succeeded Mr., now the Rev. Dr., Pennington. I afterwards taught for two-and-a-half years in Newark, New Jersey, where I was living in January 1838, when I was married to Miss Reynolds, of New York; and in October 1838 Samuel Ringgold Ward the younger was born, and I became, "to all intents, constructions, and purposes whatsoever," a family man, aged twenty-one years and twelve days.

In May, 1839, I was licensed to preach the gospel by the New York Congregational Association, assembled at Poughkeepsie. In November of the same year, I became the travelling agent of first the American and afterwards the New York Anti-slavery Society; in April, 1841, I accepted the unanimous invitation of the Congregational Church of South Butler, Wayne Co., N.Y., to be their pastor; and in September of that year I was publicly ordained and inducted as minister of that Church. I look back to my settlement among that dear people with peculiar feelings. It was my first charge: I there first administered the ordinances of baptism and the Lord's supper, and there I first laid hands upon and set apart a deacon; there God honoured my ministry, in the conversion of many and in the trebling the number of the members of the Church, most of whom, I am delighted to know, are still walking in the light of God. The manly courage they showed, in calling and sustaining and honouring as their pastor a black man, in that day, in spite of the too general Negro-hate everywhere rife (and as professedly pious as rife) around them, exposing them as it did to the taunts, scoffs, jeers, and abuse of too many who wore the cloak of Christianity—entitled them to what they will ever receive, my warmest thanks and kindest love. But one circumstance do I regret, in connection with the two-and-a-half years I spent among them—that was, not the poverty against which I was struggling during the time, nor the demise of the darling child I buried among them: it was my exceeding great inefficiency, of which they seemed to be quite unconscious. Pouring my tears into their bosoms, I ask of them and of God forgiveness. I was their first pastor, they my first charge. Distance of both time and space has not yet divided us, and I trust will ever leave us one in heart and mind.

Having contracted a disease of the uvula and tonsils, which threatened to destroy my usefulness as a speaker, with great reluctance I relinquished that beloved charge in 1843, and in December of that year removed to Geneva, where I commenced the study of medicine with Doctors Williams and Bell. The skill of my preceptors, with God's blessing, prevailing over my disorder, I was enabled to speak occasionally to a small Church in Geneva, while residing there; and finally to resume public and continuous anti-slavery labours, in connection with the Liberty Party, in 1844. In 1846 I became pastor of the Congregational Church in Cortland Village, New York, where some of the most laborious of my services were rendered, and where I saw more of the foolishness, wickedness, and at the same time the invincibility, of American Negro-hate, than I ever saw elsewhere. Would that I had been more worthy of the kindness of those who invited me to that place—of those friends whom I had the good fortune to win while I lived there—especially of those who showed me the most fraternal kindness during the worst, longest illness I have suffered throughout life, and while passing through severe pecuniary troubles. My youngest son, William Reynolds Ward, is buried there; and there were born two of my daughters, Emily and Alice, the former deceased, the latter still living.

From Cortland we removed to Syracuse in 1851, whence, on account of my participating in the "Jerry rescue case," on the first day of October in that year, it became quite expedient to remove *in some haste* to Canada, in November. During the last few years of my residence in the United States I was editor and proprietor of two newspapers, both of which I survive, and in both of which I sunk every shred of my property. While at this business, it seemed necessary that I should know something of law. For this purpose, I commenced the reading of it: but I beg to say, that after smattering away, or teaching, law, medicine, divinity, and public lecturing, I am neither lawyer, doctor, teacher, divine, nor lecturer; and at the age of eight-and-thirty I am glad to hasten back to what my father first taught me, and from what I never should have departed—the tilling of the soil, the use of the hoe.

I beg to conclude this chapter by offering to all young men three items of advice, which my own experience has taught me:—

1. FIND YOUR OWN APPROPRIATE PLACE OF DUTY.
2. WHEN YOU HAVE FOUND IT, BY ALL MEANS KEEP IT.
3. IF EVER TEMPTED TO DEPART FROM IT, RETURN TO IT AS SPEEDILY AS POSSIBLE.

ANTI-SLAVERY LABOURS, &c.

Part I

UNITED STATES

CHAPTER I

Anti-Slavery: What?

It may be thought that the biographical portion of this volume is brief and summary; but it will be seen, as we proceed, that some points, deserving more attention, belong more properly to other parts of the work. In proceeding to write about my anti-slavery labours, I may be allowed to give my own definition of them. I regard all the upright demeanour, gentlemanly bearing, Christian character, social progress, and material prosperity, of every coloured man, especially if he be a native of the United States, as, in its kind, anti-slavery labour. The enemies of the Negro deny his capacity for improvement or progress; they say he is deficient in morals, manners, intellect, and character. Upon that assertion they base the American doctrine, proclaimed with all effrontery, that the Negro is neither fit for nor entitled to the rights, immunities and privileges, which the same parties say belong naturally to *all men;* indeed, some of them go so far as to deny that the Negro belongs to the human family. In May, 1851, Dr. Grant, of New York, argued to this effect, to the manifest delight of one of the largest audiences ever assembled in Broadway Tabernacle. True, two coloured gentleman, one of whom was Frederic Douglass, Esq., refuted the abominable theory; but Dr. Grant left, it is to be feared, his impression upon the minds of too many, some of whom wished to believe him. A very learned divine in New Haven, Connecticut, declared, to the face of my honoured friend, Rev. S. E. Cornish, that "neither wealth nor education nor RELIGION could fit the Negro to live upon terms of equality with the white man." Another Congregational clergyman of Connecticut told the Writer, in the presence of the Rev. A. G. Beeman, that in his opinion, were Christ living in a house capable of holding two families, he would object to a black family in the adjoining apartments. Mr. Cunard objected to my taking a passage on any other terms— in a British steamer, be it remembered; and Mr. Cunard is an Englishman—than that I should not offend Americans by presenting myself at the cabin *table d'hôte*. I could number six Americans who left Radley's Hotel, while I was boarding there, because I was expected to eat in the same coffee-room with them, at a separate table, twenty feet distant from them, being ignorant of their presence. In but five of the American States are coloured persons allowed to vote on equal terms with whites. From social and business circles the Negro is entirely excluded—no, not that; he is not admitted—as a rule.

Now, surely, all this is not attributable to the fact that the Americans hold slaves, for the very worst of these things are done by non-slaveholders, in non-slaveholding States; and Englishmen, Irishmen, and Scotchmen, generally become the bitterest of Negro-haters, within fifteen days of their naturalization—some not waiting so long. Besides, in other slaveholding countries— Dutch Guiana, Brazil, Cuba, &c.—free Negroes are not treated thus, irrespective of character or condition. It is quite true that, as a rule, American slaveholders are the worst and the most cruel, both to their own mulatto children and to other slaves; it is quite true, that nowhere in the world has the Negro so bitter, so relentless enemies, as are the Americans; but it is not because of the existence of slavery, nor of the evil character or the lack of capacity on the part of the Negro. But, whatever is or is not the cause of it, there stands the fact; and this feeling is so universal that one almost regards 'American' and 'Negro-hater' as synonymous terms.

My opinion is, that much of this difference between the Anglo-

Saxon on the one and his brother Anglo-Saxon on the other side of the Atlantic is to be accounted for in the very low origin of early American settlers, and the very deficient cultivation as compared with other nations, to which they have attained. I venture this opinion upon the following considerations. The early settlers in many parts of America were the very lowest of the English population: the same class will abuse a Negro in England or Ireland now. The New England States were settled by a better class. In those States the Negro is best treated, excepting always the State of Connecticut. The very lowest of all the early settlers of America were the Dutch. These very same Dutch, as you find them now in the States of New York, New Jersey, and Pennsylvania, out-American all Americans, save those of Connecticut, in their maltreatment of the free Negro. The middling and better classes of all Europe treat a black gentleman as a gentleman. Then step into the British American colonies, and you will find the lowest classes and those who have but recently arisen therefrom, just what the mass of Yankees are on this matter. Also, the best friends the Negro has in America are persons generally of the superior classes, and of the best origin. These are facts. The conclusion I draw from them may be erroneous, but it is submitted that it may be examined.

We expect, generally, that the progress of Christianity in a country will certainly, however gradually, undermine and overthrow customs and usages, superstitions and prejudices, of an unchristian character. That this contempt of the Negro is unchristian, perhaps I shall be excused from stooping to argue. But, alas! *pari passu* with the spread of what the pulpit renders current as Christianity in my native country, is the growth, diffusion, and perpetuity of hatred to the Negro; indeed, one might be almost tempted to accredit the words of one of the most eloquent of Englishmen, who, more than twenty years ago, described it in few but forcible terms—"the Negro-hating Christianity." *Religion*, however, should be substituted for Christianity; for while a religion may be from man, and a religion from such an origin may be capable of *hating*, Christianity is always from God, and, like him, is love. "He who hateth his brother abideth in darkness." "Love is the fulfilling of the law." Surely it is with no pleasure that I say, from experience, deep-wrought conviction, that the oppression and the maltreatment of the hapless descendant of Africa is not merely an ugly excrescence upon American *religion*—not a blot upon it, not even an anomaly, a contradiction, and an admitted imperfection, a deplored weakness—a lamented form of indwelling, an easily besetting, sin; no, it is a part and parcel of it, a cardinal principle, a *sine qua non*, a cherished defended keystone, a corner-stone, of American faith—all the more so as it enters into the practice, the everyday practice, of an overwhelming majority (equal to ninety-nine hundredths) of its professors, lay and clerical, of all denominations; not excepting, too, many of the Quakers! How these people will get on in Heaven, into which sovereign, abounding, divine mercy admits blacks as well as whites, I know not; but Heaven is not the only place to which either whites or blacks will enter after the judgment!

In view of such a conclusion, what is anti-slavery labour? Manifestly the refutation of all this miserable nonsense and heresy—for it is both. How is this to be done? Not alone by lecturing, holding anti-slavery conventions, distributing anti-slavery tracts, maintaining anti-slavery societies, and editing anti-slavery journals, much less by making a trade of these, for certain especial pets and favourites to profit by and in which to live in luxury; but, in connection with these labours, right and necessary in themselves, effective as they must be when properly pursued, the cultivation of all the upward tendencies of the coloured man. I call the expert black cordwainer, blacksmith, or other mechanic or artisan, the teacher, the lawyer, the doctor, the farmer, or the divine, an anti-slavery labourer; and in his vocation from day to day, with his hoe, hammer, pen, tongue, or lancet, he is living down the base calumnies of his heartless adversaries—he is demonstrating his truth and their falsity: indeed, all the labour which falls short of this—much more, such as does not tend in this direction—must, from the nature of the case and the facts and demands of the cause, be defective, lamentably defective, to use no stronger term. I shall be understood, I hope, then, if I include the chief facts of my life, whether in the editorial chair, in the pulpit, on the platform, pleading for this cause or that, in my anti-slavery labours. God helping me wherever I shall be, at home, abroad, on land or sea, in public or private walks, as a man, a Christian, especially as a *black man*, my labours must be anti-slavery labours, because mine must be an anti-slavery life.

CHAPTER II

Work Begun

I shall not inflict the dry details of a journal upon my readers. Treating of my labours in the American States, in this part I shall briefly speak of the incidents which in Providence led to my entering upon the lecturing field, those connected with my settlement in the ministry, and some events occurring in the course of both, and the reasons for the termination of those labours.

That the announcement of a meeting for the formation of an anti-slavery society should create a sensation among the coloured people of New York no one will wonder. Having been abused, and befooled, and slandered, disparaged, ridiculed, and traduced, by the Colonizationists, we could not but look on, first, with very great distrust upon any persons stepping forward with schemes professedly for our good. But a young printer had suffered imprisonment in Baltimore, for exposing there what Clarkson had long before exposed in Liverpool—viz., the paraphernalia of a systematic, authorized, lucrative slave trade; and this young man being released through the munificence of one of our then wealthiest Pearl Street merchants, we could not doubt the real motives of either of these. Garrison would not suffer imprisonment in our behalf, insincerely; Arthur Tappan would not liberate Garrison from imprisonment, *on such a charge*, at the cost of one thousand dollars, insincerely; indeed, we know too well that no white man would suffer for our sakes, without more than ordinary philanthropy. These gentlemen deserved, and they received, our confidence. In 1830 I heard, in New Haven, Connecticut, at the Temple Street Coloured Congregational Church, the Rev. Simeon S. Jocelyn preach. I learned that, when a young man, a bank-note engraver by trade, he studied theology and entered the ministry, on purpose to serve the coloured people. When a lecture was announced to be delivered on the subject of slavery by that gentleman, I was but too glad to hear him. I learned to love him as a child; I now have the honour of his friendship as a man. His was the first anti-slavery lecture I ever heard, and it was delivered in 1834. In the spring of the same year Professor E. Wright, jun., who had been in the enjoyment of a Professorship in a Western College, but relinquished it, and with it surrendered a salary of eleven hundred dollars for one of four hundred, that he might be at liberty to serve the anti-slavery cause, lectured upon the same subject. I was among his many delighted auditors. The same gentleman is now E. Wright, Esq., of Boston, the Douglas Jerrold of America. A lawyer well known to fame, David Paul Brown, Esq., of Philadelphia, was always ready to render his peerless services in defence of any person claimed as a slave. On the fourth day of July, 1834, this gentleman was invited to deliver an anti-slavery oration in Chatham Chapel, and, of course, the coloured people mustered in strong array to hear so well known a champion of freedom; but the meeting was dispersed by a mob, gathered and sustained by the leading commercial and political men and journals of that great city. It was Independence Day—a day, of all days, sacred to freedom. What Mr. Brown came to tell us was, that the principles, enunciated in few words, in the Declaration of Independence—"We hold these truths to be self-evident truths, that all men are created equal, and are endowed by their Creator with certain inalienable rights, among which are life, liberty, and the pursuit of happiness"—applied as well to black men as to white men. This the aristocracy of New

York could not endure; and therefore, just fifty-eight years from the very hour that the Declaration of 1776 was made, the mob of the New York merchants broke up this assembly.

On the 7th of the same month the coloured people held a meeting in the same place, to listen to an address from one of the ablest of their number, Benjamin F. Hughes, Esq. That meeting was dispersed by a mob led by a person holding a lucrative political office in the city. This *gentleman* (I like to indulge in poetry sometimes) thought to do as he pleased with the blacks, kicking them about at will; and while Mr. Hughes was speaking, ordered other parties to come in and occupy the building. Seeing resistance made by some of the coloured people, and fearing he might receive a blow for a kick, he elevated a chair over his head, and stood witnessing the *mélée* himself had begun, when Mr. Jinnings knocked him over with a well-aimed missile. Leaving his men to fight or run, as might seem wisest, this general of the mob escaped from a window 22 feet from the ground, injuring himself so as to keep his house for a fortnight—in his own person the leader of the mob and the only man injured in the affray. The blacks were victors; every white man was driven from the place. But while a few of us lingered, a reinforcement of the white belligerents came, and, finding some few lads of us in the place, they drove us out with a rush to the door. Then they commenced beating us in the most cowardly manner. The public watchman arrested the parties beaten instead of those committing the assault, and it was my lot to be among the former number. For the crime of being publicly assaulted by several white persons, I was locked up in the watchhouse throughout the night. Shortly after my imprisonment, four others were brought into the same cell by the officers of peace and justice, for the same crime. In the meantime the mob went to the house of Lewis Tappan, Esq., broke it open, sacked it, and burned the furniture. Mr. Tappan was brother and partner of the gentleman who liberated Garrison; he also believed in the Declaration of Independence; hence the mutilation and burning of his property. My oath of allegiance to the anti-slavery cause was taken in that cell on the 7th of July, 1834. In the morning we were brought before the police magistrate, with other prisoners. Those against whom no one appeared, or whom no one charged with any offence, were discharged. None appeared against us. The watchman who arrested us had no charge to bring: he simply said, in the chaste diction of a New York official, "Thur was a row in Chatham Chapel last night, and these niggers was there." The magistrate, a sample specimen of the New York Dogberry, abused us, and, instead of discharging us according to law and custom, remanded us to Bridewell, to give parties an opportunity of appearing against us. I never knew the same course taken in any other case. To Bridewell we went, and were put into a cell with nineteen others. In a most filthy state was that cell. All the occupants, besides my four companions, were charged with crime —one with killing a man; and though *we* were searched before we were incarcerated, this man had, and showed us, the knife with which he had inflicted the murder. The murderer, Johnson, had been fettered in the same cell, and we saw the chain by which he had been fastened to the floor. When the prison cup was offered us to drink from, and when the prison food was brought us, feeling our innocence and our dignity (lads of seventeen seldom lack the latter), we refused both. About ten o'clock, my father and G. A. Ward, Esq., procured my liberation, by paying the turnkey. As an innocent subject, unrighteously doomed to a felon's prison, without either accuser or trial, when liberated, I should have gone out *free*. My fellow prisoners were liberated soon after. That imprisonment initiated me into the anti-slavery fraternity.

In July, 1837, I was selected to deliver an oration before a Literary Society of which I was a member. It was my first public attempt at public speaking. Among those present was Lewis Tappan, Esq. In August of the same year I was invited to speak in the

Broadway Taberncle. In 1839 I was engaged in Poughkeepsie, as teacher of the Coloured Lancasterian School. Anxious to pursue further studies, I applied to one or two gentlemen for aid. One of them confessed himself but a beginner in one of the branches in which I had made some progress; and he soon after gave me a deeper wound, and more severe discouragement, than any other man ever did. A debate upon the peace question was to occur, in a hall of which this gentleman and I were joint proprietors for the time. I had another engagement to speak, at some distance from home, within a day or two of the time of the debate. This gentleman urged my return in time to participate in the discussion. I complied, went to the hall. A few only attended; and after a little conversation instead of a debate, it was concluded to form a Literary Society. My friend was requested to pass a paper for the names of such persons present as would enter such a society. He did *not* solicit my name. He came to me after the proceeding had terminated, and said, "Mr. Ward, you must have noticed that I did not hand the paper to you for your signature. I omitted you on purpose, because I saw that if your name was taken several of those present would bolt." Then, thought I, what is the use of my acting uprightly, seeking to win fame, and gaining it, if in this country a professed friend, a man who goes with me to the house of God, hearing me preach, visits my house, after all treads upon me to please his neighbours? My determination was formed to leave the country. I accordingly wrote to Mr. Burnley, of the Trinidad Legislature, a relation of the late Joseph Hume, Esq., M.P., who kindly encouraged my going to that island. I wrote also to Rev. Joshua Leavitt, asking for letters of recommendation. Mr. L. deprecated my leaving America, thinking I might be of some service to the anti-slavery cause. I wrote him again, bitterly stating my utter despair of doing anything for myself or my people amid so many discouragements. The reply I received was an appointment as agent of the American Anti-Slavery Society, to travel and lecture for them. I accepted the appointment, my commission being signed by Henry B. Stanton, Esq., who was *then*, and Hon. James Gillespie Birney, who *yet* professes to be, an abolitionist; these gentlemen being secretaries of that Society; in the same capacity they came to London, to attend the World's Anti-Slavery Convention of 1840. Thus was I introduced into the anti-slavery agency.

———

CHAPTER III

The Field Occupied

In November, 1839, I made my *début* as a lecturer. It cost me a great deal of effort and self-denial. My youthful wife and my infant boy I must leave, to go hundreds of miles, travelling in all weathers, meeting all sorts of people, combatting some of the most deeply seated prejudices, and in the majority of instances denied the ordinary courtesies of civilized life. I suffered more than can be here described. At length I considered that every Christian has not only *a* cross to bear, but *his* peculiar cross; and that God, not man, must judge and decide in what shape that cross must come: aye, and he too would give grace to bear it. Thus fortified, I went forth; and from that day to this I have never been able to see this travelling, homeless, wandering part of the work in any other light than a cross. No place *can* be a substitute for home, though the latter be a hovel, the former a palace. No observer can enter into one's inner feelings, live over again one's life, as does the loving wife. In sickness, in sorrow, to be away from home adds mountain weights to what the wanderer's bosom must bear; and I may as well add, that the poisoned tongue of censure—cool, deliberate, granite-hearted censure—censure from unbridled but professedly Christian tongues, to be found alike on both sides of the Atlantic, even among brethren and others—doth not diminish the rigour of the cross.

Still, with God's blessing I went forth, making my first speech at a private house, and afterwards speaking in public places until

I become accustomed somewhat to the sound of my own voice, and a little skilled in the handling of the subject, receiving kind encouragement from one friend and another; until being transferred to the service of the New York State Society in December 1839, I had the unspeakable pleasure of making the acquaintance of some of its most distinguished members and officers, and, at the same time, of avoiding official connection with the quarrels which divided the Anti-Slavery Society in 1840, and the subsequent dissensions among them.

This same December, 1839, was eventful as the month in which I became personally acquainted with Hon. Gerrit Smith, Rev. Beriah Green, and William Goodell, Esq.—three men whose peers are not to be found in New York or any other State.

Gerrit Smith had not then been sent to Congress, but he had shown himself every way qualified for the highest seat in any legislature, for the highest office in the gift of any people. Not that office would adorn or ennoble him, but that, in office as everywhere else, the majestic dignity of his mien, the easy, graceful perfection of his manners, his highly cultivated intellect, his rich and varied learning, his profoundly instructive conversation, his princely munificence, the natural stream springing in and flowing from a most benevolent heart—and, above all, his sweet, childlike, simple, earnest, constant piety, pervading his whole life and sparkling in all he says or does—these traits would have shed lustre upon any office, and have made their possessor the most admired and most attractive as they make him one of the very best men. In spite of all that was said of this gentleman by his enemies during his short career in Congress, fourteen years after the time I speak of, the very bitterest of his foes—or, what is tantamount, the falsest of his professed friends—were obliged to acknowledge him to be one of the noblest of earth's noble sons.

Never shall I forget the first time I heard that model man speak. Standing erect, as he could stand no other way, with his large, manly frame, graceful figure and faultless mannerism,

richly but plainly dressed, with a broad collar and black ribbon
upon his neck (his invariable costume, whatever be the prevailing
fashion), his look, with his broad intelleceual face and towering
forehead, was enough to charm any one not dead to all sense of
the beautiful; and then, his rich, deep, flexible, musical voice,
as capable of a thunder-tone as of a whisper—a voice to which
words were suited, as it was suited to words; but, most of all, the
words, thoughts, sentiments, truths and principles, he uttered—
rendered me, and thousands more with me, unable to sit or stand
in any quietness during his speech. This was in May, 1838. Mr.
Smith was speaking against American Negro-hate. He is a descen-
dent of the Dutch, who have distinguished themselves as much for
their ill nature towards Negroes as for anything else. He belonged
by wealth and position to the very first circles of the old Dutch
aristocracy; he was the constant and admired associate of the
proudest Negro-haters on the face of the earth; he had for years
been a member of that most unscrupulous band of organized,
systematic, practical promulgators of Negro-hate, the Colonization Society: and yet, in Broadway Tabernacle, upon an anti-
slavery platform, in the city of New York (the worst city, save
Philadelphia, since the days of Sodom, on this subject), Gerrit
Smith stood up before four thousand of his countrymen to denounce this their cherished, honoured, they believe Christianized
vice. To mortal man it is seldom permitted to behold a sight so
full of or so radiant with moral power and beauty. Among the
things he said, I may attempt to recall one sentiment—he asserted
that, in ordinary circumstances, a person does not and cannot
know how or what the Negro, the victim of this fiendish feeling,
has to endure. Englishmen coming to America at first look upon
it as a species of insanity. We are not all conscious of what we are
doing to our poor coloured brother. "The time was, Mr. Chairman," said this prince of orators, "when I did not understand it;
but when I came to put myself in my coloured brother's stead—
when I imagined myself in *his* position—when I sought to realize

what he feels, and how he feels it—when, in a word, I became a COLOURED MAN—then I understood it, and learned how and why to hate it."

To enforce his personal illustration there was one great fact. Mr. Smith had read of One "who made himself of no reputation," and he chose to imitate Him. Long, long before the anti-slavery question agitated the American mind, Mr. Smith and his excellent lady had concluded that, by whomsoever they might be visited, no coloured person should be slighted or treated with any less respect in their mansion because of his colour. Mr. and Mrs. Smith knew that they were visited by some of the first families of the land—they were such; their relatives were such; and no inconsiderable number of them were slaveholders. They knew what would be said; but they also knew what was right, and upon that principle had Mr. Smith invariably acted—scorning, spurning, and trampling upon the vile demon of Negro-hate for twenty-years before he made that ever memorable speech. Such was his qualification to make such a speech, in such a presence. Now, a man of no position, a mere mechanic or artisan, who makes himself by means of his cause, and who earns his bread by his philanthropy, may talk cheaply enough about what he dares and suffers for the poor slave; but one who, in Mr. Smith's position, gives untold wealth in lands and money, must be judged otherwise. Mr. Smith has given 120,000 acres of land to coloured people—has sacrificed his position, and, from sympathy with the coloured people, has identified himself with them. Here then we see philanthropy, real, pure, self-sacrificing—philanthropy, indeed, such as very few in any country exhibit, and fewer still in *that* country. But, God be praised, Gerrit Smith belongs to that few. The honour and pleasure of making that gentleman's acquaintance was mine in 1839, at his house, in Peterborough. No honour I ever enjoyed do I esteem more highly than that I may call the Honourable Gerrit Smith my personal friend. Of him I say, sometimes, he is the Shaftesbury of America; and those who enjoy the pleasure of knowing both that I honour the noble Earl in nothing more highly than in speaking of his Lordship as the Gerrit Smith of England, of Europe.

The Rev. Beriah Green, President of Oneida Institute (the *alma mater* of several of my dear schoolfellows, among them Henry Highland Garnet and Alexander Crummell), was among the acquaintances I had the privilege of making in 1839. Few clergymen, of any denomination, in any country, equal the profound, the learned, the original Beriah Green. His love for humanity, especially the poorest of the poor, is of the most ardent type. Upon its altar he will lay salary, name, place, reputation, not only, but submit to all manner of abuse and misrepresentation, and toil at any kind of hard labour, "for dear humanity's sake," to use his own beautiful, expressive, emphatic phrase. Such was this devoted philanthropist, sixteen years ago; such is he now, in spite of increasing years and undiminished sacrifices. I never knew a person who put a higher estimate upon simple manhood, and who relied upon the simple truth more fully, than he. In argument, in analyzing principles, in applying metaphysical tests, I never saw nor read of his equal.

William Goodell, then the editor of the *Friend of Man*, differs somewhat from both of his contemporaries, but he is a great man in all that makes a man truly great. He has not the eloquence of Mr. Smith, nor, technically speaking, the metaphysical acumen and power of Mr. Green; but for pure, sound, strong logic— for clear, consecutive reasoning—for the keen ability to detect a fallacy, a sophism, a tendency to defect or unsoundness—for a downright refinement and sublimation, as well as an acute and well tempered use, of common sense—William Goodell has not his superior, if his equal, among all whom I have met on either side of the Atlantic. If, then, these gentlemen differ in taste, education, former pursuits, habits of thought, and intellectual character, as doubtless they do, they agree in one thing—the earnest, simple devotion of the entire soul to the love of God and the love of man.

To have formed the acquaintance of these three personages, to work under their advice and direction, to acquire their friend-ship, and to be unconscious of any diminution of it for sixteen years, was and is, to me, a priceless privilege. This is the best apology I can offer, if indeed any is needed, for occupying so much of these pages in speaking of them. To know them is to love them; and it is among the most pleasing of one's anticipations of the happiness of the future state, that eternity will be enjoyed in such excellent association. Is it not one of the highest proofs of the power of divine grace, that it can and does furnish such specimens of redeemed man, in the midst of a generation however wicked and perverse? Is it not an earnest of God's favour to the anti-slavery cause, that he calls into labour and sacrifice gifts so sound, talent so exalted, intellects so cultivated, piety so Christ-like.

CHAPTER IV

The Issue Contemplated

It is a matter of surprise to people in England that the Americans should profess so loudly the *Christian* religion, and insist so strongly upon republicanism as the only proper form of government, and yet hold slaves and treat Negroes, as they do, in the directest possible opposition both to republicanism and Christianity. The opposition which the citizens of the United States, of both the North and the South, make to the anti-slavery cause, is, to Europeans, an inexplicable mystery. Far be it from me to attempt a solution of it. I will endeavour to state the real issue betwixt anti-slavery men and their opponents; and, in doing so, I fear I shall make the matter more, instead of less, mysterious.

Those who recollect, or who have read of, the opposition Clarkson, Wilberforce, and Buxton had to encounter in their day, on the subject of the slave trade, in the British senate, and from Englishmen interested in the slave trade, know what class of arguments were used against the measures of righteousness advocated by them. Precisely the same class arguments have been made against the abolition of slavery in the United States, by American senators, and by American merchants, theologians, and politicians: indeed, I have seen where the very words used by His Royal Highness the Duke of Clarence, against the abolition of the slave trade, were uttered in the American Senate against the abolition of slavery there. When the abolition of West India slavery was urged by Brougham, Stanley, and others, they in their turn were assailed with the same sort of opposition which their anti-slavery fathers, so to speak, met; and just such opposition have Sumner, Wilson, Seward, Giddings, and others, to overcome in the American Senate now. We explain the opposition of British slaveholders and slave traders to abolition, on the ground of interest, long continued use and abuse of authority, degenerating into petty tyranny and worse than brutal cruelty. These, however, sailed under no flag of boasted freedom. They did not clamour for the equality of all men. They found no fault with other than republican forms of government. They did not set themselves up as universal reformers. They said but little—wisely about religion, for they had but little religion to talk about; and such as they had, judging from their lives, was more honoured by silence than profession.

In America the case was different. Parties having the least to do with the South, or with slavery, are among the fiercest opposers of the anti-slavery cause. Ladies—save the mark!—and gentlemen of the most amiable and benevolent dispositions, such as contribute to every local charity, listen to all the cries of misery from the Old World, and honour all drafts made upon them for the spread of the gospel among the distant heathen, are the most active and, from their high religious position, the most powerful abettors and defenders of the slave system—not as it was in some ancient country two thousand years ago, but as it is now in the United States. Northern pulpit orators defend slavery from the Bible, the Old Testament and the New; and this is not true of one here and there only, it is so of the most learned, most distinguished of them, of all denominations. The very men who cater for British popularity, are the loudest declaimers in favour of this "domestic institution." Another class of them maintain the most studious silence concerning it. If they speak at all, they condemn only "slavery in the abstract," and condemn abolition in the concrete. They neither hold nor treat slavery as sinful; and when pressed, declare that "*some* sins are not to be preached against." Such was the teaching of a distinguished theological professor to his class in a "school of the prophets" in New York State. Besides, all the machinery of the benevolent societies is so framed, and set, and kept at work, as not only not to interfere with slavery, but to pander to it. The American Tract Society not only publishes no tract against slavery, but they favour that abominable system in the two following ways:—1. If an English work which they republish has a line in it discountenancing slavery, however indirectly, it is either taken out, or so altered as to lose its force in that particular direction. Their emasculation of "Gurney on the Love of God" is notorious. 2. They refuse to publish a tract on the subject, when other acknowledged Christians and Christian ministers propose to write and prepare one, and defray the expense of publishing the same. No, poor slave: dumb as thou art, dumb shalt thou ever be, so far as this Society is concerned.

The American Bible Society distributes no Bibles among the slave population. To do so, it is freely admitted, were contrary to law in some States—not in all. It is so in nine of the fifteen Slave States, but not in the other six; and some of these laws were framed, and all of them are upholden, and many of them administered and executed, by members, friends, and patrons of this Society. Not one word ever escapes the lips of that Society, as such, against these anti-Protestant laws! In 1841 I knew of an agent of an auxiliary to that Society who was distributing Bibles in Louisiana, and, being ignorant of the laws upon the subject, asked a free coloured man if he could read, with the intention of giving or selling him a Bible if he could. Some one overheard him, and informed against him. He was arrested, tried, found guilty, but leniently discharged, on account of his ignorance of the law which he had violated. Slaveholders and their abettors belong to and are officers of the American Bible Society, and they control it. That slavery forbids the searchings of the Scriptures, which Christ enjoins, is to them not even a matter of complaint.

Albeit, they pledge themselves to give the Christian Scriptures to every American family in the Union.

The American Sunday-school Union stands in precisely the same category, and is controlled by precisely the same influences; and the American Board of Commissioners for Foreign Missions is, and always has been, both in its policy and its officers, of the very same character. The several religious bodies, with their respective branches, of all denominations, except the Quakers and the Free-Will Baptists (although the majority of their numbers are Northern men), are completely subject to the control of their slaveholding members. But the most lamentable fact is, that in Congregational New England the sons of Puritan sires are as guilty as the guiltiest enemies of the down-trodden slave. Such was the state of the case in 1839, when my labours began; such, I regret to say, continues the case at this moment: and here I will take the liberty of saying that, although my connection with the New York State Anti-Slavery Society dissevered me from the division of the abolitionists in 1840, and although I never belonged to the Garrison branch of the abolitionists, so-called, I will do them the justice to record, that the least, slightest tendency towards infidelity, or even of impatience with the Churches, was never seen or suspected in them until after the New England clergy, as a body, had taken ground distinctly and openly against the anti-slavery cause (*vide* Goodall's *History of the Anti-Slavery Clause*).

What reason is given for this strange action on the part of religious denominations, benevolent institutions, theological professors, and individual clergymen? I will state it as fairly as I can.

Their chief reason is, that it will disturb their existing harmony so to take up, discuss, and consider this question, as, it seems to abolitionists, its importance demands. In the Churches, while they maintain silence upon it, or ignore it altogether, they have nothing to cause disagreement. This question would be an apple of discord, as brethren of equal piety would range themselves on opposite sides of it. So it would be in the benevolent societies. Harmony, peace, are sought in that country by religious people, at almost any expense; slaveholders are members of the different religious denominations; in fact, one sixth of all the slaveholders belong to Methodists, Baptists, Episcopalians, and Presbyterians. To treat slavery as sinful, would offend these brethren; and what is the use of that? They are good Christians; they treat their slaves well; and so long as they give signs of piety, are regular in their standing, pious in conversation, sound in doctrine, and correct in other matters, save this one of slavery, why should they be disturbed? why offend them?

Some deny the sinfulness of slaveholding; others shelter themselves behind the faults of the abolitionists; others defend slaveholding from the Bible; but I think their love of harmony is their chief alleged reason for their present attitude. Let it not be forgotten, however, that behind all this—and going very far, I think, to explain it—is the contempt they all alike maintain towards the Negro. Surely, if they believed him to be an *equal brother man*, such miserable pretexts for, and defences of, the doing of the mightiest wrongs against him, would never for a moment be thought of.

The abolitionists, on the other hand, point out the intrinsic nature and character of slavery—not in the abstract, but in the concrete—not as one might imagine it to be, but as it *is*—not as it was (or was not) two thousand years ago, more or less, but as it is *to-day*—its brutalizing, chattelizing; buying, selling, the image of God and the members of Christ's body; its adultery, fornication, incest—and ask if religious men and ministers are really serious in declaring *this* to be no sin? If not serious, is it not a matter too grave to jest about? Violating, as it does, every part and parcel of the Decalogue, could He who gave the law from Sinai approve it? They point to the law of love, and ask, Shall not our black brother receive the treatment, the love, of a brother, as

well as the Hindoo or the Laplander? They point to the law which
denies him the Bible, and ask, Can the God of the Bible approve
that law? They hear Christ say, "Inasmuch as ye did it (or did it
not) to the least of these my brethren, ye did it (or did it not)
unto *me*." Black men are, in the estimation of these brethren who
oppose the anti-slavery cause, "the least." Should not religious
men tremble, lest the Son of Man should denounce these terrible
words against them?

When told of the piety of slaveholding professors of religion,
they point to the acknowledged piety of the Jewish Church; not-
withstanding which God denounced them for refusing "to break
the yoke and let the oppressed go free" (Isa. lviii. 1–6). When
the harmony and peace of the Church are pleaded for, against
them, abolitionists plead for the "wisdom which is from above,
which is *first pure, then* peaceable." When urged, as it frequently
is, that it is no part of the business of the Church, or her benevolent handmaids, to speak against existing social and political
evils, abolitionists remind brethren of the firm lodgment which
the evils connected with and inseparable from slavery have in
the Church; so that, as the gentle and gifted Birney hath it, "the
American Church is the bulwark of slavery:" so that, the amiable
Barnes saith, "there is no power out of the Church that could sustain slavery a twelvemonth, if the Church should turn her artil-
lery against it."

If abolitionists hear pro-slavery men say there are sins which
the Church and the Pulpit ought not and need not rebuke, they
point to the preaching of all the true prophets, to the Lord, and to
the apostles; all of whom took especial pains to rebuke and to denounce the specific forms of iniquity which, in their own times,
were most prevalent, most fashionable, most profitable. This sin
of oppression was not among the least of them: so when told that
some who denounce slavery, and at the same time inveigh against
pro-slavery Churches and ministers, are sceptics, it is with no
sort of pleasure that abolitionists recall the time when the most

prominent of this class, were as sound and orthodox in their views of divine truth as any of their accusers, and continued to be so until appalled and disgusted by seeing how lamentably the class who now cry out "Infidel!" exhibited that worst, most delusive, most practical form of infidelity—the "holding of the truth in unrighteousness," the justifying of the foulest crimes (such as of necessity enter into and form constituent elements of slavery) by God's holy Word.

Such was the issue betwixt the anti-slavery cause and its religious opposers in 1839; such was it during my humble advocacy of emancipation; and such were, on the one side and on the other, the sort of arguments I had to meet and to make; and such is the issue between those who take opposite sides of this great question in that country now—an issue neither beginning nor ending with the rights and the liberties, the weal or the woe, of the poor Negro; but an issue involving the honour of Christ, the purity of the Church, the character of God, and the nature of our religion—of Christianity—and the influence of the American people, religiously, at home and abroad. What sort of Christ is he who, while professing to die for the *race*, authorizes the exclusion of the coloured portion thereof—at least three fourths—from the commonest benefits of his salvation? Even such is the Christ of American pro-slavery religion. What is the character of that God who, giving a moral code from Sinai, right in the fitness of things, as well as because an emanation from himself and a transcript of his will, but who authorizes one fourth of those upon whom he makes that law binding to violate and trample under foot every precept and principle of that code, touching the other three fourths of their fellow men? Even that is the character of the Deity, as seen in the light—or the darkness—of a pro-slavery religion. How pure can that Church be which smiles upon, fondles, caresses, protects, and rejoices to defend, a system which cannot exist without turning out a million and three quarters of the women of the country to the unbridled lusts of the men who hold despotic power over them? some of these women, three hundred thousand, being owned by members of the Church, and some sixty thousand of these women being members of it too! Such is the purity of the American pro-slavery Church. What can be the nature of a religion with which all this is consistent, and a part of which it is? Just such is the nature of the pro-slavery religion of my native country; and, what is more grievous to add, just so far as it shall spread in heathen lands, just so far as it passes current in Europe, just so far does this blighting, withering influence go with it. Now, abolitionists—Christian abolitionists—in America, are contending as to whether the religion of Jesus, or that which is fashionable about them, shall prevail over themselves and their neighbours. They see that when a system of religion becomes so corrupt as to uphold and defend so abominable a system of iniquities as slavery, it is not to be trusted upon anything else. They know that if such a Church be not reformed it must become a sort of mother of harlots, and all manner of abominations. Whether that Church can be reformed or not is, with them, still a question; with me it is not. But I entreat the reader to look at the issue. It is not whether some men have wisely or unwisely pleaded this cause, nor whether their measures were commendable or not; nor merely, what shall be done with the Negro? It is, shall religion, pure and undefiled, prevail in the land; or shall a corrupt, spurious, human system, dishonouring to God and oppressive to man, have the prevalence? That is the issue, "before Israel and the sun."

CHAPTER V

The Political Question

In like manner, the abolitionists, such as those with whom it was my honour to be associated, inquired how far they could wield their political powers, with the parties of the day, innocently. About the time to which I was referring—viz., 1839–40 —they began to see the great fact, that the political parties of the country departed as widely from the old maxims of democracy and republicanism as did the Churches from the gospel. They saw the North divided into two great parties, wielding two thirds of the votes of the nation, each of these having Southern members who controlled them, and both of them catering for the largest share of the Southern vote, which was about one third of the entire suffrage. They saw the best, highest offices, given freely to Southern men, on purpose to propitiate the South; while the South demanded and accepted this unnatural, undue, and disproportioned amount of power and emolument, both as the price of their aid to the party giving them, and as a means of securing the interests of slavery. Hence it was that the diplomatic agents of the country were sure to be Southerners, or pro-slavery men. Who ever knew any other character at the Court of St. James, or the Court of St. Cloud? Hence it was, too, that ere a Northern man could be qualified for any post or honour in the national gift, he must prove himself to have been always entirely free from the least taint of abolitionism, or to have been thoroughly purged of it, if he had ever been so much as reasonably suspected of it.

At the same time, in Northern localities the friends and members of these parties sought to cajole and seduce abolitionists into voting with one or the other of them, under the plea that *it* was more favourable to the anti-slavery cause than its opposite, while manifestly *both* were the tools and the props of the slave powers. Abolitionists did not fail to see, that to vote with either of these parties was alike repugnant to their cherished principles and to their self-respect. Then, they must do one of two things; either refrain from voting altogether, or concentrate their votes upon candidates of their own selection—in other words, form a political party upon anti-slavery principles. They adopted, wisely, the latter. That party was formed in August, 1840, at Syracuse. I then became, for the first time, a member of a political party. With it I cast my first vote; to it I devoted my political activities; with it I lived my political life—which terminated when, eleven years subsequently, I left the country.

As the abolitionists saw the Churches were trampling under foot the fundamental principles of Christianity, touching slavery, so they saw the Government and the political parties to be false to their own sworn principles of freedom and democracy. They departed from the constitution, which was made "to secure the blessings of liberty," and which ordained that "no man shall be deprived of liberty without due process of law." The Whigs denied the faith of their revolutionary fathers, whose Whiggism was but another name for self-sacrificing love of liberty. The Democrats, claiming Jefferson as their father and boasting of his having written the Declaration of Independence, hated nothing so intensely as Jefferson's writings against slavery—and that very Declaration of Independence, when, among "ALL MEN" in it declared to be entitled by God to the *unalienable* right to liberty, Negroes were said to be included. Both professed to be admirers of the great Washington; but neither of them, like him, coveted the opportunity of using his political power against slavery in his native State. What the abolitionists then demanded, and now

contend for, is the simple application of the principles of the
Declaration of Independence to the black as well as the white,
and that the former should share the benefits secured by the constitution as well as the latter. Believing just what the Declaration
of Independence says, that the right of man to liberty is *unalienable,* they hold that no enactments, no constitutions, no consent of
the man himself, no combinations of men, can alienate that which
is by God's *fiat* made *unalienable.* They agree with England's
greatest living jurist, Brougham, that the idea that man can be
the property of man is to be rejected as a "wild and guilty phan-
tasy": neither overlooking nor neglecting other great questions
with which governments and parties have to do, they make their
basis principle the *unalienable* right of man "to life, liberty, and
the pursuit of happiness." It was to the promulgation of these
political principles, and of these religious principles to which I
referred in the preceding pages, that, as an agent of the New York
State Anti-Slavery Society, it was my duty and my pleasure to
devote myself. This duty brought me into contact with all classes
of the enemies of the cause—made me familiar with all the different objections urged against it on the one hand; and it gave me the
ever-to-be-remembered pleasure of meeting all classes of abolitionists, profiting by their suggestions, accepting their hospitali-
ties, rejoicing in their sympathies, and sharing their devotions. A
truer, a more discerning set of men, America does not hold. They
are fully alive to the issue before them. They see that, if the principle be admitted that a black man may be legally, righteously
enslaved, so may any other man; that slavery is altogether regard-
less of the colour of its victims: that its encroachments upon the
right of petition, the freedom of the press, the freedom of speech
—its whipping, tarring and feathering, and lynching, *white* abolitionists at the South—its enslavement of the light-coloured children of white men—its unscrupulous, insatiate demands, nature,
character—all make it the enemy of any and every class opposing
it, willing to jeopard and to destroy the liberties of any whom it

can crush as its victims. They see that the real political issue is, not whether the black man's slavery shall be perpetuated, but whether the freedom of any Americans can be permanent. Blessings on the men who, at all hazards, are prepared to welcome and to meet that issue, with all its sacrifices and all its consequences! Whether they succeed or not, whether there is sufficient soundness and vitality in the republic to admit of its being saved or not, they, let the worst come, will ever bear in their bosoms the satisfaction of having done their duty in times of the utmost trial. Yea, blessings on that fearless band!

Allow me once more to state, what I fear Englishmen but too seldom and too slightly consider—1. The religious issue betwixt the American anti-slavery men and their opposers is deep, radical, vital, involving the religious weal or woe of the American Church. 2. The political issue is as deep, radical, and vital, in its kind: involving the safety, the stability—not the unity alone, but the very existence, of the republic. It is not like the emancipation question in Great Britain, or the corn-law question, or the reform question. It is not, What are the powers and scope of the Government, to what limit do they extend, to what classes do they apply, and of what improvements are they capable? It is a question affecting all classes, involving the fate of the whole people, undermining the basis of their best institutions, lying at the root of all constitutional government, and in its grasp including the whole range of American rights.

CHAPTER VI

The White Church and Coloured Pastor

It was while journeying through Western New York, promulgating such doctrines as the above, that I went by appointment to the township of Butler, in the county of Wayne, on a certain Saturday in February, 1841. The meeting was attended by some steady honest farmers and others, with their wives and daughters. It was holden in the Congregational Church. As was and still is the custom in that region, the lecturer was invited to tea by a gentleman of prominence in the neighbourhood—George Candee, Esq., who had a heart warm in the anti-slavery cause. At the invitation of several members of the Church, I remained and preached the following day in the forenoon, having an engagement seven miles distant in the evening.

As they were without either a pastor or a supply, several members of the Church accompanied me to Wolcott in the evening. On the way, one of the number said something about my settling with them. Thinking it a matter which would not survive the excitement of the moment, I simply gave them liberty to write to me at Peterborough, my residence. In a few days a letter came; and shortly after, another, from Clarendon Campbell, Esq., M.D., the postmaster, one of the most pious and intelligent members of the Church, inviting me formally and officially to settle.

I went to visit them in April, and a series of meetings began which was not discontinued until several persons were converted to God, through Christ's redemption, and I had been called and had agreed to become their pastor.

The Church and congregation were all white persons save my own family. It was "a new thing under the sun" to see such a connection. The invitation was unanimous and cordial; and not one incident occurred during my settlement, on the part of any of the *living* members, to make it even seem to be otherwise. Having spoken elsewhere touching this relation, I chose not here to repeat myself; but I will add, the novelty of such a settlement attracted a great deal of notice, and a great many remarks *pro* and *con*. I understood it to be a matter of vast importance, how I should demean myself in so responsible a position; for I felt it to be such, in two very important points of view—first, in regard to the anti-slavery cause generally; and secondly, in reference to the coloured people especially. If I should acquit myself creditably as a preacher, the anti-slavery cause would thereby be encouraged. Should I fail in this, that sacred cause would be loaded with reproach. So, if I were successful or unsuccessful in this charge would *encouragement* or *discouragement* come to the people of colour. In the one case, the traducers and disparagers of the Negro would say, "Said we not truly when we affirmed that nothing could be made of, or done with, the Negro? Such a one was actually placed in such a position; but so inveterate and unconquerable were the degrading tendencies of the Negro, that he could not sustain himself." Then whoever pleaded for Negro equality would be pointed to my failure as a perfect refutation of his doctrine, and a complete and triumphant answer to his argument. On the other hand, if I did succeed, some other young black would feel encouraged to qualify himself for a position of usefulness among his own people; but while appropriately serviceable to them, he might also be so situated as to do good *to* others and *for* his own class. I was not willing to do mischief to the dear anti-slavery cause, nor to that of my beloved people. I hope God

spared me from either—from both. Or, at any rate, among the
many things wherewithal I have been reproached, this is not one
of them.

During my residence in South Butler, I was frequently called
upon to speak, lecture, and preach, elsewhere. Thus were afforded
me numerous opportunities of making known to others than my
own congregation the gospel of Jesus; and of spreading before
others than those of my own neighbourhood what were the doctrines of the abolitionists, and the duties of American citizens, in
regard to those doctrines. I had the pleasure of seeing principles
of importance taking root, springing up, and becoming produc-
tive, and scattering seed upon fresh soil. While I cannot agree
with some as to the good results and wide extent of my labours, I
certainly hope that some good was done. That hope is more based
upon the peculiar character of the people of my charge, and those
among whom I travelled, than upon anything I was enabled to do.
My own people were honest, straightforward, God-fearing descendants of New England Puritans. Living in the interior of the
State, apart from the allurements and deceptions of fashion, they
felt at liberty to hear, judge, and determine for themselves, and
to act in accordance with what the Bible, as they understood it,
demanded of them. They heard a preacher: they supposed and
believed that he preached God's truth. That was what they wanted,
and all they wanted. The mere accident of the *colour* of the
preacher was to them a matter of small consideration. Some
might ridicule: indeed, some did. But what of that? They received
the truth, and it was of sufficient value to enable them to endure
ridicule for its sake. Anti-slavery doctrines were unpopular; anti-
slavery practice was still more so. But what said the Bible about
these doctrines? Did they agree with the law of love? Were they
in agreement with the law of love? Were they in agreement with
—or, what is more to the point, part and parcel of what Jesus
taught? If so, let rectitude take the place of popularity. They
could afford to do without the latter. So this honest, right-hearted

people loved—so they stood by the pastor—so their influence spread abroad—and so the Lord God of Jacob blessed them according to his gracious promise.

When in South Butler, also, the people of my own colour called upon me not unfrequently to visit and labour among them. They seemed inclined to take advantage of my position, to make it serviceable; and I was but too happy to accede to their wishes.

In doing so, I always sought to inculcate some truth which would have a direct influence on our character and our condition. Being deprived of the right of voting upon terms of equality with whites—being denied the ordinary courtesies of decent society, to say nothing of what is claimed for every man, especially every freeborn American citizen—I very well know, from a deep and painful experience, that the black people were goaded into a constant temptation to hate their white fellow-citizens. I know, too, how natural such hatred is in such circumstances: and all I know of the exhibition of vindictiveness and revenge by the whites against *their* injurers—and the most perfect justice of the Negro regarding the white man according to daily treatment received from him—caused me to see this temptation to be all the stronger: and convinced me also, that the white had no personal claim to anything else than the most cordial hatred of the black.

How frequently have I heard a Negro exclaim, "I cannot like a white man. He and his have done so much injury to me and my people for so many generations." How difficult, how impossible, to deny this, with all its telling force of historical fact! How natural is such a feeling, in such circumstances! How richly the whites deserved it!

My course was, however, to remind them of the manner in which Christ had been treated by those for whom he died, *ourselves included;* to direct their attention to the fact, that in the face of bad social customs, and education, and religion, God enabled *some whites* to do and endure all things for our cause, in its connection with their own; to assure them that the number of such was constantly increasing in our native country, while nearly all of the white race in Europe were our friends, especially the English, the French, and the Germans; and I felt justified in calling attention to my own position, as an example of improved feeling, and as a sign of hope and a token of encouragement. Accustomed to be soothed, as are my people, by hopeful, encouraging truth, I never knew these appeals to fail of effect. In addition to the above, I urged that, as Christ forgave, so should we; and that he made our being forgiven depend upon whether we forgave our enemies; that just as surely as the whites were our enemies—a most palpable fact, of every-day illustration—just so surely we must forgive them, or lie down for ever with them, amid the torments of the same perdition! What an aggravation of our temporal torments, to be obliged to be associated with our injurers, and to be partakers with them in an unrepented, unsanctified, more fiendish state, in the pangs of an endless perdition!

I beg to state, that I never taught on this subject what I did not then, and do not now, believe. I seriously believe that the prejudice of the whites against Negroes is a constant source of temptation to the latter to hate the former. I also believe that that same prejudice will aggravate the perdition of both: and I pray, therefore, that my people may be saved from that hatred, and made forgiving; and for the whites of America, my highest wish is that they may all become like the people of South Butler, thus removing danger from themselves, and, by doing justly, remove the most insidious of temptations from my people, whom, God knows, they have injured enough already.

In pleading the cause of the blacks before the whites, while I tried faithfully to depict the suffering of the enslaved, and the injustice done to the nominally free, I never stooped to ask pity for either. Wronged, outraged, "scattered, peeled, killed all the day long," as they are, I never so compromised my own self-respect, nor ever consented to so deep a degradation of my people, as to condescend to ask pity for them at the hands of their oppressors. I cast no reflections upon, and certainly utter no censure against, those who do; but I never did, and God forgive me when I ever shall. Justice, "even-handed justice," for the Negro—that which, according to American profession, is every man's birthright— *that* I claimed, nothing less. The most savage of our tormentors could now and then shed a tear, or at least heave a sigh of pity, and go out and remain the same savage tormentor still; unchanged, only a little—a very little—softened, to harden again upon the earliest opportunity. Those who have done us the worst injuries think it a virtue to express sympathy with us—a sort of arms'-length, cold-blooded sympathy; while neither of these would, on any account, consent to do towards us the commonest justice. What the Negro needs is, what belongs to him—what has been ruthlessly torn from him—and what is, by consent of a despotic democracy and a Christless religion, withholden from him, guiltily, perseveringly. When he shall have that restored, he can acquire *pity* enough, and all the sympathy he needs, cheap wares as they are; but to ask for them instead of his rights was never my calling.

Nor could I degrade myself by arguing the equality of the Negro with the white; my private opinion is, that to say the Negro is equal morally to the white man, is to say but very little. As to his intellectual equality, Cyprian, Augustine, Tertullian, Euclid, and Terence, would pass for specimens of the *ancient* Negro, exhibiting intellect beyond the ordinary range of modern literati, before the present Anglo-Saxon race had even an origin. And the schoolmate of Henry Highland Garnett, Alexander Crummell, Thomas Sipkins Sidney, Charles Lewis Reason, Patrick Henry Reason; the friend and associate of Frederic Douglass, James William Charles Pennington, Amos G. Beeman, James McCune Smith, Madison M. Clarke, and others of like high and distinguished attainments, might, perhaps, be

deemed excusable, if he simply called the names of these gentlemen as sufficient to contradict any disparaging words concerning
the *modern* Negro.

But the cool impudence, and dastardly cowardice, of denying a
black a seat in most of their colleges and academies, and literally
and scientific institutions, from one end of the republic to the
other; and, in like manner, shutting him out of most of the honourable and lucrative trades and professions, dooming him to
be a mere "hewer of wood and drawer of water"—discouraging
every effort he makes to elevate himself—and then declaring the
Negro to be naturally, morally, intellectually, or socially, inferior to the white—have neither parallel nor existence outside
of that head-quarters of injustice to the Negro, the United States
of America.

The coloured people of New York, Philadelphia, Boston—and,
I may as well add, all other cities and towns in the American
Union—bear themselves as respectably, support themselves as
comfortably, maintain as good and true allegiance to the laws,
make as rapid improvement in all that signifies real, moral, social
progress, as any class of citizens whatever. They do not so rapidly
acquire wealth, but it must be remembered that the avenues to
wealth are not open to them. The French of Lower Canada—the
Irish, the Welsh—the Jews, throughout continental Europe—the
Poles—no people in a state of entire or partial subjection ever
bore subjection so well, or improved so rapidly in spite of it, as
this very much abused class. During the past thirty years, they
have furnished their full quota of doctors, lawyers, divines, editors, orators, and poets; these in their spheres compare most
triumphantly with their countrymen, of whatever colour. With
facts of this sort before me, how could I ask pity, sympathy,
reason about equality, or anything short of justice, for my own
people?

There are a few facts connected with the free coloured people
of America, to which I may as well ask attention here as else-

where, for they are facts gathered during the time I had the honour of being one of their public advocates.

1. They number, according to the last census, some 400,000. A majority of these live in the Slave States; the greatest number is in Maryland, where there are 70,000. They are most numerous where most oppressed, though this has nothing to do with their oppression; for instance, in the great State of New York there are 40,000, in Pennsylvania 50,000, in Virginia 52,000. These are very large (in fact, the three largest) States: while in New England—where, with the exception of despotic Connecticut, they enjoy the same political rights as white men—there are but 20,-000. The explanation of this is, no Negroes originally came to America otherwise than as slaves. All who are now free are descendants of slaves, therefore; and although slavery, in early times, existed in most of the Northern States, it was never made a permanent system in the New England States, and hence there were but comparatively few Negroes introduced into them. In the Middle States, as New York, Pennsylvania, and New Jersey, slavery was far more prevalent than in any part of New England; hence their greater number of Negroes. It may be said, that this population, as a rule, bears certain proportions to the white population; being most numerous where the latter are so, and *vice versa*. Besides, those States which border upon Slave States have received accessions to their black population from the adjoining Slave States, by the immigration of both freemen and fugitives.

2. The fact that the blacks bear generally good characters, and are making progress as rapidly as any other class—and, all things considered, more rapidly than any other class—is well known to their bitterest enemies, even to those who are most eager to disparage them. I know this remark is not very complimentary to the honour and honesty of American Negro-haters; but if their characters cannot bear truth, it is no fault of mine. I have mentioned the names of several distinguished coloured gentlemen: I

beg to say; they are well known in their own country and many
of them, personally, to defamers who in this country as well as
at home, speak of the Negro as hopelessly degraded, and inferior
to the whites. In the city of New York there are several public
schools for coloured children, taught by coloured gentlemen and
ladies. The branches taught are orthography, reading, writing,
arithmetic, grammar, geography, history, astronomy, and alge-
bra so far as quadratic equations; the girls, I believe, also learn
needlework. From the branches taught, one may judge the literary
qualifications of the teachers; in each of these schools there is
a class, the highest class, in which lads from eight to fourteen
will bear a most searching examination in any part of the
branches named, without a moment's notice. Having the pleasure
of personally knowing the gifted teachers, and having examined
the classes myself, I only speak what I know; and yet, in no city
of the Union is the intellect of the Negro so much disparaged as in
that same city of New York, under the very shadow of those
schools! James Gorden Bennett, the miserable Irish detractor of
the Negro, publishes his vile *New York Herald* within ten minutes' walk of two of those schools—within two minutes' walk of
one of the oldest of them: aye, that same Bennett who in his *Herald* says, the Negro never flourishes except in slavery! Dr. Grant,
of New York, preached the doctrine of Negro intellectual inferiority on the same platform with Frederic Douglass! Dr.
Sleigh, another Irishman, published a work to prove such allega-
tions, in the city of Philadelphia, where there are 20,000 or
30,000 blacks, a due proportion of whom are equal to any of
Dr. Sleigh's countrymen, either in America or in their fatherland. Dr. J. McCune Smith met an American in debate upon the
question of the equality or the inferiority of the Negro. His
disputant deliberately refused to call the Doctor a gentleman,
and every time he accidentally did so he corrected himself. Dr.
Smith showed himself superior, both as a gentleman and a

scholar, to this person, without making the least impression upon his manners.

The following anecdotes will illustrate my point. During the lifetime of the venerable James Forten, Esq., one of the brightest ornaments of the Negro race, a leading Colonizationist called upon him, at his residence, 92, Fifth Street, Philadelphia. Conversation ran upon the news of the day, and at that point Mr. Forten produced a newspaper in French, which he had recently received from Hayti. Mr. F. handed the newspaper to his visitor, who confessed he could not read French; whereupon Mr. Forten called his daughter, a most accomplished lady, who easily, gracefully, translated for him. That very man went to a Colonization meeting that same evening, and made a speech denying the intellectual power of the Negro to receive education!

I was travelling in a railway carriage in 1839, in company with two white persons, the one of whom was an abolitionist, the other was not. They discussed the anti-slavery question. The anti-abolitionist was a merchant, a partner in a New York house, having a branch in one of the Southern cities. His objection to abolition was the unfitness of the Negro for freedom. Among other things, he stated, that a short time previous his Southern partner came up to New York on business, and, after finishing it, asked, slaveholder as he was, to be shown the condition of the free coloured people of New York. This man said he showed him the low, dirty Negroes about Five Points—answering to Houndsditch, Rag Fair, and Petticoat Lane, in London; to the Salt Market Wynds, in Glasgow; the most immoral portions of the old town of Edinburgh; and corresponding portions in Liverpool, Dublin, and Cork. To show this slaveholder the Five Points, and its inhabitants, as specimens of Negro condition, character, and habitations, in New York, was about as fair as to go to such places as I have named, to learn English, Scotch, or Irish character. The abolitionist asked him if he took his friend to see the Rev. T. S.

Wright, the lamented predecessor of Rev. Dr. Pennington, who was then living. The pro-slavery man professed not to hear, but my friend made him hear, and he coolly answered, "No." Shortly after, Mr. Furman, the abolitionist, arrived at the place of his destination, and left us. The merchant, finding no one but myself near him, began to converse with me; and, to my utter surprise, I found him intimately acquainted, and on terms of long-standing personal friendship, with many of the most genteel, best educated, and most wealthy, of the coloured people of New York State. That was the man who took a Southern slaveholder to the lowest and most degraded of our population, to impress him with an idea of what we were. I am sorry to say, that ninety-nine in every hundred of the traducers of the Negro in America, whether Yankee born or Englishmen Yankeeized, generally act with equal unfairness, under the aggravation of equal intelligence. As a rule—such is my experience and observation—they who treat and speak of the Negro worst, are they who know him best. I could fill this book with such instances.

3. In spite of the foregoing facts, the coloured people who are intelligent and prominent make friends for themselves among the very best classes of Americans; and the same is true, in its degree, of black men in inferior positions. I have known a black man to move into a neighbourhood where it was difficult for him to rent a house to live in, because of his colour; but edging his way in, and proving himself as good a mechanic, farmer, labourer, or artisan, as anyone else, he was sure to be patronized and respected by the very best customers. I have known whites to go to hear a Negro lecture, or preach, just for the fun of the thing: they have come away saying the most extravagant things in his favour. My advice to our people always was, Do the thing you do in the best possible manner: if you shoe a horse, do it so that no white man can improve it; if you plough a furrow, let it be ploughed to perfection's point; if you make a shoe, make it to bespeak further patronage from the fortunate wearer of it; if you

shave a man, impress him with the idea that *such* shaving is a rare luxury; if you do no more than black his boots, send him out of your boot-black shop looking towards his feet, divided in his admiration as between the blacking and the perfection of its application. As one of our own poets hath it,

> *Honour and fame from no distinction rise:*
> *Act well your part*—there *all the honour lies.*

I am happy to say, such is the good sense and honourable manly ambition of my people, that such advice was always approved and followed: indeed, it was seldom needed.

Mr. Douglass, as an orator, is winning for himself and his people not only fame, but, what is far better, the power of great and varied usefulness. Among his most honest admirers are persons in the highest walks of life: distinguished alike for their high positions, and their entire fitness for them. At the risk of seeming immodest, I may say, that my own short career engaged for me the personal friendship of persons who have no superiors; and whose friendship was the more highly prized, as it was the result of my own efforts—the acknowledgment of an equality previously denied to the Negro, on their part—and a favourable sign for the future of my people. The same is true of every prominent coloured man in that country.

4. The coloured people in the United States are in no hopeless circumstances. It has already ceased to be a marvel, that a coloured man can do certain things denied to be within his power thirty years ago. A State or a National Convention of black men is held. The talent displayed, the order maintained, the demeanour of the delegates, all impress themselves upon the community. All agree, that to keep a people rooted to the soil, who are rapidly improving, who have already attained considerable influence, and are marshalled by gifted leaders (men who show themselves qualified for legislative and judicial positions), and to doom them to a state of perpetual vassalage, is altogether out

of the question. They cannot be turned back, they cannot be kept stationary; they must and they will advance. Then, it is well known that social progress is made with gigantic strides, when once a movement is made in a right direction. That impulse, a mighty impetus, has been given; and already signs of vigorous and hopeful advance have been developed as the result. Then look at the materials which the blacks have at command. They have the world's history before them. They are *Americans;* they are well taught in the history of their native country; they know the avenues to, and springs of, the most important and characteristic feelings of the American heart. They know what to say, to whom to say it, and at what time. They are wronged: their wrongs are violations of American profession, and what they know ought to be American principle. They are connected socially, by choice and by force, with the subjects of the most cruel oppression on the face of the earth. The more highly they are cultivated, the more keenly they feel their wrongs. And I add, with perfect deliberation, and with philosophical objects before me, only they are of mixed blood; and that fact, with the others, makes them at this day, to say nothing of the future, confessedly the most eloquent, the most impassioned, the most powerful, the most impressive, and, when once heard, the most popular, men in the anti-slavery field of labour. This was true many years ago: every year increases its illustrations; until now, no man is so eagerly, so tearfully, so rapturously, listened to in America, on this subject, as the coloured man. Already has the anti-slavery advocacy, for all effective purposes, passed into their hands: and America now stands in the position of a great country, nominally free, de-priving one sixth of her citizens of freedom, and robbing those not actually enslaved of an equality which God has given to all nations of men, denying them even the title to it and fitness for it; while these *coloured men,* armed with the panoply of American birth, feelings, and history—gifted with talents surpassed by none—burning with an indignant sense of their own wrongs, and the enslavement of their brethren—highly skilled in the use of their powers and talents, and having gained the ears of their fellow citizens—are demonstrating the injustice of the position which they occupy, and the arrogant hypocrisy of that of their enemies.

Now, when it is considered that (with perhaps the exception of the Welsh) the Negroes are, in feeling, the most *religious* people in the world, and that in all they do they are guided, restrained, but made the more ardent, by the religious passion within them, you cannot imagine that this people will or *can* eventually fail in either recovering their rights, or attracting the thunderbolts of divine vengeance upon their oppressors. What says all past history, upon this subject? When did God cease to hear the cry of the oppressed? What, in history, is the final result of the upward struggles of an oppressed but advancing, praying, God-fearing people? But, to do as our American brethren like to do—leave out all considerations of divine interpositions, or to calculate upon indefinite forbearance of Deity—neither of which is admissible— any one can tell that, left to themselves, these causes must produce one or two important results. The young blacks of the Republic are everywhere acquiring a love for martial pastimes. Their independent companies of military are becoming common in many of the large towns. This, with other things, shows that they aspire to anything and everything within the reach of man. And as their fathers fought bravely in the former wars of the Republic, who can deny them the use of arms? Having almost everything to contend for, it is easy to see, that what wrongs they and their brethren suffer will so stimulate them as to draw out energies which not only would not be exhibited, in other circumstances, but which even themselves would scarcely believe to be theirs. The whites have all they want, and are satisfied. They are already most rapidly degenerating: they are given almost solely to the acquisition of money and the pursuit of pleasure. They will therefore become less and less active, more and more lethargic, while in their very midst the blacks will become less lethargic, and more energetic; until the latter, for all practical purposes, will exhibit, and wield too, more of the real American character, its manliness, its enterprise, its love of liberty, than the former. I speak not as a prophet: I only speak of causes now existing and in active operation, already producing some of their inevitable results. I illustrate my idea by a fact. In 1849 I introduced a young lady into my family, intending that she should teach my children, for which she was then qualified, being older and far better educated than they. In 1851 she recited in the same class with them; in 1853 she was the pupil of one of them, and lagging behind the other. Thus will it be, in my opinion, as between the blacks and the whites in America. They are now in the relation of teacher and taught, in the matter of liberty and progress; they will reverse positions ere the struggle be over, unless sudden unforeseen changes occur.

Such are the signs of the times; nor is this the first time such signs have been seen in similar circumstances. But, aside from this, that some may regard as an extreme representation of the case, let it be supposed that the free blacks shall go on and progress as they have for the past forty years: if they should do no more than simply improve themselves, without exhibiting the lofty patriotism which now so nobly prompts them to efforts for self-elevation, their gradual improvement would draw toward them the gaze, perhaps the admiration, of all the Old World. Individuals among them would be known in Europe, and public attention would be directed to the class through these individuals; and it would be altogether vain for Americans to attempt to disparage them, as they now do, in Europe. William Wells Brown was a slave; so was Garnett. Who, that saw them in Germany, France, or England, would believe any American who should presume to deny the qualities and claims of the American Negro? William Craft was a slave: many who have heard him with intense delight (as do most who hear) will feel that the American Negro is the most outraged of men—not mere animals, but *men*. O my suffering, sighing people, there is hope for you—hope in your improvement, in your own powers; in the gathering, increasing sympathy of Europe; but, most of all, in the promises of the faithful God.

CHAPTER VII

Terminus of Labours in the United States

Having given a sketch of the nature and character of my labours in the United States, it remains that I now speak of the
events which led to their termination. It is well known, that in
defiance of law and custom, and what seemed to some the provisions of the constitution, the abolitionists refused to aid in the
capture of a fugitive slave; they rendered him all manner of
assistance in effecting his escape; they would secure for him a
place of safety; they would aid him on his way to Canada; they
would legally and otherwise protect him, if he remained among
them; they would help and encourage him in resisting his pursuers: in fact, they would do for him just what they would have
him do for them in an exchange of circumstances. This was both
illegal and unchristian, in the view of the great majority of the
American people, especially the lawmakers and the religious
teachers. There was, indeed, a regularly organized society, distinct as an organization from the Anti-Slavery Society, to aid
fugitives; and that society, called the *Vigilance* Committee, at its
head quarters, New York, annually published its report, held
platform meetings, &c. So effective was this action, that it became
almost needless for a slave to go further than the Border States.
In Boston, it was boasted, a slave could not be captured. There
were men who said the same of numerous other towns; attempts
to take them often proved utter failures. Before the anti-slavery
movement, a slaveholder or a kidnapper could take any man

he pleased, where he pleased and when he pleased. This had been done in every State but Vermont, and any justice of the peace was quite competent to settle for ever the grave question of a man's right to liberty. Now, though the law was not altered, such was the state of public feeling, generated by the abolitionists, that a slave could escape, going into an adjoining State, tell his story publicly, state who his master was, where he lived, how his escape was effected, through what places he passed, who aided him, and all about it; and the whole community would say to him, "Remain here; you are safe." Doubtless this partook somewhat of the Yankee habit of boasting; it was a profession of freedom and a promise of protection that needed some severe testing, to prove its real strength: but that such was the public feeling, that men really and truly meant what they said, there never was the least reason to doubt.

The South became exasperated: their chattels, among which were persons inheriting the blood and the lineage of their masters (this strange-sounding medley is no more incongruous than true) were escaping from them; each carried off in his own person from 400 to 2,000 dollars. There was no telling what amount of property had thus been abstracted—or, rather, stolen itself: but certain it was, that every morning some planter found, or rather did not find, some slave or slaves—they had fled. They were constantly going; and what made the matter more awkward was, when once gone, they would not return of their own accord, or for the sake of anybody else. The South knew that there is a clause in the Federal Constitution, providing for the extradition of "persons held to service or labour." They knew that a great majority of the people had been but too successfully taught the false and foolish doctrine, that those described as "persons," meant slaves. They knew as well, that Congress, in 1793, passed a law for the enforcement of this clause of the constitution, with this strange interpretation. They knew also that all the courts held the same view. In 1842 a decision was rendered in the

Supreme Court to the same effect—*i.e.*, that "persons held to service or labour" included slaves. The anti-slavery, or rather the strictly legal common-sense, objection to that interpretation, is, that in law slaves are not "persons," but "chattels"—that inasmuch as the clause described them as "persons," they had no right under that clause to capture them as "chattels." As persons and chattels were neither identical nor similar in law, but opposites, and as the clause in question calls them the former, it could not at the same time intend to describe them as the latter. A law must not be interpreted to *mean* the *converse* of what it *says!*

But what of this? Were not the Supreme Court judges appointed by a President and a senate always subservient to slavery? Were not a number of the judges themselves slaveholders? Were not those judges who were non-slaveholders among the bitterest and most cringing slaveocrats in the nation? and were they not made judges in view of that fact? Could they have been made judges without it? Then, as Congressmen (the majority of whom are lawyers), and inferior judges, and lawyers, and almost everyone else, took their legal opinions from the Supreme Court, what *it* held to be law *was* law, of course. This the South, who are the real rulers of the nation, very well knew; and knowing their advantage, they followed it up, and maintained it. They demanded that the law of 1793 should be enforced—that this anti-slavery sentiment should be suppressed, and that further agitation of the question should cease. The constitution must be understood as they understood it; and therefore slaves escaping *must be given up.* Anti-slavery sentiment was not suppressed, nor in any one thing were these demands complied with. At last, adopting a two-fold expedient, which never yet failed when once faithfully and vigorously applied—viz., threatening to walk out of the Union, if their demands were not yielded; and appealing to the cupidity, fears and ambition, of leading Northern politicians—they received a promise that something should be done.

Accordingly, such Northern men as Daniel Webster and Daniel S. Dickinson (how the name 'Daniel' can be perverted!) set themselves about the work of seeking to persuade Northern men to yield.

It should have been mentioned, that so powerful had become the hostility to the extradition of fugitive slaves, that, taking advantage of the Supreme Court decision in 1842, to the effect that States need not aid in the capture of runaway slaves, but that the *duty* of doing so rested entirely with the federal officers, some eleven States passed solemn laws forbidding any of their officers from aiding in this horrible business, any of the judges from sitting upon such cases; forbidding the use of any of their jails or public buildings for the detention of a fugitive slave, or any of their citizens doing any of these things, directly or indirectly. Mr. Webster, and the men of his class, sought to persuade the people of the North to "conquer their prejudices" against slave-catching. He advised them to perform "the disagreeable *duty*" of playing the human bloodhound. "Any one," he said, "could perform an agreeable duty." The demands of the South, the practical *masters* of the nation, must be complied with. So in 1850 a law was passed, called the Fugitive Slave Law, providing most minutely, most perfectly, for the catching and the delivery of fugitives, by processes the loosest, the most summary, most contrary to all the old law standards and maxims of the last five centuries. Its provisions abolished the inviolability of a man's house, person, and papers—the right to life, liberty, and property, without due process of law—the right of being confronted with one's accusers—the writ of *habeas corpus*—the necessity of a particular description of the place to be searched and the person to be seized—the right of trial by jury, and the right of appeal: each of which is solemnly and emphatically guaranteed by the constitution. It was a most despotic law, passed by despots and their tools, for the most despotic of purposes—the replunging of an American citizen, who had escaped therefrom, into the hell of American slavery; and the prohibition of American freemen from doing aught to aid a flying brother man, threatened with re-enslavement!

In the Senate, when this Act passed, there were as many Northern as Southern senators: in the House of Representatives there was a clear decided majority of Northern representatives. This law of barbarism was passed, therefore, by Northern men. It was taken to the President, for his signature. He too was a Northern man—Millard Fillmore, of New York. He had the right to veto it. He was sworn conservator of the constitution. It violated more principles, provisions, and express clauses, of the constitution, than any law ever framed since the constitution was adopted; it was, in fact, a revolutionary, a treasonable measure. No one knew this better than Millard Fillmore. But, pshaw! *the South must be served.* M. Fillmore owed this elevation to them; they, not the constitution, must be looked after; and, with eager "hot and hurried haste," he signed it, on the eighteenth of September, lacking but one day of six hundred and twenty-four years and three months from the signing of Magna Charta—and it became a law. Now, if a fugitive go to New York, he may be followed and brought back. If any man "harbour or conceal him, or aid and abet in his escape, or hinder or obstruct the claimant, or rescue him or attempt to rescue him," it shall cost him a thousand dollars; if he does all four of these, four times as much. Nor is this all: "for either of said offences he shall be imprisoned a term not exceeding six months." Nor is this all: after suffering and paying the above, he shall also "forfeit and pay a sum not exceeding one thousand dollars, to be collected in an action of debt."—(*Section VII.*)

Five thousand dollars—in that dollar-loving country—and two years' imprisonment, for what one might do in behalf of one poor fugitive! My mother was then living, and a fugitive. Gladly should I have done all four of these prohibited things, in her dear behalf.

But the passing of this law, striking a fell blow as it did at white men's liberties, as well as black men's, was not the worst of it. Though strong and high indignation had been expressed against the law—though the impossibility of enforcing it was insisted on and declared by numerous meetings in almost every part of the country—yet, at the bidding of the slave power, through the Northern politicians, the law was enforced: victim after victim was yielded up on the altar of this bloody Moloch. It is done until this very day.

Still, this was not the worst. The most popular pulpits of the North, of Puritan New England, even rung with preachments favouring it, and urging the people to obey it, and advising Negroes to submit to it. One doctor of divinity* said he would give up his own mother, rather than disobey the law, and endanger the Union. He now says, he said his brother. Pity that any woman ever bore such a son—that she should have given birth to two, and one be such a Cain!

I am come to the darkest page in my native country's history: I am chronicling her deepest degradation. But so it is: it stands out there, in bold relief, a part of her history. Whether she can ever be recovered from this deep, foul, *chosen* disgrace, or not, is beyond my humble ken. But that darkness was relieved by some most merciful tokens. In this time of yielding principle, forswearing faith, and succumbing to the slave power, which did more than anything ever before to debauch American morals and blacken American character—in this time when priest and Levite walked on the other side, neglecting the poor wounded man by the wayside—while these classes were horrifying all Europe, and drawing maledictions upon their country from all honest hearts—there stood a host of faithful men and women, prepared for the trial and enduring it; ready for the sacrifice, and making it. Having put their hands to the plough, they could not turn back. They

* Rev. O. Dewey, D.D. The Rev. Dr. Spring says, "a man's running away from slavery is *primá facie* evidence of his being a bad man."

loved the slave, the fugitive, the suffering black, and their
Heaven-derived anti-slavery principles, more than money, office,
caste, or honours; and now that "the furnace was heated seven
times hotter than it was wont to be heated," they were blessed
with the grace of constancy to refuse, even more resolutely than
before, to bow before the golden image to which the great majority paid obeisance. If trials do not make men, they *may* develope what they are; and, what is more, they will prove who can
endure the stern demands of principle, in the hour of suffering.
And, blessed be the God of the poor! not a few were there, in that
day, in my native country, in the senate chamber, the hall of
representatives, on the judicial bench, the ministerial office, the
pulpit, and in private walks, who, having counted the cost, were
not only unflinching, unwavering, but "waxed valiant *in* the
fight." John Parker Hale, William H. Seward, and Salmon P.
Chase, were in the Senate; Joshua R. Giddings, George W. Julian,
and a few others, were in the House of Representatives; and so
long as time shall last, so long shall the brave minority opposition
given by these gentlemen to this infamous measure be remembered wth delight and gratitude. These persons have not been
without their successors. Charles Sumner—the learned, classic,
elegant, manly, heroic Charles Sumner (whom Lord Elgin told
me he regards as a personal friend, because of his anti-slavery
principles, as well as high character and shining talents)—has
since adorned that Senate; so has Henry Wilson, the self-made
(another name for God-made) champion of freedom; and Gerrit
Smith, Channey L. Knapp, and others in the House, enough to
keep the voice of manly remonstrance ever sounding in the ears
of the guilty nation.

While, too, the religion of the country had become, if possible,
more corrupt than even its politics—while its reverend doctors
of divinity, venerable in years and in learning, were counseling
obedience to this satanic law (many of whom, by the way, would
like to pass, and, unfortunately, with too much complacency and

too little scrutiny, *do* pass, as acceptable anti-slavery men in England)—there were, in a few scattered pulpits from one end of the land to the other, as if God would have the leaven well diffused, some who ceased not day nor night, in good or evil report, to lift up their voices against these crying abominations—slavery, the Fugitive Slave Law; the yielding of the press, the legislature, the courts, and the pulpit, to these demands against God and man. They were for "obeying God rather than man." They had learned that such obedience, even in a free Christian country, might cost something: they were prepared for the cost, even though they should be called upon

To weary torturers, and to rejoice in fire.

This brilliant galaxy of God-fearing men, shining as stars of the first magnitude in the moral firmament of the country, and shining all the brighter, with a light all the more welcome, in contrast with the surrounding blackness, included some honoured names which, to be associated with, is akin to the associations of patriarchs, apostles, and martyrs. Honoured of God, they shall be honoured of men, while virtuous constancy, unpurchasable integrity, and heroic devotion to principle and truth, shall be admired of mortals or angels. My pen leaps to name some of them: I cannot mention all. To name some, and omit others, were invidious in any man, but especially ungracious in so humble a coadjutor—follower and admirer, rather—of them, as myself. I will, however, name one; one whom all the others delight to honour, the chief though not the oldest of his family, a standing living rebuke to the men of his class and profession, but an honour to *the profession itself*—the bold, the honest, the self-sacrificing, the amiable, Henry Ward Beecher.

As an humble advocate of anti-slavery principles, it was my duty, under the guidance of the great chiefs of the cause, to adapt myself to those forms and phases of slavery's progress and demands which arose from time to time to public view—to drag out

to the light secret plots and mischievous though hidden machinations of the slave power—to preach the gospel of deliverance to
the captives—and to aid, counsel and encourage, my own, the
black people, in what was needed in their peculiar circumstances.
Thus, when the annexation of Texas was on the *tapis*, that must
be exposed and denounced; when the war with Mexico was conceived and brought forth, on purpose to lengthen the cords and
strengthen the stakes of slavery, that must be made a prominent
topic; when the admission of new Slave States, as Florida and
Texas, was sought, opposition to *that* was the duty of the day;
when, as in New York State, in 1846, it was proposed to continue
the odious clause of State constitution by which black men were
disallowed to vote on terms of equality with whites, the iniquity
of that proposition must be holden up; when it was the intention
of slaveocratic politicians to give slavery "aid and comfort" by
electing to the Presidential chair some such arrant slaveholder as
Henry Clay, or some such convenient, subservient instrument of
slavery as Millard Fillmore, and to seduce abolitionists into voting for them, facts in the long, dark, pro-slavery and slaveholding history of these men must be "kept before the people"; when
the Methodist, the Episcopalian, the Presbyterian or the Baptist
Church, or some of their benevolent organizations, did as they
never failed to do, annually deliver themselves of some additional pro-slavery religious progeny, the testimony of God's Word
must be uttered against these; and when the Fugitive Slave Law
began to cast the darkness of its shadow upon us, threatening its
coming self, the country must be warned against this; and finally,
when it had passed, the twofold duty of putting on record, upon
the roll of infamy, for the gaze of an indignant posterity, the
names of the conspirators against liberty who passed it, signed it,
enforced it, and executed it, and those worst of all others, who
gave it pulpit sanction; and of giving it our *heartiest* opposition,
at all hazards and under all circumstances—must be performed.
To what effect, if any, I performed my humble share in this work,

it is not for me to say: that I laboured honestly and with good purpose, I trust few will deny who honour me with their acquaintance.

In the summer of 1851, business called me to travel in various parts of the country. I visited numerous districts of New York, Pennsylvania, Ohio, Illinois, Wisconsin, Michigan, and Indiana, as well as Connecticut, Rhode Island, Massachusetts, and New Hampshire. Smarting as we were under the recently passed Fugitive Law—and these irritations being inflamed and aggravated by the dragging of some poor victim of it from some Northern town to the South and to slavery, every month or so—of course this law became *the theme* of most I said and wrote. In October, Mrs. Ward accompanied me in a tour through Ohio. We were about finishing that tour, when we saw in the papers an account of the Gorsuch case, in Christiana, Pennsylvania. That was a case in which the Reverend Mr. Gorsuch went armed to the house of a Negro, in the suburbs of the town named, in search of a slave who had escaped from him. The owner of the house denied him admittance. Several Negroes, armed, stood ready inside the house to defend it against the *reverend* slave-catcher and his party—the latter declaring his slave was in that house, avowing his determination to have him, if he went to h—ll after him; and, intending to intimidate the Negroes, fired upon the house with a rifle. Fortunately none of the besieged party were killed; but, they returned Mr. Gorsuch's fire, and *he* dropped a corpse!

The authorities arraigned these poor Negroes for murder. They seemed determined to have their blood. Upon reading this, I handed the paper containing the account to my wife; and we concluded that resistance was fruitless, that the country was hopelessly given to the execution of this barbarous enactment, and that it were vain to hope for the reformation of such a country. At the same time, my secular prospects became exceedingly involved and embarrassed; and willing as I might be to be one of a forlorn hope in the assault upon slavery's citadel, I had no reasonable prospect of doing so, consistently with my duty to my family. The anti-slavery cause does not, cannot, find bread and education for one's children. We then jointly determined to wind up our affairs, and go to Canada; and, with the remnant of what might be left to us, purchase a little hut and garden, and pass the remainder of our days in peace, in a free British country.

Such was our conclusion on Monday, the 29th of September, 1851. Residing then at Syracuse, we went home, arriving on Wednesday, the first day of October. We found the whole town in commotion and excitement. We soon learned the cause. A poor Mulatto man, named Jerry, at the suit of his own father had been arrested under the Fugitive Law, had been before the Negro-catcher's court, had escaped, had been pursued and retaken, and was now being conveyed to prison. I went to the prison, and, in company with that true sterling friend of the slave, the Reverend Samuel J. May, was permitted to go in and see the man. He had fetters on his ankles, and manacles on his wrists. I had never before, since my recollection, seen a chained slave. He was a short, thick-set, strongly built man, half white though slave born. His temperament was ardent, and he was most wonderfully excited. Though chained, he could not stand still; and in that narrow room, motioning as well as he could with his chained, manacled hands, and pacing up and down as well as his fetters would allow, fevered and almost frenzied with excitement, he implored us who were looking on, in such strains of fervid eloquence as I never heard before nor since from the lips of man, to break his chains, and give him that liberty which the Declaration of Independence assumed to be the birthright of every man, and which, according to the law of love, was our duty towards a suffering brother.

I cannot recall the *ipsissima verba* of his eloquent pleading. As far as I can revive his sentences in my memory, he exclaimed —"Gentlemen, behold me, and these chains! Why am I bound thus, in a free country? Am I not a man like yourselves? Do you not suppose I feel as other men feel? Oh, gentlemen, what have

I done to deserve this cruel treatment? I was at my work, like an honest industrious man. I was trying to act the part of a good citizen; but they came upon me, and accused me of crime. I knew I was innocent; but I felt it my duty to go before the court, to declare and to prove my innocence. For that reason I let that little Marshal, I think you call him, put handcuffs on me. You know, gentlemen, handcuffs don't hurt an innocent man! But after they put the irons on me, they told me they were taking me as a runaway slave! Didn't I tell you I was innocent? They confessed I was. If I had known what they were about, do you think I should have *let that little ordinary man put irons on me?* No, indeed! I have told you how deceitfully they took me. When I saw a good chance, I thought it was not wrong to break away from them. I watched my opportunity: I dashed out of the door; I ran like a man running for his freedom; but they overtook me, and brought me back, and here I am like a wild beast, chained and caged.

"Gentlemen, is this a free country? Why did my fathers fight the British, if one of their poor sons is to be treated in this way? I beseech you, gentlemen, as you love your own liberty, break these chains of mine; yes, and break the chains that bind my brethren in the South, too. Does not the Bible say, 'Break every yoke, and let the oppressed go free'? Don't you believe the Bible? I can't read it as some of you can, but I believe what it says, and I ask you, gentlemen, to do for me what that book commands. Suppose that any one of you were in my position. What would you wish me to do? I beg you, gentlemen, to do for me what you would wish, were you where I am. Are not all men born free and equal? How is it, then, that I must wear these chains? Give me, O give me, gentlemen, that freedom which you say belongs to all men, and it is all I ask. Will you who are fathers, and brothers, see a man dragged in chains to the slavery of Tennessee, which I know is worse than death itself? In the name of our common nature—in the name of the Declaration of Independence—in the name of that law in the Bible which says, "do as you would be done by"—in the name of God, our common Father—do break these chains, and give me the freedom which is mine because I am a man, and an American."

What a sight! and what sounds! A slave, in a free Northern city chained as no felon would be chained, with the blood of Anglo-Saxons in his veins. Still, a slave; the son of a wealthy planter in Tennessee, and still a slave; arrested by a United States officer and several assistants, who were sworn to support the glorious Federal Constitution, serving under the freest government under the sun, the land of liberty, the refuge for the oppressed of all the world! And for what was he arrested? what was his crime? A love of that liberty which we all declared to be every man's inalienable right! And this slave was quoting the Declaration of Independence in chains! He was not the subject of some Czar, some

Turbaned Turk or fiery Russ:

no, he was an American by birth, and a slave as well; so said the chains upon him: and on his lips were liberty's and religion's great watchwords! I never saw extremes so meet. I never saw how hollow a mockery was our talk about liberty, and our professions of Christianity. I never felt how really we were all subject to the slave power; I never felt before the depth of degradation there is in being a professed freeman of the Northern States. Daniel Webster had, a few months before, predicted the execution of the Fugitive Law in that very town. The people laughed him to scorn. We now felt, however, how much better he knew the depths to which Northern men can sink than we did. While these thoughts were galloping through our brains, this manacled son of a white man proceeded with his oration in his chains, and we felt dumb and powerless. A great crowd gathered about the door; and after looking on and drinking in as much of the scene as my excitable nature would allow, I turned to go away, and at that moment the crowd demanded a speech of me. I spoke. I ceased; but I never felt the littleness of my always little speeches, as I did at that moment. Jerry had made *the* speech of the occasion, and all I could say was but tame and spiritless in comparison with his

Words that breathed and thoughts that burned.

The substance of what I said is as follows:—"Fellow citizens! we are here in most extraordinary circumstances. We are witnessing such a sight as, I pray, we may never look upon again. A man in chains, in Syracuse! Not a felon, yet in chains! On trial, is this man, not for life, but for liberty. He is arrested and held under a law made by 'Us the People'—pursuant, we pretend, to a clause in the constitution. That constitution was made 'to secure the blessings of liberty to ourselves and our posterity.' Here is a man one of 'ourselves'; and the colour he bears shows that he belongs not altogether to my race, but that he is one of the 'posterity' of those who framed and adopted our Federal Constitution. So far are we from 'securing' to him the 'blessings of liberty,' that we have arrested him, confined him, and chained him, on purpose to inflict upon him the curses of slavery.

"They say he is a slave. What a term to apply to an American! How does this sound beneath the pole of liberty and the flag of freedom? What a contradiction to our 'Declaration of Independence'! But suppose he be a slave: is New York the State to recognize and treat him as such? Is Syracuse the city of the Empire State in which the deeds which make this a day unfortunately memorable, should be perpetuated? If he be not a slave, then, he is the most outraged man we ever saw.

"What did our fathers gain by the seven years' struggle with Great Britain, if, in what are called Free States, we have our fellow citizens, our useful mechanics and skilful artisans, chained and enslaved? How do foreign nations regard us, when knowing that it is not yet three short months since we were celebrating the Declaration of Independence, and to-day we are giving the most palpable denial to every word therein declared?

"But I am told that this is a legal transaction. That it is wrong

and unwise to speak against a judicial proceeding, not yet completed: I admit it all. I make no pretensions to speak wisely. I
have heard a speech from Jerry. I feel for him, as for a brother;
and under that feeling, I may not speak quite so soberly as I
ought. 'Oppression maketh a wise man mad.' I feel oppressed in
a twofold sense. Yonder is my brother, in chains. Those chains
press upon my limbs. I feel his sufferings, and participate his
anguish. I feel, and we may all feel, oppressed in another sense.
Here are certainly five-and-twenty hundred of us, wild with excitement in behalf of our chained brother, before our eyes, and
we are utterly powerless to help him! We hear his strong, thrill-
ing appeals, until our hearts sicken and our heads ache; but there
is none among us that has the legal power to lift a hand in his
defence, or for his deliverance. Of what advantage is it that we
are free? What value is there in our freedom, while our hands are
thus tied?

"Fellow citizens, whatever may be the result of these proceedings—whether our brother leaves the court, a declared freeman
or a chained slave—upon us, the voters of New York State, to a
very great extent, rests the responsibility of this Fugitive Slave
Law. It is for us to say whether this enactment shall continue to
stain our statute books, or be swept away into merited oblivion.
It is for us to say whether the men who made it, and those who
execute it before our faces, shall receive our votes, or shall by
those votes be indignantly rebuked. Tell me, ye sturdy working
men of Onondago, shall your votes be consecrated to the latter,
or prostituted to the former? Do you swear fealty to freedom this
day? Do you promise, so help you God! so to vote, as that your
sanction never more shall be given to laws which empower persons to hunt, chain, and cage, MEN, in our midst? (cries of 'yes,
yes.') Thank you, fellow citizens, in the name of our brother in
prison! thank you for your bold, manly promise! May we all
abide by it, until deeds of darkness like the one we now lament
shall no longer mar our institutions and blacken our history."

But the crowd felt rightly. They saw Gerrit Smith and me go off arm in arm to hold a consultation, and, two and two, they followed us. Glorious mob! unlike that of 1834, they felt for the poor slave, and they wished his freedom. Accordingly, at nine o'clock that evening, while the court was in session trying Jerry for more than his life, for his liberty, the mob without threw stones into the window, one of which came so near to the judge that, in undignified haste, he suddenly rose and adjourned the courts. In an hour from that time, the mob, through certain stalwart fellows whom the Government have never had the pleasure of catching, broke open the door and the side of the building where Jerry was, put out the lights, took him out in triumph, and bore him away where the slave-catchers never after saw him.

The Marshal of the United States, who had him in custody, was so frightened that he fled in female attire: brave man! According to the Fugitive Law, he had to pay Jerry's master one thousand dollars; for so the law expressly ordains.

An assistant Marshal, who was aiding this one, fired a pistol when *entrée* was first made. He injured no one, but a stout stick struck his arm and broke it. Escaping out of a window soon after, he broke the same arm again, poor man! These two were not like a Marshal in Troy, in the same State, who, rather than capture a slave, resigned his office.

The papers in the interest of the Government, in publishing an account of this affair, connected my name with it in a most prominent manner. The Marshal with the broken arm was especially commended to my tender regard. The Government, under the advice of Daniel Webster (whose Christianity, I find, is highly lauded in this country; it was always a *res non* in his own), ordered all the parties, directly or indirectly engaged in the rescuing of Jerry, to be put on trial for *treason!* For it was the doctrine of Mr. Webster and Mr. Fillmore, that opposition to the Slave Law was "treason, and drew after it all the consequences of treason." I knew enough to understand that *one* of the "conse-

quences drawn after treason" is a *hempen rope.* I had already become hopeless of doing more in my native country; I had already
determined to go to Canada. Now, however, matters became *ur-
gent.* I could die; but was it duty? I could not remain in that country without repeating my connection with or participating in such
an affair as I was then *guilty* of. If I did my duty by my fellow
men, in that country, I must go to prison, perhaps; certainly, if
the Government had their way, to the gallows. If I did not, I must
go to perdition. Betwixt the two, my election was made. But then,
what must become of my family, both as to their bread in my
then circumstances, and as to their liberty in *such* a country?
Recollecting that I had already my wife's consent (without which
I could not take any important step of the sort) to go to Canada,
I concluded that I must go immediately. I went; and a month
or two after, my family followed: since which time we have each
and severally been, *con amore,* the most loyal and grateful of
British subjects.

Jerry lived at Kingston, Canada, until the latter part of 1853,
when he died, a free man, by virtue of living in British soil. The
courts would not entertain the charge of treason against those
accused in this case, from its manifest absurdity. They did hold,
however, that they had broken the Fugitive Law, and must be
tried for that. Luckily, but one person who was accused was ever
convicted. He died before the court, in its mercilessness, could
wreak its full vengeance upon him. He was innocent, I know.

When the accused were summoned to Auburn, twenty-six miles
from Syracuse, to attend trial, the Railway Company provided
carriages for the accused and their wives, *gratis.* Returning from
Auburn, several of those ladies were in the large carriage into
which the Government prosecutor entered. They unanimously requested his departure. They afterwards made up a purse of *thirty*
pieces of silver, of the smallest coin of the country, and presented
to him—wages of iniquity and treachery. The chains (which I
helped to file off) of Jerry were packed in a neat mahogany box,

and sent to President Fillmore. The Hon. W. Seward voluntarily
became bail for the accused. He has been Governor of his native
State. He is now one of its senators. This, however, is his highest
honour. So he esteems it.

In conclusion I beg to say, that the passage of the Nebraska
Bill, and the outrages following it under sanction of the Government in Kansas, but confirms the opinion I formed four years
ago, as to the impossibility—by any means now extant, and they
are as wise as human ingenuity can invent—of reforming that
country. The Government is too much at the mercy of 62,000
slaveholders; the people are too well content to let things remain
as they are—the Churches, generally, cling with too great tenacity to their time-honoured pollutions to admit of any prospect
of reformation at present, while the gloomiest future seems to
overhang the country. The only hopeful spot in the American
horizon is the growing, advancing attitude of the black people.
From the whites, as a whole, I see no hopes. In the blacks I see
some precious vigorous germs springing from seeds formerly
sown, watered by many cries and tears, nourished by many prayers—the seed-sowing of Richard Allen and John Gloucester,
Thomas Sipkins, Peter Williams, George Hogarth, Samuel Todd
and William Hamilton, James Forten and Theodore Sedgewick
Wright, among the departed; of Jehiel C. Beeman, Samuel E.
Cornish, James William Charles Pennington, Christopher Rush,
William Whipper, Timothy Eato, M. M. Clarke, Stephen Smith,
and others, among the older living; the latter of whom have been
permitted to outlive the darkness of a past and see the light enjoyed by the present generation.

God grant that right may prevail, and that all things shall
further his glory!

ANTI-SLAVERY LABOURS, &c.

Part II

CANADA

CHAPTER I

First Impressions: Reasons for Labours

I made my *entrée* into Canada, as a resident and a fugitive, in October, 1851, at Montreal. I had been to Queenstown, Windsor, and Kingston, as well as Niagara Falls, at various times within eleven years, as a mere visitor, then little dreaming of the necessity of my going as a settler. After spending a very few days at Montreal, I ascended the St. Lawrence, to Kingston; thence by Lake Ontario to Toronto, my present residence. It is impossible to convey to an English reader anything like a just idea of the St. Lawrence River scenery in October. This is my third autumn in Europe; but never, in the British Isles, did I witness such splendour of landscape as that river presents, in autumn. The river is large and majestic—near Montreal, where the placid Ottawa empties itself, it is most magnificent. The Ottawa, as smooth as a polished mirror, opening its ample mouth to the width of a lake, gently glides into the St. Lawrence; the latter with a quiet dignity receiving the tribute of the former, as an empress would graciously accept the homage of a courtier, rolling downward towards the gulf, as if created on purpose to convey to the ocean the tributes and the trusts committed to it, and as if amply powerful to bear both the honour and the burden.

But going upwards, while the St. Lawrence is large and noble enough, it frequently is compressed into a comparatively small size, and falls over cascades. The steamers, however, are accommodated with canals, which admit of the continuance of naviga-

tion with but little interruption. At times, the St. Lawrence takes
the form of a wide bay, studded with tiny islets, and the latter
most densely covered with foliage—which, in early autumn, after
the first few touches of the hoar frost, assume the most gorgeously
brilliant hues. The intensest crimson, the deepest brown, the most
glowing lemon colour, with occasional intermixtures of the un-
changing foliage of the evergreens, and some intermediate colours, give these islets and these bays the appearance of immense
vases filled with bouquets of unspeakable beauty and of most imposing grandeur. Those who have seen the representation of the
brightness and charms of North American autumnal foliage, in
Mr. Friend's panorama, may feel assured that it is not in the least
exaggerated or overdrawn. I doubt if a more delightful autumnal
voyage can be made in North America, than that from Montreal
to Kingston; nor do I think that any season presents so many and
so varied attractions to the lover of the picturesque in nature, even
there, as does early autumn.

The banks of the St. Lawrence are cultivated to a considerable
extent; and that cultivation both bespeaks the industry and enterprise of the yeoman, and the profit of living on the great watery
highway to the ocean, and near to large and populous growing
towns. Beautiful fields of early-sown wheat showed themselves at
intervals all along our way; neat, and in some cases elegant, farm
houses, in the midst of orchards or ornamental trees, and nice
rustic gardens, lent not a little to the beauty and interest of the
scenery: and before I knew it, I was preferring the right hand—
the British—side of the St. Lawrence, and concluding that on *that*
side things were most inviting, and trying to reason myself into
the belief of this with a sort of patriotic feeling to which all my
life before I had been a stranger, and concerning which I had
been a sceptic. Why had I interest in the British side of the noble
St. Lawrence? What gave me a fellow feeling with those inhabitants? Simply the fact, that that country had become to me, in a
sense in which no country ever was before, my own, and those
people my fellow citizens.

After a most delightful passage of two days, I arrived at Toronto. I then renewed acquaintance, formerly made, with Thomas F. Cary, Esq., one of the sincerest, most generous, practical friends I ever had the honour to call by that endearing name. The Rev. J. Roaf, whom I had formerly met in New York, took me by the hand, as he is ever ready to do in the case of the outcast. Through the kindness of this gentleman I was introduced to the Anti-Slavery Society of Canada, of which the Rev. Dr. Willis was and is President. Thus Mr. Roaf laid me under a twofold obligation, which I never can cancel, and never forget—that for his personal kindness, and that for affording me the honour and pleasure of the acquaintance, ripened into friendship (if the Doctor will allow me to say so), of the Rev. Michael Willis, D.D.

By the advice of these gentlemen and their colleagues in the Anti-Slavery Committee, I began to lecture in Canada, and finally became the agent of the Canadian Anti-Slavery Society. While in this service, it was my duty to travel all over the country, giving facts touching American slavery, seeking to awaken an interest against slavery in Canada, asking aid and kindness towards such fugitives as needed help, forming auxiliary societies, seeking to show the influence correct sentiment in Canada might have upon the adjoining States, and doing all that could be done, by advice, encouragement, and any other means, to promote the development, the progress, all the best moral and material interests, of the coloured people. What I saw, and how I saw it, while thus engaged, shall be the theme of this part of this volume.

At first sight, one would scarcely allow that anti-slavery labours were needed in a free British colony: most persons think so. The remark was frequently made to me, when proposing a meeting, or when speaking of the subject. But it is to be remembered, that Canada lies immediately next to the States of Vermont, New Hampshire, Maine, New York, Pennsylvania, Ohio, and Michigan, to go no further westward. These State produce some of the boldest pro-slavery politicians, some of the guiltiest of slavery's abettors, some of the most heretical of slavery's pulpit parasites;

and it is sorrowful to add, some of the most successful in their several pro-slavery pursuits, that ever disgraced a free country, or desecrated free institutions, or belied our holy religion and its Author. Their history is not only contemporaneous with the history of Northern pro-slaveryism, but part and parcel of it. It is easy to see that a large population, infected with a sympathy for the slaveholder, upon our very border, must either have a serious effect upon us, in corrupting us, or we must exert a good influence upon them, provided we be, as we should be, thoroughly and incorruptibly and actively anti-slavery. Unfortunately, the former is the fact, and not the latter.

Besides, there is a vast amount of intercourse with the adjoining States, and a great deal of traffic, and Canadians travel extensively in the States, as do the people of the States in Canada. Thus the spread of slaveholding predilections is both favoured and facilitated; and, what is more, there is abundant evidence that some Americans industriously use these opportunities for the purpose of giving currency to their own notions. Moreover, in various parts of Canada Yankees have settled, and for miles around them the poison of their pro-slavery influence is felt. Some of them do not scruple to make known their desire to see Canada a part of the Union, and thus brought under the control of the slave power, and made a park for slaveholders to hunt human deer in. In the time of the Rebellion these things were said without concealment; and I have known cases where Yankees, living in Canada for fifteen years, have shown themselves hostile to our Sovereign and our free institutions until they wanted office, and then, all at once, they took the oath of allegiance!

It is not to be forgotten, on the other hand, that in the States bordering upon us are some of the most thorough out-spoken abolitionists in the American Union. Having had the honour of being one of their humblest coadjutors, I could bear testimony to their zeal and trueness; and I felt, in living so near them, I was not entirely separated from them, though in another country, so far as political relations were concerned. I knew very well, and so did the society, that co-operation and sympathy with these benevolent men and women was an object well worthy of our labours. Our fugitives passed through their hands. They conducted the underground railway. The goods were consigned to us. When they reached us they ceased to be goods, and became men *instanter*. For that purpose they sent them; for that purpose we received them. On that account they rejoiced in the true practical freedom of our country; on that account we deemed it a mercy to be permitted to live in such a country. They wrought and rejoiced on one side of the line; we did the same on the other side of the line. We were yokefellows, why should we not recognize each other as such? We did; we do yet. They attend our annual anti-slavery gatherings, we attend theirs.

But I may as well come to some more unwelcome facts, showing the need of anti-slavery labour in Canada. I class them under two heads—1st, Pro-slavery feeling; and, 2nd, Negro-hate.

1. I do not now speak of Yankee settlers, visitors, or travellers: enough has been said of them. I now speak of British-born subjects, who in Canada exhibit these two sentiments in a manner that no Yankee can excel. There are men and women in our midst who justify slavery, out and out. Some of these were heretofore planters in the West Indies. The victims of their former power being translated by the law of 1834 into freemen, they never can forgive Lord Grey, Lord Derby, nor the British Cabinet and the British people, for the demanding, advocacy, and passing, of that law. Their property, their power, their wealth in human beings, are all gone, or nearly so. They are almost all of them friends of slavery, or enemies of the Negro, or both.

Others were slaveholders aforetime in the United States. Circumstances of one sort and another have induced them to change their residences, and they now abide in our midst, participating in our freedom, and seeming to enjoy it; but they cannot forget the "leeks and the onions" of that Egypt in which they once luxuriated as small-sized, very small, Pharaohs. They are not wont to say a great deal about it, for that is not exactly the latitude for the popularity of such sentiments; but they say enough to show who and what they are. And, "tell it not in Gath!" some of both these classes of Canadian slaveocrats are coloured men!

Another class were poor in former days, and, going out to seek their fortunes, alighted upon Southern plantations, where they found lucrative employment, in slave-driving; or they have contracted marriage alliances with the daughters of slaveholders, and thus become sons-in-law and brothers-in-law to slaveholders and to slavery. Such self-seeking, pelf-seeking, devotees of the institution, are always the most clamorous in its behalf. These obey this rule with all their might.

Others still—like many, too many, Englishmen—without direct or indirect, present or past, interest in slavery, have travelled in the South; and, belonging to that extremely clever class of persons who possess the extraordinary facility of going through a country with both eyes wide open, and seeing nothing but just what they wish to see, return ignorant of any evils in slavery. "Fat, sleek, well contented slaves," were the only ones *they* saw. There were none but the kindest masters in any part of the country through which *they* travelled. They cannot distinctly remember to have heard of a slave auction, of the separation of a slave family, of a case of severe flogging, of a chained coffle gang, of murder, incest, fornication or adultery, during all the tour: in fact, they cannot believe that such things do occur! Slavery, in their eyes—sightless eyes, in chosen circumstances—is a very innocent, happy affair. True, they never wore the yoke, they never even tasted any of those sweets which they are sure were from *necessity* in slavery; but they know (that is, they know nothing) and are prepared to testify (albeit their testimony is good for nothing) that slavery is only bad, if bad at all, either in the exaggerated view of the abolitionists, or as the result of the exasperations of the amiable slaveholders by the intermeddling of the abo-

litionists. Yes, our sacred soil is polluted by the unholy tread of
pro-slavery men. Fortunately, but few of them, so far as I know,
are ministers of the gospel. Two bishops, one a Roman Catholic
and the other an Episcopalian, have the name of it. I doubt if
they are falsely charged; but still I cannot say, certainly. Some,
I know, are very chary of doing anything against slavery. I know
of one, an Englishman, in Hamilton (the Yankeeist town in Canada), who is especially cautious; and another, a Scotchman,
"canny" to the last degree, lest he should be suspected of anti-
slaveryism. And fame says—no, it was a doctor of divinity who
told me—that there is at least *one* now in Toronto, who was once
in Hamilton, who favours the pro-slavery side of the case. But the
very difficulty I have in recollecting these few, after having
travelled all over the colony, shows that, with us, anti-slavery is
the rule, pro-slavery the exception, in our clergymen, while in
the States the converse is true. That is something. But I shall not
leave this truth, so gloriously creditable to the ministry of my
adopted country, to be merely inferred from the foregoing. I shall
by and by have the great pleasure of asserting it in direct terms,
as I do now by implication.

2. Canadian Negro-haters are the very worst of their class. I
know of none so contemptible. I say this in justice to the Americans from whom I have suffered, in the States, and to whom I
have very freely alluded; and in justice, too, to such Yankees as
are now resident in Canada. And I beg to say, that I write no more
freely than I have spoken, to the very faces of those I am now
describing.

This feeling abounds most among the native Canadians, who,
as a rule, are the lowest, the least educated, of all the white population. Like the same class in England, and like the ancestors of
the American, they have not the training of gentlemen, are not
accustomed to genteel society, and, as a consequence, know but
little, next to nothing, of what are liberal enlightened views and
genteel behaviour. Having no social standing such as gentlemen

feel the necessity of maintaining, they suffer nothing from doing an ungentlemanly deed; and having neither a high aim nor a high standard of social behaviour, they seem to be, and in fact are, quite content to remain as they are. It is obvious, too, that such a class will maintain a poor petty jealousy towards those coming into the country who give any signs of prospering, especially if they are, from colour or what not, objects of dislike. In saying this feeling abounds most among native Canadians of the lower order, I do not mean that it is confined to them; nor do I mean to say that it is universal, without exception, even among this class —others exhibit it, and some of that class are among the freest from it. Still, its chief seat is in their bosoms. A few facts will make my meaning more clear.

In many cases, a black person travelling, whatever may be his style and however respectable his appearance, will be denied a seat at *table d'hôte* at a country inn, or on a steamer; and in a case or two coming under my own observation, such have been denied any sort of entertainment whatever. A gentleman of my acquaintance,* driving a good pair of horses, and travelling at leisure, with his ladylike wife, was one night, in the winter of 1851–52, denied admittance at some dozen public taverns. His lady, being of lighter complexion than himself, on one or two occasions was admitted, and was comfortably seated by the fire, and politely treated—until her darker-skinned husband came in, and then, there was no room for either. It was a bitterly cold night; and being treated—maltreated—after this manner until nearly midnight, they were at length obliged to accept of a room in which they could *sit up* all night.

In December, 1851, a black man arrived at Hamilton. He proposed going into an omnibus, to ride up from the wharf at which he landed, to Week's Hotel. The servants on the omnibus declared it was full. This being false, and it being pointed out to them,

* Mr. Peter O'Banyon.

they declared the empty seats were engaged to persons whom they were to take up on the way. After the black had been refused a passage in the omnibus, numbers of whites were freely admitted —in fact, solicited to enter it. The Negro had no means of getting up with his luggage until a kind-hearted Irishman took him in his waggon. Upon reaching Week's Hotel, he applied for lodging, but was distinctly refused a bed, solely on the ground of his colour. Such were Mr. Week's express orders.* Some six months after that, I heard of the destruction of a large amount of Week's property by fire, without shedding a single tear! Two cases like these I have not known in the States for twenty years. While these Canadian tavern-keepers have been apeing the bad character of their Yankee neighbours, they have not participated in some better influences on this subject, which the repeated droppings of the anti-slavery streamlet have caused to take place on the Yankee rock of Negro-hate. In that respect Canadian is beneath and behind Yankee feeling.

The instances which have come before me of such occurrences at taverns would be too numerous to mention. I will give two steamboat cases, of many. A gentleman of colour,† who graduated at King's College (now the university) at Toronto, was going to Kingston. He took a first class ticket, and was accordingly entitled to first class fare. When the dinner bell rang, he presented himself at the table. He was forbidden to sit down. He paid no attention to the prohibition, and was about sitting down, when the captain approached him menacingly, and was about to draw the chair from under him; when the black drew another chair, knocked the captain down, and then sat down and eat his dinner in peace. On their arrival at Kingston the captain complained of him for assault; and he of the captain, for interference with his rights. The Court fined the black gentleman five pounds and the captain twenty. And here is the grand difference betwixt Yankee

* The black person is the Writer.
† Peter Galego, Esq.

and Canadian Negro-hate—the former is sanctioned by the laws and the courts, the latter is *not*. In either of the tavern cases to which reference has been made, the parties could have had legal redress. In my own case, I went to a law office, and looked up the law upon the subject, and found it as plain as daylight; but I did not prosecute.

The other steamboat case was that of a coloured woman, with her sister and three children, coming to Canada from New York State, in 1851. The brutal captain, a Scotchman, by the name of Ker, refused them a seat anywhere else save on the deck, and refused even to take money from them for a cabin passage. His lying plea was, that it would be offensive to the passengers. Every one of them distinctly denied it; and, what is more, another coloured lady, with her husband, had and enjoyed a cabin passage! Tell me not that I speak too strongly about this case. The woman is my wife, the children ours! God forgive Captain Ker! I was stating this case one night in a lecture, and afterwards learned that among my hearers were several of the relatives of this same recreant Scotchman. Glad was I that the case was told so near home.

Speaking at Paris, in the Rev. James Vincent's church, on this subject, one night in February, 1852, the Rev. Mr. Clements, of the Wesleyan denomination, arose after I had done, and testified to the truthfulness of my statement by giving a case that had come under his own observation. The case, briefly, is this. A Scotchman, named Buchanan, one of Her Majesty's postmasters, refused to allow Mr. Clements admittance into his house, on a certain night, although Mr. C. was his pastor, and the night most stormy, and other friends distant. For what reason, think you? Because Mr. C. had been reported to have eaten at the same table with a black!

I have known several instances in which coloured children were denied their legal right to attend the public schools, by their Canadian neighbours. When Rev. Mr. King applied to Lord Elgin for the land upon which Buxton Settlement now is—a credit to all connected with it—his Lordship was besieged with petitions and remonstrances against allowing land to be sold to Negroes. I never shall forget the cool quiet manner in which the noble Earl told me that he disregarded the prayer of these petitions. I knew he had, for I had been upon the land more than once; but to hear it from his Lordship's own lips, in the presence of his Grace the Duke of Argyll, was more than an ordinary privilege. I recollect to have read of a case in the township of Gosfield, county of Essex, in which the whole mass of coloured voters were driven away from the polling place, and disfranchised for the time, by a low set of Gosfield Canadians. The injured parties had recourse to law— British law, thank Heaven!—and triumphed.

Now, far be it from me to complain of any white man's denying any Negro a seat at his table, or the association of his family. I am free to confess that, so far as a majority of them are concerned, *that* would be, to me, no honour—in many cases I could not reciprocate it, consistently with my own self-respect: and I know I speak the sentiments of my black fellow Canadians, generally. I know, too, that every man has a right to reject whom he pleases from his own social circle. Exercising this right as I do, I should be the last man in the empire to complain of it in any other man, white or black; but when it comes to ordinary public, purchased rights, legally enforced, I say I not only may complain, but am entitled so to complain that my complaint shall be both heard and felt, by the aggressor and by all concerned. When at home, I do not scruple to say, as also says the Rev. Hirnam Wilson, "he who, to gratify his petty prejudice, flies in the face of British law, to deprive any Negro (or any other man) of his rights, is a REBEL, and as such ought to be treated." Happily for us, we have equal laws in our adopted country; and I know of no judge who would sully the British ermine by swerving from duty at the bidding of prejudice, in a case coming before him as betwixt a Negro and a white man. I know of more than one instance in which our Canadian judges have acted with the most honourable impartiality in such cases; indeed, I know of no case in which they have done otherwise.

In the foregoing cases, it is seen that Canadian Negro-hate is not confined to native Canadians: others share it as well. One thing I have here the greatest pleasure in saying: I never saw the slightest appearance of it in any person in Canada recognized there, or who would be recognized here, as a gentleman. Either that class do not participate in the feeling, or their good sense and good taste and good breeding forbid its appearance. Perhaps it would not be deemed immodest in me to say, that I have had as ample opportunities to know "whereof I affirm" as any black man who ever was in Canada; and I have not observed a solitary fact contradictory to what I am now stating. I do not expect any one to understand how great is my pleasure in saying that, so far as my experience goes (and that is considerable), *the British gentleman* is a gentleman everywhere, and under all circumstances. Therefore, in every town of Canada, and especially in Toronto, I see what I saw in but extremely few and exceptional cases in the States—viz., that among gentlemen, the black takes just the place for which he is qualified, as if his colour were similar to that of other gentlemen—as if there were no Negro-crushing country hard by—as if there were no Negro-hating lower classes in their midst.

And now for an anomaly. Fugitives coming to Canada are, the majority of them, young, single men. Many more young than old, may more male than female, come. Then, these look about them for wives. Coloured young women are comparatively scarce; and, in spite of the prevalent prejudice, they marry among this very lower class of whose Negro-hate I have said so much. Hence, while you get so much evidence of the aversion betwixt these classes, you see it to be no strange thing, but a very common thing, for a black labourer to have a white wife, of a like class. In other circumstances, one would not wonder at it; but considering the bitter feeling of the whites, it is, to say the least of it, an anomaly, that blacks should propose on the one hand, and that whites should accept on the other. However, the history of poor human nature and its actions is full of these anomalies. It is certainly without pain that I add, these matches, so far as I know, are happy ones. How far this anomaly may tend in future to correct the prejudice, I cannot tell. How powerful, how wide-spread, how speedy, will be its operation, are matters upon which I do not even venture to speculate. That it is a condescension on the part of the white, that it at all elevates the individual Negro, I of course deny. That the progeny of such marriages will be physical and intellectual improvements upon the parental stock of both sides, admits of no doubt: whether a corresponding moral advantage will result, is quite another thing. That is a question *of* posterity; and *for* posterity, and *to* posterity, I beg to leave it.

I am sure I have said enough to demonstrate the need of anti-slavery labour in Canada. My experience, everywhere, confirmed the views I previously held on the matter. I went at the work under such auspices as I have mentioned, and with such obstacles as I have descanted upon. I will close this chapter by stating briefly the class of encouragements afforded me in this field of labour.

1. The hearty co-operation and earnest paternal sympathy of the Committee of the Anti-Slavery Society of Canada.

2. The very ready and very kind reception and aid I received from ministers of the gospel, of all denominations, and other individuals, almost without one exception. I may say in this place, that, as a rule, the officers and members of the Churches, and the congregation, gave a most ready response to the claims of our cause upon them. I have before my mind's eye some exceptions, no doubt; but they are in themselves and in their principles unworthy of further notice either from myself or from you, kind reader. And how do I know but, ere this, they may be converts to our principles?

3. I must be allowed once more to advert to the strong British feeling pervading the better classes, and, in this connection, to

refer to many noble Americans, resident in Canada, whose anti-slavery principles admit of neither question nor compromise.

4. The co-operation of all the better class of the coloured people, and the evident and well defined signs of improvement in the other classes of my own people. Some facts illustrating the last shall be hereafter introduced.

———

CHAPTER II

Resistance to Slave Policy

There are supposed to be in Canada some 35,000 to 40,000 coloured people. One reason why we cannot get at the actual numbers more accurately is, that in taking the Census, designations of colour, though provided for, were not made. It is only possible, therefore, to give the approximate number, from the best sources at command. The number, as I have stated it, seems to be generally regarded as correct by those who know best. The majority of these are refugees from American slavery: in fact, I do not believe that, with the exception of the children born in Canada, there are 3,000 free-born coloured persons in the whole colony. There are, however, some, and in truth many—and they are constantly increasing—of the very best classes of the free blacks of both the Northern and the Southern States, who have cast in their lot among us. There is enough to draw them. There is our impartial British liberty—the

Liberty to feel, to utter, and to argue freely—

such as they cannot have (as some of us know from dear-bought experience) in any of the States. Then, the climate is the most pleasant and the most salubrious on the American continent. I speak now particularly of Upper Canada, or Canada West. The winter there is not so severe as in Lower Canada, or Canada East. Yet, with its clear, cloudless, smokeless, fogless atmosphere—its bright blue sky, its white snowy drapery enveloping the earth—

even winter is a most beautiful season. Add the sleighing, and an English winter is thrown into the shade completely. The summers are not so hot as in Lower Canada; and, surrounded as a large portion of the Upper Province is by vast lakes, we have both the heat and the cold most agreeably modified. I never knew, or heard, or read of a more healthy country. It would seem as if Providence designed it for a vigorous people. Abundantly watered, beautifully diversified, gradually rising and as gradually falling, very regularly undulating, with but few unhealthy marshes, and, when somewhat damp, becoming dry upon the first felling of the forests, it would seem as if nought but health could abide, nought but vigour could abound, there.

And the land is so excellent. None better, to use an Americanism, "lies out of doors." Skilled, persevering labour, is remunerated upon that soil with an unequalled abundance. Besides, Canadians (especially since the Reciprocity Treaty) enjoy the best markets, near and distant, on the continent. And, lastly, the land is so cheap. The Government sells the best lands in the country at from six to eight shillings the acre, and allows ten years' credit at annual payments. There are companies and private individuals as well, who are selling lands at most reasonable prices. These advantages prove alluring to some of the best of our people in the States; and they see, too, that all other branches of business flourish as does agriculture. Hence, with that restless and resistless desire for improvement which the coloured man in all parts of America is now making manifest, many of them "shake off the dust" of the persecuting cities of their native land, and come to us. The condition, prospects, progress, enterprise, manhood, every way exhibited by this class, make them what they deserve to be, the esteemed of all classes whose good opinion is worth having. I see a recent traveller says, "there is not a respectable coloured family in Toronto." That is like "Sam Slick" (Judge Haliburton) saying, "a Negro gentleman is out of the question." I would say to that bold false writer, and to that Negro-

disparaging judge, what Robert Emmett said to Judge Norbury
—"There are men united with me * * * * * who are superior to
your own conceptions of yourself, my Lord."

But, as I have said, and as is well known—too well known
in the Slave States—the mass of our Negro population are
refugees from American despotism. So early as 1824* the attention of the American Government was turned to the numbers then
escaped and escaping to Canada. In 1827 the Secretary of State†
spoke of it as "a growing evil." The same year, the British Government were besought to make a treaty for the extradition of
slaves. In 1842, when the Ashburton Treaty was made, they
wished to smuggle into it a provision to this effect; and a little
while after, an effort was made to pervert the tenth article of that
treaty, to make it authorize the delivery of fugitives from slavery,
as felons. But the British Government consenting to none of these
propositions, this "evil," as Mr. Clay called it thirty years ago,
continues to "grow." Its "growth" is giving us a most vigorous,
most royal, most useful population, whose presence and increase
amongst us is every way most welcome.

It is a matter of great difficulty for them to reach Canada. It
follows, that *but few* comparatively can come. There is no country
in the world so much hated by slaveholders, as Canada; nor is
there any country so much beloved and sought for, by the slaves.
These two feel thus oppositely towards our fair province for the
same reason—IT IS A FREE COUNTRY. As Cowper said of England,
so is true of Canada. There, too,

> *Slaves cannot breathe.*
> *They touch our country, and their shackles fall.*

Miss Martineau was told by a gentleman, that the sublimest
sight in North America is the leap of a slave from a boat to the
Canadian shore. That "leap" transforms him from a marketable

---

* *See* Judge Jay's "View of the Action of the Federal Government in behalf of
Slavery."

† Honourable Henry Clay.

chattel to a free man. Hence that "leap" is far more sublime
than the plunge of the Niagara River from its natural bed to the
deep, deep, receptacle of its voluminous waters, far below. But
when it is remembered how much of difficulty the poor American
slave has to encounter, in preparing for his escape, and in making it—how every step of the way is beset with peril and threatening disaster—then one could see in that "leap" so much of the
consummation of long and fondly cherished hope, hope nurtured
on the very brink of despair, so much of real true manhood, as
to give a better insight into its real "sublimity" than a mere
casual glance could afford. To the better feelings of our common manhood, it is most gratifying to see a man made free by
an effort of peaceful though energetic heroism; but to know how
much that effort has cost him, and to know that he has both
counted and paid the cost, is more gratifying still. The one gives
us, it may be, but a momentary thrill of delight; the other
awakens and fixes our admiration.

When I say that our immigrant and oft-coming* fugitives are
a most welcome accession to our population, the reader may
smile and say, "That is all very well in one Negro to say of others
of the same class." But I say it in view of the wants of our colony,
and of the character of these people. What the former are I will
state in few words—labourers of real sterling industry; what the
latter is shall be inferred from what they show themselves to be,
as slaves, as fugitives, and as freemen. I use this peculiar nomenclature for the sake of perspicuity and logical correctness.
The fugitive is different on the plantation from what he is flying.
When he reaches Canada, he is no longer either a slave or a
fugitive, but a freeman.

1. I hesitate not to affirm, that the class of slaves who escape
to Canada are generally the most valuable of the whole stock.
Ordinarily, as Jefferson says, "men are more apt to bear evils

---

* Since the enactment of the Fugitive Slave Law they have increased rapidly.
Those who had been in Free States for years, many of them, were obliged to flee.

than to put themselves to the peril and trouble of getting rid of them." Ordinary men submit to, and try to make the best of, what they suffer. Besides, oppression cramps and dwarfs the mind so as to make it mean enough, most frequently, to submit to what is imposed upon it, if not without murmurings and re-pinings, at least without very vigorous efforts, either in the mass or in individuals, to better themselves.

I hope I need not say, that Negroes do not furnish the only or the worst illustrations of this fact. Around the American slave, however, are placed all manner of obstacles to his escape, and over him the most vigilant surveillance is constantly exer-cised. The fear of his running away is constantly present to the mind of his master, and against it all manner of precautions are used. The slave may not learn to read or write—it would better prepare him to make his escape; he may not be out after ten o'clock at night, "without written permission"; he may not be absent from his master's premises after nightfall, at all, "with-out written permission"; he may not be away, any distance from home, day or night, "without written permission." If found otherwise, he is apprehended, imprisoned, and advertised, as a runaway. If detected as actually guilty of running away, or of being liable to reasonable suspicion of the crime (for it is such), he will receive the severest possible punishment. His punishment is more than ordinarily cruel for the fault—desire for freedom, in the freest country under the sun—both to cure him of any such desire or tendency in future, and to intimidate other slaves.

All this the slave knows before he starts—indeed, before he determines to start. Then, he occasionally receives a lecture on the bad climate and worse customs of Canada. All manner of bug-bears are put down before him, touching this country. Sometimes, however, they go too far in this direction. I have heard slaves say, "We knew Canada was a good country for us, because master was so anxious that we should *not* go there." Such have learnt to in-terpret their masters' pretended solicitude in their behalf as the

Irish interpret their dreams, "by conthraries." In case a Negro
has the stubborness (it would be called bravery and fortitude in
a white man) to go to Canada, in spite of his master's contrary
wish, in spite of all he has heard against it, and in spite of all he
has heard and seen of punishment—and, it may be, has felt of
it too—then he must consider what he is about. He must impart
his secret to no one; not even his bosom friend may be trusted.
Then, what he does by way of preparation must be done most
stealthily. At that time, of all times, he must appear best satisfied
with slavery, least anxious for freedom. He has no means of purchasing the articles he needs for his journey. His conscience may
be tender as to whether he should appropriate to himself what
he deems necessary for his escape, from his master's possession,
without leave. Sometimes their consciences give them far less
trouble than the vigilant eyes of their masters. It is true, however,
that there are slaves so completely under the control of religious
scruples, as to refuse to appropriate not only what they need for
their escape, but what they need to live upon. Frederick Douglass
says, that while a slave, for a length of time he felt conscientiously
opposed to the taking of such food or animals as he really needed
for his sustenance. An old Negro preacher, however, who was
more skilled in casuistry, determined to convert him from his
needless scruples. On one occasion he reasoned with him after the
following manner:—

"Frederick, are not *you* master's property?"

"Yes," said Frederick.

"Well; is not yon pig master's property also?"

"Yes, I see that."

"Well then; if you take a pig, which is master's property, and
put it *inside of Frederick*, which is master's property, has not
master got both pieces of his *property together*?"

"Yes," replied Frederick, perfectly reconciled, and relieved
of all doubts on the subject from that day forth.

Some do, and some do not, become entangled with such difficulties; whether they do or not, thousands of obstacles surround them. Any one may betray their secret, if knowing it, and hence everything must be kept to themselves.

A man entrusted with a plan of importance grows with it. If it be the fruit of his own thoughts and one if his own purposes, he is more of a man for having conceived it. If it must be wrought out with his own unaided hands, it improves him to entertain the intention of doing it. If in the way of his resolution—and, still more, in the way of executing it—there stand many mighty obstacles of which he is well aware, but the existence of which appals him not, he has in him all the elements of your moral or physical hero, or of both. Now, the slave intending, planning, determining to escape, is one of that class. He knows he must lie in the woods all day—that he can only travel in the night—that he must not be seen in any public thoroughfare—that no animal of the earth is so much to be dreaded and avoided as *man*—that cold, and wet, and hunger, and thirst, and approaching naked-ness, are among the most ordinary adjuncts of his toilsome jour-ney. Worst of all, he knows that the keen scent of the well-trained bloodhound—a dog educated like an American, and by an Amer-ican, to hate and worry a Negro*—a dog bad enough naturally, but made ten thousandfold worse by his republican, Bible-defended† training: as well as the swiftest hunter, the most ferocious of all, the human professional Negro-catcher—will be upon his track. They may over-take him; they may overpower him, and drag him back! Then the hottest part of the hell of slavery is to be his portion. Still he holds on his purpose, defies the dangers, battles the obstacles, stills the palpitations of his own trembling heart, and makes his preparations and—his *exit.*

Now, not only the philosophy of the case declares this man to be superior to those generally surrounding him, those he leaves behind him, but, as in the case of other refugees, the history of

---

* These dogs are trained by being set upon young Negroes, in their puppy days.
† The divines who defend slavery from the Bible, defend this practice as well.

the case agrees with its philosophy. The slaves advertised as having run away, or as having been arrested upon suspicion of being runaways—as any one may see in any Southern newspaper, political or religious—are men and women of mark. "Large frames" are ascribed to them; "intelligent countenances;" "can read a little;" "may pass, or attempt to pass, as a freeman;" "a good mechanic;" "had a bold look;" "above the middle height, very ingenious, may pass for white;" "very intelligent." No one who has seen such advertisements can fail to be struck with them. A mulattress left her master, Mr. Devonport, in Syracuse, in 1839, who "had no traces of African origin": as advertised. Mr. D. said she was worth 2,500 dollars, nearly £500. Such are the slaves who run away, as a rule. I do not deny that some of "inferior lots" come too, but such as those described from the *rule*.

Then, as fugitives, when we recollect what they must undergo in every part of their *exodus*, we can but see them as among the most admirable of any race. The fugitive exercises patience, fortitude, and perseverance, connected with and fed by an ardent and unrestrained and resistless love of liberty, such as cause men to be admired everywhere—that is, *white men everywhere*, but in the United States. The lonely, toiling journey; the endurance of the excitement from constant danger; the hearing the yell and howl of the bloodhound; the knowledge of close, hot pursuit; the dread of capture, and the determination not to be taken alive—all these, furnaces of trial as they are, purify and ennoble the man who has to pass through them. All these are inseparable from the ordinary incidents in the northward passage of the fugitive: and when he reaches us, he is, first, what the raw material of nature was; and, secondly, what the improving process of flight has made him. Both have fitted him the more highly to appreciate, the more fully to enjoy, and the more wisely to use, that for which he came to us, for which he was willing to endure all things, for which, indeed, he would have yielded life itself—liberty.

Let me illustrate these points by a few facts. A Negro, Madison Washington by name—a name, a pair of names, of which he was well worthy—was a slave in Virginia. He determined to be free. He fled to Canada and became free. There the noble fellow was dissatisfied—so dissatisfied, that he determined to leave free Canada, and return to Virginia: and wherefore? His wife was there, a *slave*. Freedom was too sweet to be enjoyed without her. That she was a slave marred his joys. She must share them, even at the risk of *his* losing them. So in 1841 he went back to Virginia, to the neighbourhood in which his wife lived, lingered about in the woods, and sent word to her of his whereabouts; others were unfortunately informed as well, and he was captured, taken to Washington, and sold to a Negro-trader. One scarcely knows which most to admire—the heroism this man displayed in the freeing of himself, or the noble manliness that risked all for the freedom of his wife. One cannot help thinking that, as his captors led Madison Washington to the slave pen, they must have been smitten with the thought that they were handling a man far superior to themselves. When a load of Negroes had been made up, Madison Washington, with a large number of others—119, I think—was put on board the schooner "Creole," to sail out of the mouth of the Potomac River and southwards to the Gulf of Mexico, up the Mississippi, and to New Orleans, the great slave-buying port of America. But on the night of the 9th of November, 1841, Madison Washington and two others, named respectively Pompey Garrison, and Ben Blacksmith, arose upon the captain and crew, leading all the other slaves after them, and gave the captain the alternative of sailing the vessel into a British port, one of the Bahamas, or of going overboard. The captain, wisely and safely for himself, chose the former; and these three brave blacks, naturally distrusting the forced promise of the Yankee captain, stood sentry over him until he *did* steer the "Creole" into the port of Nassau, island of *New Providence,* touching which they became freemen. The United States Government, through the Honourable Edward Everett,* demanded of Lord Palmerston gold to pay for these men. The Court of St. James entertained the demand—not one moment. What lacked these men of being Tells, Mazzinis, and Kossuths, in their way, except white or whitish skins?

* This was during the time when the Honourable Daniel Webster first was Secretary of State. It was the first time the British Government had rejected such a demand, I am sorry to say.

CHAPTER III

Fugitives Evince True Heroism

Among the many who come to us from slavery, it cannot be expected that all, or many, should be such as the three described in the closing part of the last chapter. I do not pretend any such thing. Slavery is not the sort of institution for the training and producing of such men. Many, too many, bear with them the indelible marks of the accursed lot to which they have been doomed, in early life. It is almost impossible to spend youth, manhood, and the greater part of life, in such a condition as that of the American slave, and entirely escape, or to any great extent ever become free from, the legitimate influences of it upon the whole character. It is so with slaveholders. They never, during life, lose the overbearing insolence, the reckless morals, the peculiarly inelegant manners, and the profligate habits, which distinguish too many of them. Why should slaves be expected to be better than what they have been made, by the institution which has crushed them? Indeed, though I recollect nothing of slavery, I am every day showing something of my slave origin. It is among my thoughts, my superstitions, my narrow views, my awkwardness of manners. Ah, the infernal impress is upon me, and I fear I shall transmit it to my children, and they to theirs! How deeply seated, how far reaching, a curse it is!

All I claim for the Negro settler is, that as a slave, a fugitive, and a freeman, he is equal to other poor immigrants, superior to many, and from among the very best of his own class; and that, take him all in all, he is just such a man as our new country needs —a lover of freedom, a loyal subject, an industrious man.

I fear that I should leave an unfair impression upon the minds of my readers, if I did not give other instances of the class and condition of fugitives, than the case of Madison Washington and his compatriots. Some are not nearly so fortunate. One poor man came to my house, in Toronto, who had fled from North Carolina, leaving behind him a wife and four children, whom he had no expectation of seeing again on earth. He was four-and-thirty years old; and at *that* age, while enjoying freedom, and having shown the manliness to escape, bearing all the perils of his flight most bravely, his poor heart must be sunken in sorrow by the gloomy recollection that all dear to him were 1,400 miles away, in *slavery*. Few men, of any race, would retain sufficient energy of body, or soul, or mind, to bear up under such evils; but this poor fellow went to work in the service of a friend of mine, who wrote me in 1853 concerning him that "he spends his leisure in learning to read, in which he is quite successful."

Another came to me at the age of sixty-one. He had spent his best days in the service of a man who had frequently sent him with six horses, as a teamster, to Pennsylvania (thereby making him free, though the poor man did not know it), and whom he had served till his death. His master's sons sold him to a Negro-trader. Returning to the house at the close of his day's labour, one evening, he was informed of his being sold. He could not believe that lads to whom he had been so kind *could* sell him. Poor man! little did he dream of the ingratitude of a slaveholding Yankee. He was called to his supper, which, instead of being set in the kitchen as usual, was set in a small room to which there was but one door, and the table stood behind that door. Woodfolk, the Negro-trader, was in an adjoining room, viewing him with professional interest. The presence of this demi-demon, the arrangements for supper, and the appearance of matters generally, but too clearly revealed to him that the information he had received was quite correct. He saw that, should he sit down *there* to supper, Woodfolk and the young men could, like tigers, spring upon him; and there being no chance of escape, he could be overpowered and borne off, in spite of any resistance he might make. Wisely concluding that "discretion is the better part of valour," he went out as if to look after the horses he was accustomed to attend, *and never returned.* His wife lived some two miles distant: should he visit her, to bid her farewell? No! for so soon as they missed him, they would suspect he was gone to see her, and therefore that would be the first place to which they would repair in quest of him. Besides, was it not wise to gain time by taking advantage of this fact? He adopted the latter plan, kept the barn behind him, went to the woods, followed the North Star, and journeyed patiently until he arrived, in the character of a freeman, the first time in his life, upon the soil of a free country.

At first, I could not make the old man believe that he was really in a free country; but the kindness shown by the Ladies' Society for the Aid of Destitute Fugitives brought the fact gradually, like the approach of dawn to his vision, and then he came to me in haste, demanding to be sent away to work. He needed no more rest; he was not ill, as he had supposed; he could scarcely believe he was old and weak—he was *free!* that was youth, health, rest, strength, all things. He was sent to the county of Lincoln, where he obtained employment; and he is now working out the problems of his maintenance as successfully as any man of his years, in that part of Her Majesty's empire.

Another was so unfortunate as to be obliged to travel in the winter. I met him at a ferry on the Niagara River, crossing from Niagara, on the British side, to Youngstown, on the New York side. It was a bitterly cold day, the 11th of January, 1853. Crossing the river, it was so cold that icicles were formed upon my clothes, as the waves dashed the water into the ferry boat. It was difficult for the Rev. H. Wilson and myself—we travelled together—to keep ourselves warm while driving; and my horses, at a most rapid rate, travelled twelve miles almost without sweating. That day, this poor fellow crossed that ferry with nothing upon his person but cotton clothing, and an oilcloth topcoat. Liberty was before him, and for it he could defy the frost. I had observed him, when I was in the office of the ferry, sitting not *at*, but *all around*, the stove; for he literally *surrounded and covered it* with his shivering legs and arms and trunk. And what delighted me was, everybody in the office seemed quite content that he should occupy what he had discovered and appropriated. I yielded my share without a word of complaint. There was not much of the stove, and we all let him enjoy what there was of it.

The ferryman was a bit of a wag—a noble, generous Yankee; who, when kind, like the Irish, are the most humane of men. Upon asking the fare of the ferry, I was told it was a shilling. Said I, "Must I pay now, or when I get on the other side?"

"Now, I guess, if you please."

"But suppose I go to the bottom, I lose the value of my shilling," I expostulated.

"So shall I lose mine, if you go to the bottom without paying in advance," was his cool reply.

I submitted, of course. When partly across, he said to me, "Stranger, you saw that 'ere black man near the stove in the office, didn't you?"

"Yes, I saw him, *very near* it, *all around* it—*all over* it, for that matter."

"Wall, if you can do anything for him, I would thank you, for he is really in need. He is a fugitive. I just now brought him across. I am sure he has nothing, for he had but fourpence to pay his ferry."

"But you charged *me a shilling*, and made me pay in advance."

"Yes, but I tell you what; when a darky comes to this ferry from slavery, I guess he'll get across, shilling or no shilling, money or no money."

Knowing as I did that a Yankee's—a good Yankee's—*guess* is equal to any other man's oath, I could but believe him. He further told me, that sometimes, when they had money, fugitives would give him five shillings for putting them across the ferry which divided what they call Egypt from Canaan. In one case a fugitive insisted upon his taking twenty-four times the regular fare. Upon the ferryman's refusing, the Negro conquered by saying, "Keep it, then, as a fund to pay the ferriage of fugitives who cannot pay for themselves."

While I was upon the journey in the course of which the foregoing occurred, a man arrived at Toronto who had come from the South, travelling on foot, wearing out his shoes, and freezing his feet so that for a fortnight he could not stand upon them. He, as are all others in like circumstances, was attended to and provided for at the expense of those "Sisters of Mercy," the Ladies' Society, to which I referred in a preceding page; and being a stonecutter by trade, so soon as he was able to stand he found employment in one of our best stonecutter's yards, and proved to be a most serviceable skilful workman.

I will give one or two instances of the difficulties which beset them on their way. Andrew Jackson, a well known and dearly beloved man, was, after he started, beset by five slave-catchers, who were determined to take him back. Andrew told me, that when they demanded his surrender and return, he pointedly refused, and placed himself in an attitude of defence and defiance. He says, "they came upon me, and I used a hickory stick I had in my hands. Striking them as hard and as often as I could, with each blow I prayed, 'Lord, save! Lord, save!' Now," said he, "had I simply cried, 'Lord, save!' without using my hickory, they would have taken me. Now I know that faith and works go together." He conquered; flogging the five, as he said, by God's blessing upon the energetic use of his hickory. I believe him. Who does not?

Another man, of whom the Rev. Mr. McClure (as true a friend to the Negro as ever drew breath) told me, ran away in the absence of his master, not knowing whither he had gone. He arrived at the Niagara River without serious mishap, and was just about to cross, and make the "leap" of which Miss Martineau speaks.

But he cautiously approached the river's brink, and looked up and down before *borrowing* a boat, there being no ferry very near, and he preferring to cross quietly and privately, in that manner: but down the river he saw a man fishing, whose appearance he did not particularly like. He hesitated. The man turned his face towards him. It was the face of his master! In an instant, he ran—almost flew—from the margin of the river, to gain the suspension bridge close at hand, and cross it. His master pursued. On he flew: he gained the bridge; so did his master. He ran for life, and liberty—the master ran for property: the former had freedom to win, the latter feared the loss of a chattel. On both ran, the Negro being ahead by some few "lengths," and showing a most practical disposition to keep so. The keeper of the tollgate encouraged the Negro, who, though breathless, redoubled his energies and almost multiplied his speed at every bound, until he reached the Canadian end of the bridge—when he suddenly stopped, his haste being over, the goal having been reached, the prize won. He looked his former master, who had just "arrived in time to be too late," calmly in the eye, with a smile of satisfaction and triumph overspreading his features. The two were equals: both were free. The former slave knew it right well. Hence that calm triumphant smile.

I heard of one who, like the man just spoken of, reached the Erie River at Black Rock, near Buffalo, and in sight of that Canada which had been the object of his fondest desires, and had actually gone upon the ferryboat to be conveyed to his much-wished-for free home. The ferryman was loosing the boat from the shore, when, to his utter dismay, up rode his master upon a foaming steed, and with a look

> *Like the sunshine when it flashes on steel,*

drew his loaded pistol, and plainly told the ferryman—"If you loose that boat to convey my Negro to the opposite bank, I'll *blow* your brains out!"

The Negro in an instant seized a handspike, and, holding it menacingly over the ferryman's head, said, "If you don't loose the boat and ferry me across, I'll *beat* your brains out!"

The ferryman, one of the best of his class, a Yankee, friendly to the Negro, looked a moment, first at the one and then at the other, seeing both equally determined and decided, and expressed his decision. He said coolly, "Wall! I can't die but *once;* and if I die, I guess I would rather die doing right. So here goes the boat."

He loosed it and shoved it off. While this was being done, the slaveholder, seeing his slave, who had always

Fanned him while he slept, and trembled when he woke,

defy him, with a threatening gesture at a white man, was thunderstruck. He sate in mute astonishment. His countenance reflected the state of his surprised mind. He was transfixed, as it were, to his saddle. He gazed with a stupid glare, as if he saw not, while the boat sped her way Canada-wards. The Negro, on the other hand, watched every inch of progress which widened the distance betwixt the two shores, until, not waiting for the boat to touch, he ran back to the stern, and then, with a full bound like a nimble deer, sprang from the boat to the shore in advance of the boat, and, rising, took off his poor old hat, and gave three cheers for the British sovereign.

From my native State, Maryland, in 1853, four young men started, under the following circumstances. One of them was to be sold—a doom which the slave dreads next to perdition. He at once concluded that he would meet the perils of running away before he would suffer himself to be sold from his somewhat comfortable home. He imparted his secret, unhappily, to some few, as he supposed, trusty friends. Arming themselves, they started together. They travelled every night, they concealed themselves during the days, until they reached and crossed the border of Pennsylvania. One morning, as they were entering a place of safety for the day, a dog came to them, barking; the dog was quickly followed by a biped. The latter, assuming the language of a Quaker for his base purposes, addressed them kindly, offered them a breakfast, and bade them follow him into his house. They did so. He gave them the first hearty meal they had eaten since leaving home. After breakfast, he showed them a place of safety, in his barn. He left them, and returned a few hours after, and brought with him eight men, to take them as fugitive slaves! Two of them yielded at once. The other two fought until one of them was overpowered. The other continued to fight until his right arm was riddled with shot, and fell powerless at his side; then he threw his pistol at them, and they took him. This was the leader, the one who first proposed the escape. His captors found his arm needed the care of a surgeon before he could be safely removed. They therefore, instead of taking him back to Maryland immediately, as they proposed to do with the other three, caused him to be put to bed in the second story of the inn where they lodged, and obtained surgical aid for him.

Having achieved so signal a victory—these eight brave Anglo-Saxons—over four Negroes, two of whom did *not* fight! they felt that both their valour and their victory (to say nothing of their stomachs) were worthy of a celebration. A celebration, with free drinking of wine, &c., they had, and in it they got into a state of *sublimity*. The Negro, knowing what was going on, and, though foiled, not defeated, arose stealthily from his bed, took the bed-cord out of his bedstead, fastened it to the window, and let himself down, by his left hand and his teeth, to the ground. He dragged himself away to the woods, and made good his escape to a town that shall be nameless—found a friend in the gentleman who gave me the facts, and was finally sent to Canada, where he arrived safely, a crippled but a free man.

This may remind the reader of the case of William Thomas, a fugitive, of whom we read in the London *Times* in August, 1853. This man had fled from Virginia to Pennsylvania, and was waiter in a hotel at Wilkesbarre, in the beautiful Wyoming Valley, on the banks of the Susquehannah River. He had lived there some years; but being traced by the agents of his master, *five* men came to the hotel and called for food. William waited upon them. They eat and paid; and while he was going to his master with the money, these cowards came behind him stealthily, and struck him a stunning blow, which brought him senseless to the floor. They then put handcuffs on him, and arrested him as a fugitive; this being the first intimation they gave that such was the purpose for which they had come. In a few minutes poor William recovered partially from the effects of the blow, arose quickly, and with the handcuff flogged his five captors; and then, not before, ran to the river.

He went into the water up to his chin. His pursuers followed him to the bank, and commanded him to come out. He plainly declared that he preferred drowning to being carried back to Virginia, a slave. The slave-catchers then shot him in the head. He sank; the blood from his wounded head commingling itself with the waters of the Susquehannah. He soon afterwards rose to the surface, and was about to approach the shore, as the brave men who were in quest of him had left the river, saying that it was "scarcely worth while to take a dead nigger to Virginia"; but as he came near the shore they returned to take him. He went back into the river, sunk beneath its surface, and, while under, made the best of his way unobserved down the stream; then, after a little while, got out, and stealthily reached the cottage of a poor black woman in the neighbourhood, who kindly took care of him until he was well enough to be sent to Canada. What would such poor fellows do, if it were not for the British American possessions? Can the reader blame me for believing, that the All Merciful One has preserved that land from the hands of the Americans, almost on purpose to shelter the outcast?

I am sorry to be obliged to add, that the United States Circuit Court decided that these five men used no undue, unnecessary, or illegal severity, in their attempt to take William Thomas. So pronounced his Honour Judge Grier, an elder in a Presbyterian Church!

A poor fellow, having escaped one day, was pursued in the afternoon by professional man-hunters, Negro-catchers, with bloodhounds. They were upon his track, gained upon him, and would surely have him if he did not resort to some artifice. Fortunately there was, near by, a morass. He knew that in the water the dogs would lose the scent. He therefore went into the morass, sunk down to his neck, threw his head backward beneath some bulrushes, and thus concealed himself while he could see and hear all that passed. The dogs were at fault. The horses could not enter the bog; or, if they did, they might find it not so easy to come out. The men were vexed. They knew he was there somewhere, but exactly where they could not determine. Had they seen him, they would in all probability have shot him. They shouted, they swore, but all to no purpose. At last, night came on, and they were far from home; they must therefore return, and, to their mortification, they must go without the Negro. After their departure he came out, but so benumbed that he was scarcely able to stand. By extraordinary exertions, however, he recovered warmth, and pursued his journey until he reached a land of freedom. In his native country, there is not a square inch of territory where either he or poor Thomas could be free and safe. He told me, he thought his case *somewhat* resembled that of Moses; he had been hid in the bulrushes, and thus saved!

One more case must suffice, both to illustrate my position and to close this chapter. It is that of a poor pious man who was a slave in Maryland, some twenty-seven miles from Baltimore. His master was a lawyer—a free and easy sort of person, who generally visited his plantation but once a fortnight, having his office in Baltimore. The slave I speak of had a wife, and they had a child some few months old, all of whom were the property of this young lawyer. These slaves, and some others in the vicinity, had resolved upon being free. They made their arrangements for going to Canada, and wisely arranged to start on the Saturday night on which the master of the man, wife and child, was not to be at the plantation. They were to meet a waggon at a place some few miles distant, to which they were to travel on foot. They slept in a bedroom next to that in which their master slept. A window, looking out of their bedroom upon the road, was near the partition, and therefore near the master's room; but besides this, a like window was equally near the partition, in his room. Their arrangements were all made; the time was approaching; the Saturday came; evening drew on; and with it, contrary to his custom and to their expectations, came their master.

Ordinary persons would have given up, or at least postponed, this journey. Not so did this couple. They consulted, and determined to proceed with the plan. The wife was especially determined. At length the hour for starting approached. They listened: all was still in their master's room, save the noise of his deep breathing, as he slept soundly. It was a clear, frosty, starlight night, peculiar to an American autumn—it was November. In silent prayer this pair bowed, and, rising, felt what seemed to them new inspiration. Perhaps it was the calmness of soul resulting from an earnest trust in the God of the poor and the needy; perhaps it was the foreshadowing of new evils to come, and a sort of gathering up the soul's energies for a new conflict; perhaps—but why speculate? They had committed themselves to God, "as to a faithful Creator," and they set about what they felt to be duty. Softly they raised the window, and then listened to ascertain whether the sound of it had attracted attention. They heard nothing but the deep breathing of the sleeper in the next apartment, within, and the chirrup of the cricket without. The man went out of the window: did any one hear? No. Now comes a difficulty. Out of the warm bed, where it had been nestling in its mother's bosom, into the cold frosty air of a November night, must this child of a few months be taken, and so passed from the

hands of the mother to those of the father. A cry from that child—
and how natural that a child should cry, in the circumstances!—
would betray them. Could it be taken out silently? They must try;
they did try; they succeeded. The babe was still, and lay in a
sleep almost motionless, in his father's arms outside the window.

Safely, as speedily and silently, the mother moved out, low-
ered the window. No one heard, all was still; and they started
with hearts beating almost audibly, and leaping almost into their
throats. They walked to the place of rendezvous; but so high were
their hopes, so cheerful was their conversation, that they almost
realized my friend Joseph Payne, Esq.'s, favourite quotation—
"A good companion on a journey is better than a coach." Almost
ere they knew it, they were at the appointed place; but the waggon and the other parties were not there. There were no footprints,
no wheel tracks: they had not yet come. They could afford, they
thought, to wait, and they did wait. But, to their grief and disappointment, neither the waggon nor the rest of the party appeared;
and they, alternating between hope and fear, remained shivering
in the cold, until it became but too evident that the others must
have met with some hindrance which had prevented their departure. The night advanced, morning began to approach. They saw
that they must return, and that speedily, or they would not be able
to enter their bedroom without awakening either their master or
some of the neighbours. To make sure of returning under cover
of the night, they must retrace their steps at once.

As they returned, one would naturally enough think, their
minds would dwell somewhat gloomily upon this sad disappointment. Their conversation, however, was animated, for they were
in a dispute. The wife insisted upon a proposal to which the husband would not listen. But she was eloquent: wives, when in earnest, always are. The opposition grew feebler and feebler, until at
last he sought peace, as discomfited husbands generally seek it,
by saying, "Well, my dear, if you insist upon it, with the help of
God I'll try." The victory overcame her: she was silent, tearful,

and they walked on, until, collecting herself, she threw her arms about his neck, as he held the child, and said with a full heart, as none but a wife can say, "God bless you, my husband!" Why had they been disputing, and about what?

After the disappointment, the wife, with a tenacity peculiar to the sex, found it impossible to give up the idea of freedom for *some* of the party. She could not endure the idea that *all* of them should return to hopeless bondage. Like other women, she thought she could endure more than her husband could at home, while she had no doubt of his ability to meet trouble abroad. She therefore proposed that he should go on and seek freedom, while she, with the child, should return. Opposing this, as we have seen, without success, he yielded the contest, but insisted upon accompanying her back to the home they had left a few hours before. They reached it in safety, lifted the window; the mother listened, took the child, bade her husband adieu, and sank upon the bed in the solitude of disconsolate sorrow, while he commenced his journey alone, towards the land of freedom. He said to me, in the artless but pious language of a confiding heart, as he pointed upward, "I think the Father kept the child still; don't you think so, Mr. Ward?" "Certainly," said I.

Poor man! He never saw his wife again. He died ere he received tidings of her. But those two simple hearts, reciprocally confiding in each other, and mutually trusting in their God, shall be again united. Indeed, are *hearts* ever dissevered? However this may be, they shall be *one* again when they, and those who oppressed them, shall stand before a common judgment-seat!

CHAPTER IV

Canadian Freemen

It but remains for me to speak of our people resident in Canada as freemen. Once more, let me remind the reader that slavery is the worst school of vice in the universe. I am ashamed to plead so much on this subject, bearing as it does the unpleasant appearance of special pleading. I will just give my apology for it. When I go to Glasgow, Scotland, and see along Argyle Street, and near the Tontine, and in High Street, specimens of low, dirty, degraded population, I am told that the parentage, early education, and low origin, of these people, ought to be taken into the account, in making up my estimate of them. When I complain of the beggary, the want of self-respect, which show themselves in Ireland, in every street and lane of every town, and at the doors of every country tavern, many circumstances, some of them simply historical, others purely imaginary, are made answerable for all this, and I am reminded of past condition and present improvement. So, when I turn out of Fleet Street, the Strand, or Regent Street, London, and express my disgust at what I find within a stone's throw of those fashionable thoroughfares, Englishmen point to the inadequate education of these people, their deep poverty, their degrading and constant toil, the long neglect of them by better classes, and the very many gin shops to be found in their midst.

Now, the reasonableness and the force of all this I most freely and cheerfully admit; but why does it not apply with equal force and reasonableness to the case of the formerly, lately, enslaved Negro? I hear him censured as if he and his ancestors had been civilized, evangelized, highly educated, and especially favoured, for the past fifty generations. His faults are set down to the viciousness of his nature. Mr. W. Chambers, the London *Times,* everybody, English, Scotch, or Irish, as well as Yankees, can find fault with the Negro; but few will do him the justice to judge of him, his faults, and his virtues, by the same rule that they would apply to other classes, to their own class. What I affirm *of* the Canadian Negro is, that he bears himself equal to English, Irish, Scotch, Dutch, or French Canadians, although he *has* and they have *not* been slaves; all I claim *for* the Canadian Negro is, that same fair rule and standard of character which is applied to other peoples, and by which they are estimated. Let us stand or fall by such a rule, and I am content.

As any one would judge, the mass of our population are labourers. Some are most excellent mechanics and artisans; others are farmers, yeomen. Too many of them live in and about large towns. That is always unwise in poor people, in my judgment. In these towns they pursue the means of livelihood common to other poor people, and in what they do they are as expert and efficient as any other class: in some things, I think, they excel. A few in large towns are servants in hotels. A small number of the same class are servants on steamers. Exceedingly few of either sex, as compared with the coloured people of the neighbouring States, are household servants. This last fact, in connection with another I am about to mention, speaks well both for their independence and for the degree of equality existing betwixt whites and blacks in Canadian towns. There are a great many, as compared with what one sees in the States, engaged in other than menial or semi-menial employments—fewer barbers, bootblacks, and more porters, carters, cabowners, &c. Small shopkeepers, also, are far more numerous, in proportion to their relative numbers, in Canada than in the States. Some of the grocers' shops, as well as those of other tradesmen, are on a very respectable scale, considering the wants of the populace; many are equal to any in the colony.

If any class excel, it is our mechanics and artisans. We have the best and most clever of the Southern population, white or black, in this respect, and they add not a little to our stock of industrial wealth as a colony. I know of no better builder in St. Catherine's than a coloured man to whom I was introduced there, in 1853. The best cordwainers in Middlesex and in Kent respectively are Nelson Moss, of London, and Cornelius Charity, of Chatham. James Madison Jones, of Chatham, has not his superior as a gunsmith in Canada, if indeed in North America. Charles Peyton Lucas, in his trade as a general blacksmith, will compare with any man in Toronto, where he resides; but as a horse shoer, it is impossible for any man to exceed him. Before he went to Canada, I knew him to stand at the head of his trade in this respect. The most skilful bricklayer I ever saw, was a person as black as myself, whose name I have not the pleasure of knowing.

We now have the good fortune to number among us some gentlemen of education and property, who have turned their back upon the States, and "who are not mindful of the country from whence they came out." These are educating their children, and fitting them to occupy any position which Providence may call them to fill, as all posts of honour and profit are as open to them as to any other class. They now see many persons taking the positions for which they are fitted, irrespective of complexional distinction. That is an earnest of what they may enjoy, as they shall be qualified for like situations and honours. Indeed, Negro-hate cannot do them the mischief it does in the States, for the reasons before stated: it has not the sanction of our laws, the spirit of our institutions, or the countenance of our better, more fashionable, more powerful—in a word, our ruling classes.

I shall now briefly detail what I have seen in the settlements of the blacks, in Canada. I must express, however, my regret that

I have not had the pleasure of visiting two of them—one situated in the township of Oro, county of Simcoe, seventy miles from Toronto, and another in Peel, county of Wellington, about the same distance from Hamilton. The Wilberforce Settlement, in Middlesex, near London, has become extinct, having proved, from some cause, a failure.

In 1840 a farm was purchased in the township of Dawn, now Gore of Camden, in the county of Kent, by several gentlemen under the guidance of Rev. Hiram Wilson, for the purpose of establishing a Manual Labour School. Around this nucleus have gathered several coloured families. It was *then* an unbroken, undisturbed forest; *now*, some of the best farms, approached by as good roads as have been made in Canada, are in that settlement. There are about 150 families in the neighbourhood, among whom resides George Cary, Esq.—as intelligent and enterprising a man, as fit for a magistrate or any other like office, as any person in North Kent. Here lives, too, quite at his ease, in a large farm comprising several hundred acres of most excellent land, the gentlemanly, noble-hearted Dennis Hill, Esq., one of the best educated yeomen in Canada. Peter Johnson, now living independently on his ample property, was an ordinary labourer fifteen years ago, carrying a bag of meal fourteen miles through the forest, on foot. Now, persons come to him from the surrounding towns, to make purchases. Over the same road that he travelled fifteen years ago on foot, with his bag of corn meal as the result of a week's work, he now drives his well fed horses to market, with large supplies. In his neighbourhood, one of the earliest and most prosperous settlers, beginning with nothing, mutilated by his brutal master while a slave, coming to Canada when he was forty years old, with a large family—now reposing in comfort upon the produce of eighty acres of as good land as Canada contains—is the honest, the venerable, the beloved Josiah Henson—"Father Henson," as most persons affectionately call him.

The school to which I refer, in this settlement, proved a failure. Like other failures, it involved all connected with it in pecuniary loss, and rendered them liable to a great deal of censure. Of the merits of the matter one can scarcely judge, from the criminations and recriminations of contending parties. I am sorry to say, that when I visited the settlements, in 1852, neither the school, nor the buildings, nor the farm, reflected the least possible credit upon any party concerned. I fear that little or nothing has been done since, to improve the affair. It is in the hands of certain gentlemen of great eminence in London, but why nothing is done I know not.

That the settlement should succeed so well without the school, and by the unaided and energetic efforts of the settlers, many of whom were once slaves, all of them from the Southern States, with an exception or two, does them the highest credit. It will not be long before that part of Kent and the southern part of the county of Lambton, adjoining it, will be in the hands of coloured men, chiefly. Most of the whites in the neighbourhood are very respectable persons, treating their coloured neighbours as neighbours ought; some few are among the most indescribably offensive wretches I ever saw. They have no claim to sense, manners, morals, character, reputation, nor anything else than what, for them, supplies the lack of all these—a skin which, when clean (as fortunately it is occasionally), if not submitted to too rigid an examination, would, among folks not very discriminating, pass for white, or at least approaching white, though rather dingy. The Sydenham River, which empties into Lake St. Clair, runs through this settlement. It is so deep, though narrow, that steamers and schooners can come to the wharf to load and discharge. Thus the Dawn settlement is brought within water communication of Detroit, the metropolis of the neighbouring State of Michigan. The outlay of a little capital, the continuance of such energy as has brought the settlement to its present state, and the yet further increase (for which there is ample occasion and encouragement in the resources of the country), will make the "Dawn," as it is called, a very flourishing town not many years hence.

At the risk of giving offence, as I may perhaps by my freedom, I will here record my opinion as to one of the most lamentable defects I found while visiting "Dawn." It is, the general, almost universal, want of energy and enterprise among the young people. It is really painful to see the sons and daughters of fathers and mothers who dared the perils of flight—defied the discomforts of what an ornament to Canadian society, perhaps the most attractive of Canadian authoresses,* calls *Roughing it in the Bush*—partaking so little of the traits of their parents' character, as to suffer such appearances to strike the eye and wound the heart, as their neglect makes but too apparent to the most casual observer. Much of the lands *professedly* tilled in that settlement, if *really* tilled, would bring twofold, fourfold, more abundant crops; while the plough and the axe, the scythe and the cradle, should do much, more, out of doors—the needle and its accompaniments, within. I know I am liable to be reminded that such are not *my affairs*. In a certain sense, that is quite true. I do not own a square inch of land there; I am not personally affected by any of the evils to which I refer. But when I see what is done on the farms of Messrs. Carey, Johnson, Hill, and others, I cannot but deplore that several persons, whom I refrain from naming, do not profit from such business energy as these gentlemen display, especially as they have the advantage of their good example.

Besides, I write as a black man. I write no more than I have publicly said, in speaking on the subject, in Canada. I have a right to complain. "I do well to be angry" with any black man who throws discredit upon our people. I denounce any son of a black man who dishonours his father and mother—breaking the fifth commandment—by neglecting to improve what they, at the

* Mrs. Moody.

expense of great toil and sacrifice, have earned for him. In this sense, these young gentry are doing what it is my business to speak of; and were my children to walk in the same negligent way, he who would rebuke them I should hail as a friend. Some poet says,

> *Boys will anticipate,*
> *Lavish and dissipate,*
> *All that your busy pate*
> * Hoarded with care:*
> *And, in their foolishness,*
> *Passion, and mulishness,*
> *Charge you with churlishness,*
> * Spurning your prayer.*

I fear more than one of the sturdy, settlers of "Dawn" have such "boys," and, alas! girls too. Such things, in *that* settlement, are incapable of justification or apology. But, with this one draw-back, I think any one who visits it will call "the Dawn" a very successful settlement. It speaks well for the energy, perseverance, and economy of the settlers. It shows that the old pro-slavery story, that the Negro can only work well when under a taskmaster —or that he is a poor weakly creature, unfit for any position lacking the sterner virtues of our nature—is quite consistent with other falsehoods told against him. No one knows how false such assertions are, so well as the slaveholder. Does not the slave at his feet endure all manner of sufferings and privations from the hands of his master? Are not the slaves of the South the mechanics and artisans thereof? Does not the slaveholder, when offering a slave (especially if the latter be his OWN CHILD) for sale, boast of these qualities, by way of obtaining a larger price for him? When bought, is not a high price paid for the slave because of his possessing these qualities? As one of the many good results growing out of the residence of 40,000 fugitives in Canada, I hail the refutation of this calumny. As one of the many facts which practically demonstrate the falsity of the disparaging re-marks concerning the Negro, made by his enemies, I hail "the

Dawn" settlement, its present success and its prospective prosperity.

I know not that I shall "travel beyond the record" in speaking
of Chatham as a settlement. It certainly contains a large proportion—some say, and I think correctly, one third—of coloured
people, and most of them live in a portion of the town which might
not unjustly be called a coloured village; and, I may make a
remark or two, applicable alike to this and to other towns wherein
our people live in districts by themselves, I will introduce to the
reader Chatham as a settlement. If as a rural district "the Dawn"
is prosperous, so is Chatham as a town. About one third of the
town plot is owned by black men. Here they have two coloured
Churches—one a Baptist, presided over by Rev. Mr. Hawkins,
son-in-law of the late Rev. Benjamin Paul; and a Methodist
Church, supplied according to the itinerant system. The cottages,
and the buildings of a more pretending character, in the vicinity,
are of creditable size, and, though quite destitute of architectural
grace or beauty, compare most favourably with what one generally finds in young villages in the West. Their gardens are not
filled with ornamental exotics, but, like the gardens of their
paler neighbours, they contain most of the substantial comforts
generally grown in village gardens. Greater neatness, and more
general good morals, are not to be found in the settlements of any
class in the colony, as a rule. The industry and enterprise of the
majority of the settlers are most commendable. They are peculiarly fortunate in the mechanics and artisans. The three best
blacksmiths in Central Kent are the three coloured blacksmiths
of Chatham. Mr. Thomas Bell, a builder of that town, makes his
work so speak for itself that his hands are always full. If he
lives to the ordinary age of man, he will have the proud satisfaction of knowing that no small portion of Chatham was of his
own building. He is destined to make and to leave his mark on
the town of his adoption. I was delighted to see, too, that when
he desires to employ bricklayers, plasterers, joiners, or other

mechanics, he finds expert and skilful ones at hand, among our own people. I have already spoken of Mr. Charity and Mr. Jones, of this town.

And yet, there is not a town in Canada, in which the feeling against Negroes is stronger than in Chatham. Most of the white settlers in Chatham were low, degraded persons, in early and former life. They are the Negro-haters. The more gentlemanly, as is true almost everywhere, treat blacks according to their character and position. There are some excessively lazy, idle black persons in Chatham—they are a positive disgrace to the class; but they have their equals among the whites. There are two distinct classes, distinguishable according to character, among the one as well as the other. Some very clever travellers pass through Chatham exercising only the faculty of seeing the low, degraded Negroes, and the more respectable whites. Somehow or other, their vision does not extend so far as to see any low, dirty, drunken whites, nor any respectable Negroes; and when they speak of Chatham and its inhabitants they speak according to what they saw—but that was only what they *chose* to see. Happily for the blacks of Chatham, they are known and appreciated by all whose good opinion is worth having, or whose bad opinion is worth dreading. As to the others, no matter about them or their opinions.

A steamer, belonging to a firm in Chatham, plies betwixt that and other ports, down the Thames to Windsor and to Detroit. No coloured person is allowed a cabin passage on board this steamer. What is needed is, that some wealthy and respectable person of colour should give the owners of the boat a chance of testing the validity of their rule by British law. That opportunity doubtless they will have, before they shall be many years older, in their offences against their coloured fellow subjects. I regret that I cannot recollect the names of these owners: I should like to hold them up to infamy. The class of rebels to which they belong would, if they could, rob us of all our British rights and privileges; but,

to the praise of our Heavenly Father be it spoken, there is a limit
to their power.

I first visited Chatham in 1852, in August. I was simply passing
through it on my way further west. Though personally a stranger
to everyone in the place, I had not been long there before a requsi-
tion, in due form, but in terms much too flattering, was presented
to me by Mr. J. C. Brown, one of the most active of the coloured
men of the county, desiring me to speak to them that evening.
Though I had not intended to remain so long, I could not very
well refuse, and therefore consented. A numerous auditory, convened upon a few hours' notice, greeted me; and they both listened kindly to what I said, and contributed most liberally to the
funds of the Canadian Anti-Slavery Society, whose agent I was.
My next visit was but six months afterward, when I was struck
with the noticeable progress my people had everywhere made
during the time intervening. That I was cheered and encouraged
by this agreeable fact, I hardly need say. At that time, too, though
at mid-winter, their voluntary contribution, following so soon
upon the former one, gave me a most welcome surprise.

Chatham is emphatically the point of *entrée* into Western Canada. Before the railway was opened, it was, from its position on
the Thames, conveniently reached by steamers from Detroit. It
was then almost exclusively *the gate* to the Western interior.
Hence fugitives from the South-Western Slave States, and free
coloured people from Ohio, Pennsylvania, Michigan, and other
North-Western States, are almost daily arriving there. This is one
circumstance which draws to it a large black population; and
being already the residence of so many, makes it attractive to still
more. Besides, it lies midway, or nearly so, between Dawn on
the north and Buxton on the south, the two principal rural settlements of our people in the colony. Those therefore who desire
to settle in a town, or those wishing to go to either of these two
farming districts, usually land at Chatham.

There are fugitives—no, free persons—in that town whose

history would form a most enchanting romance. I can scarcely deny myself the pleasure of presenting some of them; but I must forbear. Suffice it to say, that there are persons here who have escaped from their own parents—some of them as white as the whitest Europeans; others who ran away from the men by whom they were treated, in some respects, as wives—escaping with the children which were the fruits of those connections. Some of these, having been favourite slaves, were allowed some accomplishments, and are therefore well skilled in music, drawing, &c. Their appearance and demeanour but too plainly show, that the system from which they escaped includes some of the most debasing immoralities in the whites, quite equal to what it forces upon the blacks. What a sunken community must that be, in which men belonging to the Church can beget children contrary to the seventh commandment, without needing to blush! What a religion must that be, which declares that the system, of which these deeds are part, is ordained, sanctioned, owned and blest, of God! And, apart from all moral and religious considerations, how wretchedly depraved, how unnatural in his feelings, how near the level of the lowest heathen—not to say, of the brutes that perish— must be that man who complacently sells the children of his own body! Ah! the slaveholders are publishing, as in so many legibly written volumes, in the faces of their mulatto offspring, the sad, sickening evidences of their abominable immoralities. As a tree is known by its fruits, so is slavery by this, one of its most common results.

Now let me suggest where fault may be found with one or two things.

1. I do not agree with the policy of coloured people settling themselves together, in a particular part of a town or village. Some of their white neighbours need to be taught even the first ideas of civilization, by being near to enlightened progressive coloured people, such as are not few in Canada. And where there are no legal difficulties in the way, as there are not in Canada,

their is no reason why we should not buy, build, live, die, and be buried, just where other of Her Majesty's subjects live.

2. I have just the same to say about coloured Churches. The day was, in the United States, to their everlasting disgrace, when the whites so maltreated the blacks, in their places of worship, that the latter could not be comfortable in the same congregations with them. Being subject to a universal odium, and having no legal *locus standi,* there was no other way at that time apparent, but to worship separately from the whites. Thus have grown up coloured congregations in the States, until they have become, both from custom and from the circumstance alluded to, *almost* —I must be excused from saying, *quite*—matters of necessity, in those States. However, we were shut up to such poor ignorant teachings as our own preachers alone could give us, and our ignorance was greatly perpetuated thereby. True, this fact furnished occasion for the exhibition of one of the most remarkable facts in the history of any oppressed people. I refer to their discovering such a thirst for knowledge, in the midst of the greatest discouragements, as to compel their preachers to give them better instructions. Now, many of them compare very favourably in education with white preachers; and as *honest* expositors of God's holy Word, they by illimitable odds excel them. They never use the Bible to justify any of their sins. I do regard this as one of the most remarkable facts in the history and progress of the Negro race. I regret exceedingly, that the great lights of our generation have not brought this fact out in bolder relief. In this fact the black people of America show greater advancement than any other oppressed people, than any unenlightened class of people not oppressed, in the world.*

But we of Canada are in far different circumstances; and even such results as above referred to, in a country like ours, may

* It is true that the coloured preachers are many of them ignorant men; but it is also true, that this ignorance is so felt and complained of by a great many of their hearers, that they have been compelled to acquire education. Is not this a very creditable fact?

be purchased at too dear a rate. In Canada we are not on trial as
to whether we shall have our rights: we have them. We cannot
afford to be confined to the ignorant teaching of our poor brethren,
just from the plantations, because other and better teachings are
at our service. We cannot afford to wait for the success of such
slow steps as have brought about the improvement of our people
in the States, for we must *now*, without delay, fit ourselves and
our children for the responsibilities of free British citizens—
responsibilities which are already ours, whether we be fit for them
or not. I beg, therefore, to record here my opinion, as far as it may
have weight, against all and singular of the Negro Churches, not
only of Chatham, but throughout British America. I speak the
more freely from having uttered the same sentiments to those
concerned, who were kind enough to hear me patiently, and who,
I know, would be the last to suspect me of anything else than the
most fraternal feeling for them personally.

3. I must be allowed to express my regret that some of the
black men of Chatham—men, too, of wealth and position, as
compared with many others, white and black—are wanting in
manliness. They do not bravely, manfully, stand up for themselves and their people as they should. They cower before the
brawling demagogue Larwill—a man well known as an enemy of
the Negro, but a man beneath any manly Negro's contempt—a
recreant Englishman, of low origin but aspiring tendencies, not
knowing his place, and consequently not keeping it. He has some
little property, some coarse vulgar talent, which, with a good
degree of dogged boldness, makes him—especially as his principles are of most convenient changeableness—popular with his
class. It was he who moved, as an appendix to the vote ratifying
Lord Elgin's Reciprocity Treaty, a provision against fugitives entering Canada except under onerous Negro-catching conditions.
He avowed his object to be, to please the slaveholders of America.
English readers will pardon me for obtruding so unworthy a man
upon their notice; but I am sure they will at the same time

approve my scolding black men for cringing to him, much more for voting for him, when a candidate for office.

I say, this man and all like him should be taught that the self-respect of every black man, imperatively forbids his having anything to do with them; much less seeking their favour, by anything like fawning upon them. But there are noble blacks there, who will never do anything of the sort. Take it all in all, Chatham, as a settlement, is most successful; its influence upon our cause cannot but be most healthful. Take them all in all, the coloured people of Chatham are an honour to the race of Ham.

In the town of London (which, I beg to inform the reader, is on the Thames, in the county of Middlesex; its principal church is St. Paul's; it has a Blackfriars and a Westminster Bridge; the town immediately west of it is Westminster) there are some coloured families and individuals who are not only equal, but superior, to many of the inhabitants, of whatever colour. Here, our people do not live so much in distinct districts as in Chatham and some other towns. Abel Bedford Jones has his shop, his residence, and most of his town property, in one of the best streets, in the centre of the town. His brother, Alfred Thomas Jones, a druggist, is in one of the best business positions in the town. The same is true of others whom I could name. There is not a town in Canada where the respectable coloured people enjoy more of the esteem of the best classes, than London. Here, too, the lower classes are, according to their custom, Negro-haters.

I cannot speak of London without recollecting the lamented John Fraser, Esq., whose personal acquaintance and whose very great kindness I had the honour to enjoy, a year or two before that deplorable accident which deprived him of life and London of one of her most useful, most honoured citizens. Standing in the first rank of London society, Mr. Fraser was always ready to use his great name, his commanding influence, his ample purse, and his shining talents, in behalf of the poor—among others, of my own people.

I now come to one of the most gratifying parts of my work.
It is, to speak of the Buxton Settlement, township of Raleigh, in
the southern part of Kent. I will not repeat what I have said elsewhere concerning the early origin of this settlement. It seems that
the Rev. William King (one of the most single-minded, straightforward, energetic and philanthropic Scotchmen I ever knew)
being, in the right of a relative—perhaps his wife, I do not
know exactly—a slaveholder, and seeing the evil of it, determined
to free slaves. In such a mind as his, it was natural *that* thought
should give rise to another; that was, to settle them in a free country. Hence he brought them to Canada for that purpose. But while
settling these, why not found a settlement for other free coloured
people? Why not purchase a tract of land, and open it for any who
might come? And then, they would need some one to look after
them, guide them, teach them, and preach to them: why should
not *he* undertake this? He did: and immediately formed a Company, called the "Elgin Association," in honour of the then
most excellent Governor-General of Canada; raised money,
bought lands, settled his own freed men, invited others, founded
a colony, opened a school; and, having been appointed a missionary by his own (the Free Scotch) denomination, he organized
a Church, formed a Sabbath School, and is going on most successfully with the settlement of Buxton.

There are about 150 families in the settlement. It is now about
six years old. Each family purchases fifty acres of land, paying ten
shillings sterling the acre. To accommodate their circumstances,
the land is sold to them for the price the Association gave for it.
The payments are divided into ten of equal amount; and upon
making the first payment, the settler enters upon his land. Certain
moral qualifications must be processed to fit one for an opportunity of purchasing. This wise rule is adopted for the purpose of
securing to the community none but persons of good character.
As a result, I did not learn of one immoral person, among the
150 families. No drunkard—and, indeed, no person who uses

alcohol as a beverage—is among the whole mass of those settlers.

They commenced when the whole tract was an unbroken forest. They now have comfortable houses, of the primitive description; clearings growing more and more extensive, good crops, a fair proportion of stock, and as many signs of present comfort and future prosperity as any settlement of the same age in Canada. I am now speaking merely of their physical circumstances, the best feature of which is their genial cheerfulness. This is the more remarkable, as some of them never lived on farms, much less on new bush farms, before. Some of them are immediately from large towns, where their occupations were any other than would fit them for such residences; some were from the far South, where they never felt the rigours of such winters as we have in Canada: but these are as cheerful as any others. I was there, the first time, in the summer; my next visit was in the middle of the winter. On both occasions I had the pleasure of seeing with what peculiar satisfaction they enjoyed and imparted the fruits of their own toil, the products of their own labour.

In the higher matter of intellectual manhood, these Buxtonians are making most commendable progress. Mr. King has established a school that would compare well with most of the grammar schools in the country. In it are taught the ordinary English branches, and Latin as well. Two of the most proficient pupils are a boy and a girl formerly Mr. King's slaves. So much more efficient is the school than those of the Government in the neighbourhood, that the latter are abandoned, and the whites of the vicinity gladly avail themselves of the superior advantages this school offers them. Hence, white children and black children sit, recite, and play together, without distinction. Hence, also, in the Sunday-school, are some white and some coloured teachers; and some of the one race are teaching those of the other, and *vice versa*, in the different classes. So also the Negro and the white man worship and commune together, a coloured lad setting the tunes. In the winter a night school for adults is taught. I have seen a mother and her two sons in the school during the day; and I have seen men, who worked hard at woodcutting all day, spend their hours, after walking by torchlight through the forest for miles, in the evening school. Aye, I have seen the same mother who was a day scholar take her place among the evening scholars, as well. Indeed, the young men and young women generally spend the winter in acquiring education; it is their chief, chosen pastime. Persons whom I knew to be careless about it in the States, are anxious and persevering to learn, now that they live in Buxton.

The fact of the physical and the intellectual development of the settlers, along with their high-toned moral character, already makes that settlement a model one. *There* is a living refutation of all that is said against us. It is not a matter of speculation, it is a matter of history. It is not something about which learned men may differ touching the ancient Negro; it is fact concerning the modern Negro, the Negro of the nineteenth century. It is not a question about what the Negro is capable of; it is an undeniable truth in demonstration of what he has done and is doing. The best country tavern in Kent is kept by Mr. West, at Buxton. Mr. T. Stringer is one of the most enterprising tradesmen in the county, and he is a Buxtonian, a coloured man. I broke my carriage near there. The woodwork, as well as the iron, was broken. I am particular about such things; so I am about the shoeing of my horses: but I never had better repairing done to either the woodwork or the ironwork of my carriage, I never had better shoeing than was done to my horses, in Buxton, in February 1852, by a black man, a native of Kentucky—in a word, the work was done after the manner of Charles Peyton Lucas. They are blest with able mechanics, good farmers, enterprising men, and women worthy of them; and they are training the rising generation to principles, such as will give them the best places in the esteem and the service of their countrymen at some day not far distant.

But I know of no community (I have travelled all over the United Kingdom) where stricter, better attention is paid to religion, than in Buxton. The whole population attend church. Their attention—their deep, serious interest—their intelligent love of the gospel—their decent, dignified demeanour—their freedom from gaudiness in dress, their neatness of person, and best of all, the lives they exhibit in daily transactions—render them a most agreeable congregation, either to worship with or to address. I speak from experience, having had the pleasure of both.

When Mr. King proposed this settlement, such a hue and cry was raised against it! The Mr. Larwill before spoken of headed a petition against allowing Mr. King to purchase the land. They said that "nobody would live near a Negro settlement. Land would become good for nothing in the neighbourhood. The Negroes would never cut down the trees and clear the land. They would be constantly committing depredations. In short, they knew the whole thing would prove a failure; at least they hoped it would." They even went so far as to threaten to pull down the Negroes' houses, if they should have the temerity to build upon the land, when purchased for them and sold to them. Mr. King, armed with the warrant from Her Majesty's representative to that effect, purchased the land, and, not having the fear of man before his eyes, settled his family upon his own farm, in the neighbourhood. The first purchaser was a strong-minded, bold, courageous black man, a native of Tennessee. He purchased a farm, erected his cabin, and on one Saturday removed his little family into his house. On Sunday, according to the fashion of the times *then*, a number of ill-featured, wild-visaged, unwashed, unshaven, scape-gallows-looking fellows, were out shooting, and came to the house of Mr. Riley, this Negro. He was near his door when they approached. Coming up to him, one of them, a wolfish-looking customer, said gruffly, "Haint you heard that if any of you niggers built a house here, we would put it down?"

Putting himself into a defiant attitude, Riley replied, "Yes,

I have heard so; and if *you* are here to pull my house down, *I* am here to see you do it."

That was the last of that threat. Now, these persons are not only content to live near their coloured neighbours, but they like it: now, no shooting is done on Sunday, in that part of the township. Such is the moral influence of the settlement and its excellent minister. Land sells all the higher because in that neighbourhood. These blacks are spoken of as good customers, good neighbours, good farmers, &c. Two farms were offered me, in the neighbourhood, by white persons. They asked round prices for them. I complained. "But you see, sir, they are so close to the King Settlement. First-rate neighbours, good customers, good preaching, *tallest kind* of a school; do you see?" I saw. (The preceding is the Western method of setting forth all manner of advantages in one breath.) Thus has that little community lived down more falsehoods than even its enemies ever told about it; and I hesitate not at all to say, that no subjects of the British Crown reflect more honour upon the liberty, the equality, the institutions, of Canada, than do the inhabitants of Buxton.

These settlements all happen to be in Kent. There are others, some of the most densely populated, in the county of Essex. They are flourishing in a high degree, but my limits will not allow of my mentioning them in detail. Dawn represents fairly, I think, the average condition of the three before mentioned; what I say of Chatham applies to towns in which we live generally; and Buxton is both a model for other settlements, and a proof of what can be done by judicious right-minded men.

In conclusion, I beg to say that I do not think that exclusive settlements for coloured people are to be considered desirable. Experiments have been made; they have proved triumphantly successful: now we need no more of them. In a country like Canada, whose population must of necessity become more or less mixed, the maintaining of distinct nationalities is certainly exceptionable. Anything exclusive, except so far as education and morals go (and perhaps, in future days, rank and wealth, provided they be open alike to all), is certainly unwise and unfair. After all, you can better teach by intermingling than isolation, to those who deny the Negro's capacity, what he can do. It is by constant, every-day contact with the Negro, that his character—his faults as well as his virtues—can be learned; and if anything in the way of settling is to be done, it were far better to do it by fusion than by any exclusive plan or scheme. I think just the same of French settlements, or Dutch, or Irish, or any other.

However this particular point may be viewed, I think no one can look at the black population of Canada, with its great energy, increasing intelligence, moderately but certainly increasing wealth, skilful industry, high moral character, aspiring aims, and great loyalty (as was shown in time of the rebellion, and will be again, whenever needed), increasing numbers and in all respects growing importance, without agreeing with me, that a most important future is before them. The attraction of freedom, spite of fugitive laws and bloodhounds, will draw them to us from the Slaveholding States. Those who are residing in the North, and feel alarmed, will come to us. Thousands of others, who were never slaves, will join us—as many have during the past year or two. Can the South afford the drain of her most energetic men, the very lifeblood of the country, year after year? Can the traducers of the Negro refute the fact—so contradictory to their assertion, as having come from Dr. Bacon twenty years ago, and from Ex-Governor Hunt but the other day, "that blacks and whites cannot live together on amicable terms as equals in the same community"? Here is a demonstration, a *quod erat demonstrandum*, to the utter confusion of that oft repeated untruth. It is not far off, it is right at their very doors. If we point to our West India Islands, they have two refuges to fly to: 1, The superior number of the Negroes—as if that altered the case! 2, The ruin that emancipation is said to have wrought. But here is no preponderance of blacks; no ruin, especially no ruin in the settlements and villages of the blacks. If they point to Hamilton, or some other town where immorality among coloured persons is but too common, it can be most triumphantly replied, that there are no women of bolder lewder character, no men who give more trouble to the magistracy, in that and like towns, than the low whites thereof; and while Negro degradation is, I am sorry to say, too apparent there, some of the most enterprising, and in every way most honourable, men of that town and vicinity, are coloured men.

And if the South cannot afford the draft upon her population which her oppression drives and our freedom draws, what can she do to help it? What can the North do? Talk of annexation or conquest! Why, when there were but a handful of inhabitants in Western Canada, the invaders were driven out. "Yes, but York was burnt!" So was Detroit! The rebellion gave intermeddlers a "taste of our quality," as Negroes; and there are more of us now. But annexation would not dispose, and could not compel, a single Negro to return to the South: it would, however, if the extradition were attempted, drench the soil of Canada with blood, for we should resist quite as firmly as we resisted British bayonets, when we fought for Yankee liberty in both wars, and there are yet some living who recollect how that was done. But since the passing of the Fugitive Law, Canadians who were once foolish enough to be friendly to annexation see so clearly what American freedom is (or is *not*) for both white and black—they see how perfectly the whole Union is chained to the car of slavery (and not helplessly, but cringingly, basely, because willingly dragged at its wheels)—that they prefer real British freedom to the specious, despotic, misnamed Yankee substitute.

To the silent but powerful operation of those causes, therefore, must our neighbors submit, while the onward progress of the Canadian Negro shall exhibit the workings of American despotism, and British freedom, in their opposite results, before the eyes of an overlooking world.

The cause of the free coloured man in the States, and of the

British American Negro, is one. On both sides of the line that cause is in the hands of those most concerned. May they work in harmony; may the work prove successful! May each of us, in his sphere, do his part! And may God give the victory, and to him be the glory!

I have given what I deem the truth, concerning the character of the slaves who come to Canada. I have also spoken of what I have ventured to call "the improving process" of their flight. Some facts have been presented, touching their progress, their skill in their employments, their general industry, and the prosperity of their settlements. I beg to add, more definitely than heretofore, a statement of what is, to me, one of the most gratifying facts connected with our population: I refer to the very high standard of morals among them.

From my long residence and extensive travels in the United States, I may, I think, claim to be pretty well acquainted with the moral and religious character of my people. I am free to say that, from the ample opportunities afforded me of judging, the coloured people of Canada, as a whole, are the most moral and upright of our race in America. I am aware that in the States, North and South, they compare well with their pale-faced neighbours. I believe that the fair and the impartial will admit, that while in property and education the Negro in the Republic is, from causes beyond his control, inferior to the more favoured class, in morals, in character, he is not a jot or a tittle beneath the best of his neighbours. Whether others do or do not admit it, such is the fact.

But I know of no community of coloured people, in the States, where moral character is so pure as it is in Toronto. There, the least breath of suspicion against a person's moral character is the signal for his being universally avoided. It matters not what be his wealth, he is shunned and abandoned, if his character be spotted. Former position, powerful friends, nothing, can give him admission to society, if once a moral stain be fixed upon him.

The consequence is, that persons who are the least doubtful in this respect, find it impossible to impose themselves upon society, while a greater circumspection than I ever saw elsewhere is most studiously observed by all. The good influence of this state of things upon the young cannot be over-estimated. This, I know, is a point of great delicacy; but it is one of so much importance, and of such great credit to my people, that I am sure I should be wanting in duty and faithfulness if I did not mention it.

What I say of Toronto, where the largest coloured population is, applies equally well to London and to all other towns which I have visited. It is but true, that to this rule there are some unfortunate exceptions; some towns have larger proportions of the immoral class than others: but what I have just said is true of our people in Canada as a rule.

I know of cases in which persons not the most circumspect before they removed to Canada have come amongst us, and have put on such behaviour and exhibited such morality as they never did when residing in the States. I have known others, who passed current in the States, who thought to be admitted into society among us as they were at home, without amendment. They were most wretchedly disappointed. They were obliged to associate only with those of their own low level. In other instances, I have known of persons saying, "We are free and equal here. Our manhood is recognized, and we must live up to our responsibilities." The freedom of my adopted country works as an antidote to the moral poisons of the slavery and the prejudice of my native country. While the latter degrades, the former elevates.

> *The day*
> *That makes a man a slave takes half his worth away.*

The day that makes him a freeman, if it does not restore "half the worth taken away" by slavery, restores a part of it.

That this very important population may go on improving, and, by improving, reflect honour upon our race and justify the institutions under which it is their blessing and privilege to live, is, I am sure, a wish in which all benevolent hearts, on both sides of the Atlantic, will join me. I know of no better method of rebuking, practically and powerfully, the attitude and the conduct of our American neighbours, for their evil treatment of the slave and the free coloured man, than the improvement and development of the British Negro; and I beg to repeat, that what is done in this direction is practical co-operation with the abolitionists of the States in their laudable work. Success to the work, on both sides of the line!

ANTI-SLAVERY LABOURS, &c.

Part III

GREAT BRITAIN

CHAPTER I

Voyage, Arrival, Etc.

After I had travelled in the service of the Anti-Slavery Society
of Canada from December 1851 until April 1853, they desired
to take advantage of the well known anti-slavery feeling of Great
Britain, quickened and intensified as that feeling had recently
become by the unprecedented influence of Mrs. Stowe's master-
piece, *Uncle Tom's Cabin*, by sending me to England, to plead
in their behalf, and in behalf of my crushed countrymen in America, and the freed men of Canada. Accordingly, I took the good
steamer "Europa" on the 18th of April, 1853 (having bid adieu
to Toronto, and the precious ones within it, the day before), for
my first voyage across the Atlantic. This voyage was, to me, of no
ordinary interest. It was my first departure from my native continent. I was on my way to a strange land, thousands of miles from
family, friends, relatives, or any one who cared for me. I confess
to no little nervousness on this account.

Then, I had scarcely gone on board before a fact occurred that
did nothing to increase my mental comfort. And, while I am about
it, I may as well state two facts of like character. The first is, that
Louis Tappan, Esq., in procuring a passage for me, had, with his
characteristic straightforward manliness, told the agents that I
was a black man. For this I was grateful: it saved me much inconvenience. They sold Mr. T. a ticket upon the back of which
was the following indorsement:—"This gentleman's passage is
taken with the distinct understanding that he shall have his meals

in his state room.—E. C."* Mr. Tappan, both as my personal friend and as a Christian man, remonstrated; but it was of no avail. As if this were not enough, so soon almost as I touched the deck of the ship, a fine gentlemanly-appearing *Englishman* accosted me—

"Mr. Ward, I believe?"

"The same."

"You are going out to Liverpool?"

"I am."

"When Mr. Tappan took your passage, I was obliged to say to him, that you would take your meals in your state room; for you know, Mr. Ward, what are the prevalent feelings in this country in respect to coloured people, and if you eat at the cabin table Americans will complain. We cannot allow our ship to be the arena of constant quarrels on this subject; we avoid the difficulty by making the rule that coloured passengers shall eat in their state rooms, or we can't take them."

I replied, "I desire, Mr. Cunard, to be in London by the 4th of May. If I wait for another steamer, I shall be too late. For that reason I *submit* to that to which, I wish you to understand, I do not *consent.*"

"I am an Englishman," said Mr. C.: "I entertain no such feelings; but I must see to the comfort of the passengers. I will see that you have a comfortable state room; and indeed, you shall have a room, if possible, on deck, which will be more pleasant for you; and the steward shall have directions to make you as comfortable as possible; and I wish you a pleasant voyage, sir."

Well, thought I, here is an Englishman perverted, according to his own showing—like the Yankee, making the dollar come before right, law, or anything. He does not "share" Yankee feeling —he only accommodates, panders to it! that is all! His passengers must be made "comfortable"; that is, if they be white. If

---

* The initials of Mr. Edward Cunard.

not, why, the ship must not be "an arena for public discussion," &c.!

This was not exactly sea sickness, but no one will be surprised that it did not add to the pleasure of going to sea. I could not but reflect upon the arrogance of the Americans. They are for freedom, but they must enforce their own views of matters upon other people. They believe in equality; but it must not be exhibited, even in a British ship, in a form different from their way of showing it. In a word, the arrogance of Yankees amounts to this— "Wherever we go, and over whomsoever we meet, *our* peculiar views, feelings and customs, shall be made the supreme rule." Worse, however, than Yankee arrogance, is the easy accommodating virtue of a Yankeefied Englishman.

The other fact came to my knowledge soon after. It seems that the second steward, having some "flesh in his heart," and seeing that, with one or two exceptions, the second-cabin passengers (of which class I was) were Englishmen, proposed that I should be invited to join my fellow passengers at the table. All agreed *but one*, and that one was a small-sized Welshman! He had been to Texas, forgotten his Welsh breeding, become a slave-holder and a Negro-hater, and his pro-slavery spoiled dignity couldn't endure my black presence at table. I knew that no passenger, nor even the owners, could legally deny me my right to enter the second cabin. I knew that I had submitted to quite enough, in allowing them to put me into a superior state room, abaft the wheels, 20 feet further aft than second-cabin passengers are allowed to go, as a compromise with Negro-hate. Now, to be kept out of the cabin by a little fellow about "four feet nothing and a half" tall, was quite too much. I therefore entered the cabin when I pleased, defiant of my *little friend*, who, I am bound to say, became quite civilized in a few days; so much so, that ere we parted, he invited me to a small entertainment, in that very second cabin within which he could not at first endure my presence. What an ever-present demon the spirit of Negro-hate is! How it haunts, tempts, wounds, the black man, wherever his arch-enemy, the American, goes!

In Mr. Cunard's case, in its likeness to and connection with those of many other Englishmen, of such character, I found occasion for serious reflection, that has driven me to a conclusion which shall hereafter control my life. It is a conclusion to which my excellent friend, Mr. J. N. Still, of Brooklyn, came long since. I never really differed from him, but I confess that not until I came to Europe did I see it in its full importance. Mr. Cunard is a man of business; so are the mass of Englishmen. What interferes with or threatens a diminution of the gains of business must be avoided. What is right or wrong, if not set aside altogether, must at least be merged in or be made subservient to business considerations. What is peculiar to an Englishman's feelings, what is accordant with the spirit of British law, what is included with a British subject's rights, in my case, must all give way to the mere question of business: *i. e.*, Yankees pay largely, as passengers on the Cunard line. True, there are three Yankee lines competing with it; and it is equally true, that the rights of a black subject are as sacred in the eye of the law as those of a white subject (though Yankees are not subjects, by the way); so it was true, that what were my rights on British soil were my rights in a British ship. It was also true, that Her Majesty's Government retained so much control over that line as to have the power, when necessary—as has since been done—to send half the vessels comprising it to the Baltic, in the transport service. It was equally true, too, that if any one made a disturbance on board of the "Europa," *that* was the person to be deprived of his rights, and not an innocent person; besides, in my case, the matter was prejudged, and I was made to feel the weight of the regulation, in advance of any disturbance arising from my presence. But, pshaw! This is simply the right and the law of the case. It must be viewed, Mr. Cunard thought, in a business light. Yankees are frequent customers; Negroes are not. Now, could not the thing so be managed as to retain the £50,000 given by the Government for carrying the mails, retain the patronage of the Yankees, and, if some few Negroes occasionally go on the steamers, partly conciliate them and partly sacrifice them? That is the *business* view of the matter—that is the view of Mr. Cunard; and I am sorry to say, about ninety-nine out of every hundred Englishmen in America view such matters in the same light. What is a Negro made for, but to be kicked about for a white man's convenience?

Then I saw, that the *chief*, almost the *only* business of the Negro, is to be a man of business. Let him be planter, merchant, anything by which he may make his impression as a business man. Let a fair representation of us be found, not in servile and menial positions, but in business walks—on 'change, in Lombard Street, at the Docks, anywhere; but let it be in active prosperous business life. Let us become of some value as customers; then, when such devoted men of business as Mr. Cunard have before them the question of treading under foot some Negro, they will conclude differently. They will say, "Yes, it is true he is black, and our taste is like yours, gentlemen—a taste wonderfully improved by living with you under the 'stripes and stars' of republican freedom and equality; but then, looking at the matter with an eye to business, the fact is, we cannot very well afford to lose the custom of this class." Yes; black men must seek wealth. We have men of learning, men of professional celebrity, men who can wield the pen, men of the pulpit and the forum, but we must have men of wealth; and he who does most to promote his own and his neighbour's weal in this regard, does most to promote the interests of the race.

Could we speak of wealthy blacks as we fortunately can of Robert Morris and Macon Bolden Allen, of Boston, as lawyers; James McCune Smith, of New York, and John V. Degrasse, of Boston, and Thomas Joiner White, of Brooklyn, as medical men; Charles L. Reason, William G. Allen, and George B. Vashon, as college professors; James William Charles Pennington, William

Douglass, William Paul Quinn, Daniel A. Payne, Alexander Crummell, Henry Highland Garnett, Amos Gerry Beeman, and William H. Bishop, as divines; James M. Whitfield and Miss Watkins, as poets; Frederick Douglass, William Howard Day, John J. Gains, Charles Mercer Langston, and William J. Watkins, as orators—we should be looked upon and treated in altogether a different manner. But as we have produced such men as I have named—or rather, as they have, under God, *produced themselves*—so let us hope and be assured that the day is not far distant when, like the Quakers and the Jews, we shall be well and widely known for the pecuniary prosperity and independence of our class.

With the exception of the two annoyances referred to, I had a most delightful voyage, and became a most capital sailor—that is, in the passenger's sense of the term, which simply is, to be able *to do nothing*, comfortably and perseveringly, without sea sickness. I ate, drank, and slept, well—great comforts, at sea. I had the honour of daily visits from the excellent physician of the vessel, whose acquaintanceship I have the pleasure of still enjoying. Mr. W. M. Thackeray did me the honour to spend an hour daily in my state room. He, too, still honours me with his friendly acquaintance. The Lord Bishop of Montreal called upon me, the day after our first Sunday. Perhaps his Lordship was looking after me as a stray sheep, for I did not attend the service conducted by him on the day before. The service was in the after-cabin. I was not a passenger in that cabin. I was partly proscribed, because of my colour, to accommodate the passengers. To be a fellow worshipper with them, on sufferance, was more than my self-respect would allow. I therefore remained in my state room, where, I trust, I found and worshipped the omnipresent, the impartial Jehovah. For the kindness shown me, as well as for the manner of showing it, by the gentlemen referred to, I shall ever be grateful. There were several Americans on board, not one of whom came to me. Of course I did not seek them.

On Saturday, the last day of April, we saw land on the coast of Ireland. We then moved gracefully along the coast of Wales, telegraphed our approach at Holyhead, took a pilot early on Sunday morning, and, at eleven o'clock precisely, anchored in the Mersey, after a passage of ten days, fifteen hours, and fifteen minutes, mean time. I was in England—the England of my former reading, and my ardent admiration. I was at Liverpool—that Liverpool whose merchants, but sixty years before, had mobbed Clarkson for prying into and exposing the secret inhumanities of their slave trade. I was in a land of freedom, of true equality. I did not feel as some blacks say they felt, upon landing—that I was, for the first time in my life, a man. No, I always felt that; however wronged, maltreated, outraged—still, a man. Indeed, the very bitterness of what I had suffered at home consisted chiefly in the consciousness I always carried with me of being an equal man to any of those who trampled upon me.

My first experience of English dealing was in being charged treble fare by a Liverpool cabman, a race with which I have had much to do since. Acting upon the advice given me by John Laidlaw, Esq., I went to Clayton Square, where I found good quarters at Mr. Brown's very genteel Temperance Hotel. The Rev. Dr. Willis had very kindly given me a note of introduction to the master of the Grecian Hotel; but I found no reason to desire a change, and therefore remained, while in Liverpool, where I first lodged.

Several things arrested my attention upon the first day of my being in England. One was, the comfort and cleanliness, not to say the elegance of appearance, presented by the working classes. I had always, in the United States, heard and read of the English working classes as being ground down to the very earth—as being far worse in their condition than the American slaves. Their circumstances, in the rural and the factory districts, I had always heard described as the most destitute. That they wrought for sixpence a day I had been informed by I know not how many Americans, who had visited England. How many times have I heard from the lips of American protectionists, and seen in the columns of their journals, statements such as this—"If we do not maintain a protection tariff, English manufacturers, who pay their operatives but sixpence a day, will flood our markets with their products, and the factory operative in America will, in consequence, be compelled to work for sixpence a day, as the English operative now does"! When I was an American protectionist, how I used to "take up that parable," and, believing it, repeat it! How others with me believed the same too often told falsehood! Here was before me, in Lancashire and her noble port—Lancashire, the headquarters of British, if not European, factory interest—almost a manufacturing kingdom in itself—a most abundant refutation of what, on this subject, I had nearly a thousand times heard, read, believed, and repeated.

But this was Sunday. The next day, having occasion to cross the Mersey, I saw nearly as many well-dressed working men, with their wives and sweethearts, enjoying the holiday of that Monday, as I had seen the day before. This led me, as I travelled further into the factory district, to make definite inquiries into the condition of the operatives; and, as I may not again recur to it, I will put down here, in few words, a sort of summary of the information I obtained. I learned—indeed, saw with my own eyes—that throughout Lancashire the young women in the factories dress as well as the young women I had seen at Lowell, Dover, Manchester, Nashua, and other manufacturing towns in New England. I had been in those towns but a year and a half before; and now, at Manchester, Bolton, Preston, Wigan, &c., had a fair opportunity of comparing them. I learned as well, that the wages of the different grades of operatives varied from highest to lowest, each respectively being about the same as in New England. The hours of labour were no greater; and upon visiting several factories (among them that of Sir Elkanah Armitage, at Pendleton, Manchester), I found the work as easy, and the health and cheerfulness of the operatives as good, as I had seen in the same class on the other side of the Atlantic. What was true, comparing the English with the American *female* operative, is equally true of the *male*. I was agreeably surprised to learn that the condition of these people, as I had heard of it at home, was a misrepresentation of the condition in which I found them. Formerly, the operatives had suffered much from the want of care exercised by themselves, and more from the want of humanity on the part of their employers; like some persons of other business, of whom we have been speaking, humanity was made to succumb to business: but, by the perseverance of Lord Shaftesbury (then Lord Ashley) and others, Government exerted an influence between the employer and the employed, and led to the adoption of many very important improvements.

Here were two truths which the pro-slavery portion of the Americans did not at all like to tell, and therefore cleverly and conveniently forgot them: 1, That the improvements referred to do exist. 2, That the British Parliament shows an interest in behalf of these people, who "are worse off than our slaves." It better suits their purpose to state matters as they *were*, than as they *are;* and to state the truth, that the Government of Great Britain, through its legislature, looks after these people, would *rather* spoil the parallel between the British free labour and the American slave! It is a clever thing to *forget* just what one chooses *not to recall!*

Another thing that attracted my attention was, the beautiful twilight of this latitude. Forgetting that I was eleven degrees further north than ever before, I wondered why at eight o'clock it was so light. I then learned how to join Englishmen in the enjoyment of that most delightful part of the day. But when I went to Scotland, subsequently, I was still more charmed, especially at midsummer, in the far north, with this pleasing feature of a northern residence.

I wondered, also, that I could not realize the vast distance I had come, and the mighty space between me and those loved ones

I had left behind. I seemed to be simply in a neighbouring town, when in Liverpool. I sould see in this town, and in the appearance of many of its inhabitants, some resemblance to Boston and the Bostonians. Nothing wore, to my view, the strange aspect which I had expected. This, I think, was owing partly to my having travelled so much before, constantly visiting strange places and constantly seeing new faces; partly to the strong resemblance of the New England people to those of Liverpool; but, more than either, to the fact that in Canada, especially in Toronto, we are English in habits, manners, &c.

I beg to add, too, that I could not have anticipated how much my faith would be strengthened, by trusting in God amid the exposures of a voyage. Faith grew stronger by its own exercise. For nine consecutive nights I had lain my head upon my pillow at sea. In the midst of the vast deep, where our great vessel and all it contained might, like the "President," go to the bottom in an hour, leaving none to tell the story of our fate, and no traces of even the whereabouts of our destruction—to trust God in these circumstances—to hear the rolling heaving ocean, at deep dark midnight, and still to trust him—to listen to the hurried commands, and the rattling of ropes and sails, and the hundred and one accompaniments of a storm, and still to trust him—give faith a strength peculiar only to its trial amid dangers. I could not help writing to Mrs. Ward, that, having long before learned to trust our Heavenly Father as the God of the land, I had now learned to rely upon him as the God of the ocean. I know not how far this accords with the experience of other voyagers, and have now no means of knowing whether the same feeling will continue with myself; but I do know that it at present is far from being one of the least striking or the least pleasing incidents of my first voyage.

CHAPTER II

Commencement of Labour in England

The object of my coming to England has been stated. So soon as I began to speak of it, I found persons responding to it most readily. After presenting my letters at Liverpool, I took the train for London, for the purpose of meeting the great leaders of England's unrivalled benevolent movements, during the May Meetings. Finding most agreeable travelling companions, and seeing England in her first of May dress, to my very great delight, I reached London at about 4 P.M., in the midst of a pouring rain. Unfavourable as was the day for seeing London, yet London has some things, many things, innumerable things, to show, on any day. Here, I was much more impressed with my being a stranger than at Liverpool. There was no such thing as learning my way. There was neither rational beginning nor ending to the streets. They were so tortuous, that, starting in one of them in a certain direction, I soon found myself going in the opposite direction in the same street! Still, even London can be learned, with all its intricacies; and after a while I became, in this respect, a Londoner.

Delivering my letters to the persons to whom kind friends had commended me, and finding myself expected at the Anti-Slavery Office, I set about the *work* of attending the May Meetings. I am sure people must have been amused with my exceedingly awkward, backwoods appearance. A backwoodsman in London is sure to be conspicuous. The more he tries to hide the fact that he is such, the more apparent he makes it. But I adopted the easiest, quietest mannerism I could command, and confessed myself a mere colonist, asking no one to take me for more than I was, while I cared not how much they underrated me.

Exeter Hall I had often heard of, and went there the first thing after my arrival. A meeting was in progress—with speeches, cheering, passing resolutions, and all that sort of thing, to which I was not an entire stranger. A large fine-looking person was in the chair. I took a seat near to a most affable gentleman; and wishing to know who the chairman was, I wrote on a card and handed it to my neighbour, "Who is the gentleman in the chair?" "The Marquis of Cholmondeley," was his reply, on another card. I had seen a nobleman, a lord—for the first time!

The Rev. Thomas Binney, to whom I brought letters from Rev. Mr. Roaf, my pastor, received me most kindly. Mrs. Binney acted as if we had been acquainted for the preceding six-and-twenty years; and, being the first London lady with whom I had the pleasure of acquaintance, I saw in her what I have since seen in English people of all ranks, who are really genteel—a most skilful and yet an indescribably easy way of making one feel perfectly at ease with them. I cannot tell how it is done. I saw it in all good English society, but how they did it I know not; at any rate, they are most successful in making one feel it. I think a part of it is, in being perfectly at ease themselves; and another part is, the perfectly captivating kindness that is seen in all they say and do. In this respect, really genteel people, of all ranks, are perfectly alike; in this you cannot distinguish a nobleman from a commoner: but the most ridiculous blunders are made by those assuming it to whom it is not habitual, natural, or educational.

My first introduction to any portion of the British public was at the meeting of the Colonial Missionary Society, on the evening of its anniversary, at Poultry Chapel. To the Rev. Thomas James, its excellent Secretary, I had brought letters. On their presentation, this gentleman, as a sort of "Minister for the Colonies," took me by the hand most warmly. At his invitation I attended the meeting in question. The Rev. Mr. Binney kindly introduced me, in a manner which, I fear, my effort did not at all justify. At that meeting the Lord Mayor Challis presided. I had never before seen a Lord Mayor. His Lordship kindly invited me to the Mansion House, in company with several ministers of the Congregational denomination, a few days after. About the same time the meeting of the Congregational Union occurred, and I was formally introduced to the body by the Secretary, Rev. George Smith, in company with Rev. Charles Beecher, whom I had not met before. Then came a dinner for the ministers and delegates at Radley's Hotel, at which I was called upon for a speech.

The amiable Rev. James Sherman, at that time minister of Surrey Chapel, with his accustomed kindness took me in his carriage to the dinner; and afterwards, for four months, not only made me his guest, but made his house my home. I never lived so long with any other person, on the same terms. While I live, that dear gentleman will seem to me as a most generous fatherly friend.

It was at his home, the best place to study a man's character, that I learned who James Sherman is, and how and why to appreciate him. If I love him more than some persons do, while all admire him and multitudes love him, it is because I know him better and am more indebted to him. His is not the friendship of the passing hour; it is not that which only smiles when everybody else does, and deserts one in the hour of trial and need; it is not the friendship which easily exhausts itself in a few courtly, complimentary phrases, and common-place, costless, worthless because heartless, flatteries. The friendship of James Sherman is that of a man of feeling, as well as a man of honour; it is that which places at one's disposal whatever he has, whatever he can do, and rejoices in any sacrifice to accommodate whoever may have the good fortune to be admitted to his intimate acquaintance. Since the demise of my dear father, I have seen no man whom, in adversity and prosperity, in sunshine and in storm, I could so safely trust, in whom I could so implicitly rely in any and all the varying and trying circumstances of life and fortune, as James Sherman. This, I know, is no honour to one so exalted, from one so humble. But gratitude and affection, it seems to me, are not out of place here; and I wish to convey to the friends of the Negro on the other side of the Atlantic, what they have a right to receive, my deep and humble though ardent sense of obligation to that gentleman, both in my own behalf and in behalf of my people.

Once introduced to their meetings, kind brethren found enough for me to do, Sunday and every other day, until the meetings were over, and I had formed a list of acquaintances well worthy of my crossing the Atlantic. Having served several other causes, it became time to launch my own, especially as I had not dragged it upon other people's platforms.

I had arrived in England at a fortunate time—not merely because of the May meetings, but because of the twofold fact that *Uncle Tom's Cabin* was in every body's hands and heart, and its gifted authoress was the English people's guest. For anti-slavery purposes, a more favourable time could not have been chosen for visiting England. I may be allowed to dwell upon this for a moment. The book came in the very best time, as if by an ordination of Divine Providence. A year before, the expected invasion of England by the French absorbed so much attention, that it could not have been so patiently and attentively read, nor could it have made so deep an impression; a year after, the war with Russia engrossed universal attention; but the issue of that work during a sort of lull in public affairs, between these two events, was most opportune. I regard it, I repeat, as a special ordination of Providence.

Uncle Tom's Cabin had so impressed the anti-slavery people of the aristocratic classes, as to lead to the celebrated address of English women to the women of America, in behalf of the enslaved. This with its powerful effect, was the theme of universal discussion when Mrs. Stowe arrived in England. The book from the one side of the Atlantic, the address from the other side, and the arrival of her whose gifted pen had been the occasion of the one and the origin of the other, awakened more attention to the anti-slavery cause in England, in 1853, than had existed since the agitation of the emancipation question in 1832. It was my singularly good fortune to meet Mrs. Stowe at the house of Rev. James Sherman, in May; indeed, we were dwellers under his hospitable roof, along with Rev. Dr. Stowe and Rev. C. Beecher, for some three weeks.

By the advice of Rev. T. James, I invited several friends of the anti-slavery cause to a meeting at Radley's Hotel, on the 7th of June, to lay before them the objects of my mission. Having been honoured with the acquaintance of Lord Shaftesbury, I ventured to ask him to take the chair on that occasion; to which, with his Lordship's ordinary kindness, he consented. The meeting, approving of my objects, adjourned to Freemasons' Tavern, on the 21st. In the meantime, Lord Shaftesbury kindly procured for me the names of the following noblemen to attach to the call for that meeting: the Duke of Argyll, the Earl of Harrowby, the Earl Waldegrave, and Lord Brougham. Mr. Sherman procured for me the names of Sir James K. Shuttleworth, Mr. Sheriff Croll, and Messrs. Bevan and Tritton the bankers. On the 21st the meeting was held, the Earl of Shaftesbury in the chair: and a Committee was formed, of which that distinguished nobleman consented to be Chairman; Rev. J. Sherman, and S. H. Horman-Fisher, Esq.,* Honorary Secretaries; and G. W. Alexander, Esq., Treasurer.

Thus, in a manner neither anticipated by myself nor by those who sent me to England, was my cause launched, so to speak, upon the broad sea of public British munificence, under such auspices

---

* A most devoted friend of the Negro, and a gentleman who honours me with his personal friendship, tested in hours of trial and darkness.

and with such a prestige as favour the missions of but few colonists coming to this country, on any errand whatever. Deep and lasting are the obligations under which I was laid. I never *shall* forget those obligations; I never *can* cancel them. It is to me a great relief, in view of my own unworthiness of them, to know that they had infinitely less to do with me than with my people; and that, however unfortunate the latter were in the selection of their representative, they themselves are far more worthy of the distinguished consideration they received through him. I may be permitted to add, I have the satisfaction of knowing that the Anti-Slavery Society of Canada, who sent me here, have, on more occasions than one, testified their high appreciation of and cordial fraternal thanks for the manner in which the distinguished personages who contributed to our cause, and gave it the sanction of their great names, and laboured in its Secretariat and upon its Committee, served and forwarded the objects of my mission.*

As I was under no agreement to labour for the Committee on Sunday, I accepted of an offer kindly made me by the Committee of the Colonial Missionary Society, through its excellent Secretary, Rev. Thomas James, to urge the claims of that very important charity, on the first day of the week. Thus the field of my labours and circle of my acquaintance were enlarged greatly; and as my appearance anywhere, as I understood the matter, brought the *slave* to mind, I hope that, in that service, I did not mar the great chief object of my coming hither. Occasionally, too, I was honoured by invitations to speak for the London Missionary Society; while kindred charities, along with these, seemed to regard me as public property; and, ere I knew it, I had the name of a respectable successful beggar. The duty of travelling in these causes called me into almost every county in England, into the pulpits of the most distinguished Dissenting divines in the land,

---

* The noble Earl of Shaftesbury had made his honoured name fragrant among all the lovers of freedom on the other side of the Atlantic, before this. His Lordship is now revered in every cabin in Canada.

into company with some of England's noblest sons and daughters, into contact with representatives of the different classes of pro-slavery men in England, whether exotics or natives—in a word, into a sphere of active usefulness which I had before never dared to covet.

It is, as it should be, in America and in the colonies, regarded as a matter of importance, for a man wishing to improve both his head and his heart, to visit England. There is so much to be learned here, civilization being at its very summit—society, in consequence, presenting every attraction, and every form of social improvement and instruction. Here, too, is so much of historic recollection. England, indeed, is a book, ancient, mediæval, and modern, in itself. One cannot but agree with those who hold the opinion that the best specimens of the Colonial or the American gentleman need European travel for their finishing. English travel, in more ways than one, is the best, choicest portion of European travel. I came to England knowing this, and hoping to enjoy and appreciate it in some degree; but to be associated with that band who have no equals in this world and no superiors in any age, the leaders of the benevolent schemes of England—to be acknowledged by them as a coadjutor—to be permitted to share with them in those smaller, lighter portions of their work, for which alone I had any sort of even seeming qualifications—was what I had no right to expect, but what I felt the honour of all the more. Before I had been one month in England, I had been upon the platforms of the Bible, Tract, Sunday School, Missionary, Temperance, and Peace, as well as the Anti-Slavery, Societies. To the last, in my native country, Negroes are freely admitted, invited, as a matter of course. Who ever saw one of sable hue upon the platforms of *the others?* Never, as an equal brother man, was I welcomed to the national platforms of any of them, until I became a resident of Canada.

After ten months' service for the Anti-Slavery Society of Canada, through the Committee in London, its affairs were wound up, some £1,200 having been kindly given to its treasury by the philanthropists of England and Scotland. A large meeting was holden at Crosby Hall on the 20th of March, 1854, the venerable and philanthropic Samuel Gurney, Esq., in the chair; Rev. James Sherman, Samuel Horman Horman-Fisher, Esq., L. A. Chamerovzow, Esq., Rev. James Hamilton, D.D., Rev. John Macfarlane, B.A., Josiah Conder, Esq., together with others, being on the platform; and Joseph Payne, Esq., gracing the occasion with his presence, a speech, and a piece of poetry, the last of which he kindly gave me. I hold it as a memento of its beloved author, and as a remembrance of the friendship wherewith he has been pleased to honour me.

I shall not, I am sure, be expected to give the dry details of a journal, nor a formal account of the meetings I attended, much less the speeches I made—if speeches they deserve to be called. Nor, I hope, shall I be considered wanting in gratitude (a charge brought against too many Americans, with but too much justice, it is to be feared), if I do not mention the name of every town in which I received kindness, and every family and every individual to whom I am indebted. The reason why I shall not do so is simply this: this book must have an end. Where that end would be, were all those recorded, it were impossible for author, publisher, or printer to say; but I am very sure no reader would have patience to seek it by consecutive reading.

Several incidents—some of the principles I sought to promulgate—a few reflections upon what I saw, heard, and felt—with the mention of some names, which must be taken as representatives of all their class—I shall give: this, I am convinced, is all that can be expected of me. As my time and labours were not exclusively devoted to anti-slavery advocacy, *in forma*, my remarks will not be restricted to that subject.

CHAPTER III

Pro-Slavery Men in England

On a former page I spoke of "pro-slavery men in England, whether natives or exotics." There is no use in concealing that there are such, of both classes. The latter do not always choose to be called pro-slavery men; but that is their position, nevertheless. For example: the Rev. Dr. Cox would like, in England, to pass for the friend of the slave; but at home he is a justifier of slavery. The Rev. Dr. Baird can lecture eloquently about the oppressions the Hungarians suffer at the hands of the Austrians: his lips are sealed, his tongue is dumb, on the oppressions of American slavery. The Rev. Dr. Anderson can inveigh against "Englishmen's singling out slavery for rebuke, passing by other sins:" at home, he has yet to treat it *as a sin, for the first time.* The Rev. S. J. Prime, D.D., likes well enough to be seen among British abolitionists, but he scorns the company and the principles of Christian abolitionists at home. His paper, *The New York Observer,* with which I have been acquainted, more or less, for twenty years, is, without exception, the most persevering pro-slavery paper in the country in which it is published.* Such gentlemen, I repeat, come to this country anxious enough to have an anti-slavery *reputation here;* when, like the Rev. Dr. Chickering, of Portland, Maine, they have no anti-slavery *character at home.* This is certainly the most dangerous, and perhaps the most numerous, class of exotic

* I cannot except even *Bennett's Herald,* or *Webb's Courier and Inquirer;* no, not even the *Journal of Commerce.*

pro-slavery men. I did not meet any of them personally, but I had the pleasure of seeing them writhe under the earnest, loving, anti-slavery passages in the speech of the Hon. and Rev. Baptist Wrio-thesley Noel, at Exeter Hall; and I saw how they looked while the Rev. Thomas Binney, upon the same occasion (the anniversary of the British and Foreign Bible Society, to which the Bishop of Ohio and the Rev. Dr. De Witt, both pro-slavery, were American delegates), poured upon them his huge pity for being "unable" to give the Bible to the slaves: and, as I travelled about, I could every now and then hear of their pro-slavery deliverances. Still they never came out in the face of day and avowed themselves what they are proved to be at home—the friends of slavery, the enemies of anti-slavery, the revilers of the Negro, the supporters of the Fugitive Law.

At times, however, in private circles, one would meet a Spanish slaveholder, or a person who had been a slaveholder in the British West Indies, who would utter, in a very quiet way, denials of anti-slavery truth. I will give a few instances of what I mean by native pro-slavery men, and by exotics.

Among the former are such Englishmen as the editors of the London *Times*, who did their utmost to write down *Uncle Tom's Cabin*—who ridicule and misrepresent the Negro—and, when respectfully asked to publish a dozen lines in their defence, contemptuously refuse to do so. Among such, also, is a lawyer of London, who, when hearing of a movement for the education of Negroes in the West Indies, wrote a pamphlet against the movement—of which pamphlet I had the inexpressible pleasure of hearing Lord Robert Grosvenor say, that in all his life he never had seen so many pages of letterpress contain such "an infinite deal of nothing." To the same class belongs a young physician, who, in a pamphlet concerning Jamaica, published a few weeks since, and which received a favourable critique from the *Morning Advertiser*,* says all manner of bitter things against the

---

* I regret exceedingly that Mr. Grant should have given currency to so ill-tempered and truthless a pamphlet.

Negro. As a specimen of this person's candour and veracity, he says, "a nigger cannot speak English." One would almost think that the writer proved it to be more difficult for himself to write truth *in any language,* than for "a nigger to speak English." And lastly, to this class I set down those Englishmen who, like Mr. Baxter (successor of the late Joseph Hume in the representation of the Montrose burghs), travel in America, see slavery, and return with honied words in its favour, to garnish their speeches and adorn their books. I may be pardoned for sparing no more space to them.

Among the latter are to be included such colonists as are always seeking to make it appear that prejudice against Negroes is quite natural and unavoidable, and that a Negro becoming anything else than a mere "hewer of wood and drawer of water" is out of the question. Belonging as I do to one of the humblest classes of colonists, I cannot but feel ashamed of any one from the distant dependencies of the Crown, who, in spite of what Negroes are in the Colonies, can give utterance to an assertion so utterly contradictory to historical truth. I give a specimen of colonial pro-slavery obliquity.

In June, 1853, the Rev. Mr. Dowding, a most excellent clergyman of the Established Church, favoured me with a most cordial invitation to attend a meeting for the promotion of Negro education in the West Indies, by the revival of Berkeley College, in Bermuda. I was but too happy to comply. At the time, I had not an inch of property in any part of the West Indies, nor was it then among the most distant of my intentions to go there to reside; but it was enough for me to know that some of the most exalted in the land, at the head of whom stood the venerable and benevolent Primate, were determined that to this population, along with freedom, education should be given. The meeting was held in Willis's Rooms; the Earl of Harrowby was in the chair. Among the personages present were the Earl of Shaftesbury, Lord Radstock, Lord Robert Grosvenor, Captain the Honourable Joseph Denman, the Honourable Charles Howard, the Rev. J.

Hampden Gurney, the Rev. Dr. Vaughan of Harrow, &c.; there was also the Honourable C. S. Haliburton, of Nova Scotia. One of the speeches was made by this gentleman. In the course of his remarks the learned Judge said, that inasmuch as the Bishop of New Brunswick approved the plan, and as he had the highest confidence in the judgment of that right reverend Prelate, he felt pleasure in giving it encouragement and wishing it success. But he ridiculed the idea of *a college* for Negroes. A school of an ordinary sort would have met his approval, but a college was generally understood to be a place for the education of a *gentleman*—a gentleman, among that race, was entirely out of the question. He was neither an Englishman nor an American, having been born "along shore," in Nova Scotia: but he was free on that occasion to say, that he shared in the prejudices generally entertained by Americans in regard to Negroes; and could not regard such feelings as unnatural or unjustifiable, but as inevitable. The idea of mixing with Negroes was naturally, to a white man, altogether and unconquerably repulsive.

I do not profess to give Judge Haliburton's words,* but I think those who heard them will admit that I give his ideas. He made another point, about the ruin of the West India planters by emancipation, which showed but too plainly that, to the heart's core, he was entirely with and for slavery, and that it was next to impossible to find a more malignant enemy to the Negro than the Honourable C. S. Haliburton. There were present some exceedingly genteel persons, whose embrowned complexions told plainly enough that they were not only West Indians, but that they shared African blood with me, though in a far less degree.

We are sometimes amused, if not disgusted, by vulgar persons trying to put on genteel manners, for the sake of inducing the belief that they belong to genteel classes, while their airs and

---

* S. H. Horman-Fisher, Esq., was present, and so was J. Gurney Hoare, Esq. I think either of those gentlemen will attest the general correctness of my version of the speech.

assumptions betray them. So Judge Haliburton, on the occasion referred to, in speaking contemptuously of a class whom his superiors on that platform were seeking to benefit—by the very effort to demonstrate that the Negro could not possibly be a gentleman, proved that, of all things, he himself most needed the qualities of a gentleman. Lord Harrowby, the chairman, had commended the object; Lord Shaftesbury had spoken of the object, and of Negroes (some of whom he named) who, in his Lordship's opinion, had made and merited a name. I dare not repeat what this distinguished nobleman said. Now for Mr. Haliburton, in such a presence, to give an implied, if not a direct, contradiction to these noblemen, was far more ungentlemanly than anything done by any coloured person in that meeting.

As Judge Haliburton is the representive of a class, and as he is a man of some local popularity, holding opinions in common with other accidentally elevated men of low origin, I beg, without repeating exactly what I was permitted to say on that occasion, to make a remark or two on this matter.

1. It is to be hoped that Englishmen, especially English noblemen, will not suppose that Mr. C. S. Haliburton, the author of *Sam Slick* and some other such productions, is a fair specimen of colonial judges, nor of colonial feeling. His Honour only illustrates the fact that, in the North American colonies in former days, judges were made rather hastily, and of rather singular materials. Such a personage as Mr. Justice Draper, of Toronto, or Sir John Robinson, the Chief Justice of Upper Canada, or Mr. Justice Jones, of Bruntford, or the eminent Ex-Chief Justice Marshall, of Nova Scotia (who devotes himself to the temperance cause, at his own expense, in Canada), would neither offend a platform of noblemen, nor show the *bravery* of attacking an absent prostrate people with expressions of heartless approval of their sufferings, and sympathy with their tormentors—for the plain reason that each of these personages is incapable both of the indecency and the inhumanity to do so. Judge Haliburton is

not: his Honour is most abundantly equal to any such task. Therein he differs, I am proud to say, from colonial judges generally.

2. Admitting that Judge Haliburton's speech (I mean that part of it which was a wholesale disparagement of the Negro; hoping to say something about the subject matter of the other part at some day, not long hence) may have been as beautiful (doubtless it was, in his own eyes) as Vulcan's wife, it was, at the same time, as false as that unchaste daughter of Jove. Within six-and-thirty hours' sail of Judge Haliburton's residence are the cities of Portland and Boston. Five hours more would bring him to New York; and four more, to Philadelphia. The Rev. M. Dowding has published the names and opinions of several distinguished coloured *gentlemen,* in the last-named of those cities, having visited them; and Judge Haliburton could have acquired information concerning them quite as easily: indeed, one cannot believe that a man of letters, wealth, and leisure, a man in a learned profession, did not know of coloured gentlemen so near him as are many in those cities, especially in Portland and Boston.

But Mr. Haliburton spoke as a British colonist. Could he be ignorant of the names of the Honourable Edward Jordan, the Honourable Richard Hill, and the Honourable Peter Moncrief, of Jamaica? Could he fail to know that those eminent personages had, like himself, practised at the bar, worn the ermine, and adorned the legislative hall? Lord Harrowby knew it; why should not Judge Haliburton? An older lawyer, and a far more eminent man, Sir Allan MacNab, of Canada, told me he had seen with great pleasure these and like gentlemen, in the Jamaica Legislature. But Judge Haliburton says, "the idea of a black gentleman is out of the question!"

What lamentable ignorance, to use no harsher term, does such an assertion as Judge Haliburton's betray, in respect to the historical Negro! Euclid had a black face, wooly hair, thick lips, flat nose, and crooked ankles. He was the father of geometry, but Judge Haliburton had never heard of him, or he could not have said that "the idea of a black gentleman is out of the question." One of the objects of Berkeley College is to teach modern Negroes the science whereof the Negro Euclid was father. To this Judge Haliburton objected. To his learned vision, it was perfectly absurd! Was Terence, the black poet, a gentleman? Were Tertullian, Augustin, Origen (of whom Archbishop Sharpe, the grandfather of Granville Sharpe, speaks as "among the most extraordinary lights of the Church of God"), gentleman? But let me not do injustice to Mr. Haliburton. I may not know what his idea of a gentleman *is*. Judging from his appearance, his writings, the taste displayed in the only speech I ever heard him make, the sort of rudeness with which he treated his superiors on this occasion, and the utter destitution of any semblance of liberal feeling then and there shown by him, I am tempted to believe that the standard of a gentleman, holden by Judge Haliburton, is one according to which it may be, after all, no discredit to the Negro race if they do not produce many *such* specimens.

A word as to the naturalness and inevitable necessity of Negro-hate: that word is, *"truthless."* In proof of it, the language of every speaker on that occasion, with the single exception of Mr. C. S. Haliburton, in respect to the Negro, was most abundant, most triumphant.

3. I beg to say, that sometimes the unfortunately disproportionate number of Negroes in prisons is pointed out to me as evidence of the very great criminality of my people. I ask any one to say, what chance of a fair and just trial a Negro could have, before such a judge as Mr. Justice Haliburton, when a white man was prosecutor? (I happen to know how Negroes have suffered in such cases.) For it is impossible for a man, when he puts on his judicial robe, to put on another nature: the man and the judge will be very much the same. I know nothing of Judge Haliburton's character, or rather of his history, in this regard; but judging from his own words, and from the likeness of feeling to himself on the part of his fellow citizens, I do not at all wonder

that the blacks of Nova Scotia are deprived of many of their rights by them.

The explanation of all this is, that Judge Haliburton, and all like him, whether on Yankee or British soil, do not wish to know better. A fair illustration of the class was given me by G. Ralston, Esq., in the case of an American lady who was at the Clarendon when Her Majesty's Secretary of State for Foreign Affairs gave a complimentary dinner to his Excellency the Honourable Benjamin Roberts, President of the Republic of Liberia. President Roberts, it is known, is an American by birth, and of African origin. Seeing—and, though an American, so far above the contemptible prejudices of his countrymen as to enable me to say, with great pleasure, with delight—that President Roberts was the "admired of all admirers," Mr. Ralston proposed to introduce his fair country-woman to the guest of England's noble Secretary. With real American feeling, this proud republican dame declined. So do all of the class. They choose not to know coloured persons of distinction, when they might; or, knowing them, they choose to misrepresent them.

I must be allowed to record, just here, the very great delight I had in hearing the *real* gentleman and nobleman speak, at the meeting referred to, in such terms as they were pleased to use, concerning the Negro. Doubt of the Negro's capacity was scouted, as a brainless, senseless thing. Rejoicing in such an opportunity of forwarding such a movement was, common to all lips, as it flowed from all hearts; but the expression which struck me with greatest force was the one which conveyed the idea of their indebtedness to the Negro. Upon this Lord Harrowby and Lord Shaftesbury strongly insisted, and the meeting received their words with marked approbation. The Honourable Charles Howard, brother of Lord Carlisle, and Lord Robert Grosvenor, brother to the Marquis of Westminster, dwelt upon this thought as if it were one to which they were no stranger. The Honourable Captain Denman, brother to the present Lord Denman, declared that "we had sinned against the Negro in the West Indies; and while he could not agree with Mr. Ward, that no evils had followed emancipation, he did trace a natural connection between those evils and the sins which preceded them." The Rev. J. Hampden Gurney, the Rev. Dr. Vaughan, and all the other British *gentlemen* present, expressed like sentiments. I need not say, that on my people's behalf I was but too proud of the opportunity kindly afforded me, of thanking such benefactors for such words. If any one should infer that the author of *Sam Slick* appeared awkward and out of place in such company, I am quite willing to bear the responsibility of this inference.

Leaving this meeting, and that member of it upon whose words I felt myself called upon to say so much, it may not be inappropriate to say some other things, in this chapter, on this subject. It is not to be denied that a history of the Negro race is unwritten; no, it is written in characters of blood! It is a very compact, succinct chronicle: it comprises but one word and its cognate—*slavery, slave trade.* There is the history of the Negro, at least for the last seven centuries, while what is said of him before that time is interspersed among the annals of other peoples. It would seem from this fact, at first sight, that those who know nothing of the Negro, except as they see him in slavery and in menial positions, are quite excusable. But scholars deserve no such extenuation. They know what is written of the ancient Negro—from which they might, if they chose, infer something concerning the modern Negro. Travellers, too, are inexcusable; for they frequently see in other than slave countries, and in some slave countries too, the descendant of Africa in positions anything but servile or menial. True, there was none who cared for us sufficiently to write our history, in modern days —we were unable to write it ourselves—in the lands of our captivity; and in our fatherland, alas! our condition is far from favourable for the furnishing of historical data. Scraps, patches, anecdotes, these are all that bear record of us. We have now,

fortunately, some living men among us who illustrate our manhood, and live down the disparagements of our enemies; but as
a rule, our history is that of the chain, the coffle gang, the slave
ship, the middle passage, the plantation-hell!

If, however, it be true that honourable mention is made of
many of our fathers, and if, in spite of the most adverse circumstances, we have produced some worthy sons of such sires, ought
we not to have the benefit of these creditable facts? And yet, I
honestly confess that I fear what I say on this subject will, by
some professedly anti-slavery persons, be regarded as somewhat
objectionable, or as a point upon which it is not best to say a
great deal. But if we do not vindicate ourselves, who will do
it for us? Alas! who indeed? for we are not without experience
in that matter.

I will venture upon a few points to which I have had the honour
of calling public attention in a lecture on this subject at Cheltenham, Liverpool, Glasgow, Ulverstone, and Dundee, and before
two metropolitan literary societies.

In the sacred Scriptures, no mention is made of the son of
Ham which in any respect represents him as at all inferior to the
sons of Shem or Japhet. I know that "cursed be Canaan"* is
sometimes quoted as if it came from the lips of God; although,
as the Rev. H. W. Beecher says, and as the record reads, these
are but the words of a newly awakened drunken man. There was
about as much inspiration in these words, as there might have
been in anything said by Lot on two very disgraceful nights in
his existence. I admit, of course, that the descendants of Canaan
have since been the "servants of servants"; but I do deny that
God is responsible for the words of Noah at that time, and I also
deny that there is any sort of connection between his prediction
and the enslavement of the Negro. The Scriptures nowhere allude
to it in that sense: indeed, I see no more sanction to that prediction
than I see approval of his debauch, in the Scriptures. Besides,

* Genesis ix. 25.

how many other than Africans have been enslaved, oppressed, and made "servants of servants," since the time of that prediction!

Aside from this one point, however, is the fact that the first person made a slave, of whom we read in the Bible, was sold *to* Egyptians. Joseph was sold into Egypt. The Israelites were oppressed by Egyptians. Moses was called the son of Pharaoh's daughter, and was thus heir apparent to the Egyptians, the most powerful throne in the world. After the exodus, and the establishment of the Jewish empire, frequent mention of an honourable kind is made of the Egyptians, with whom Solomon was on the most friendly terms. He took the daughter of the Egyptian monarch as a wife; he received the Queen of the South as a distinguished guest, and treated her so, during her royal visit to the Jewish capital.

The Assyrians, with their great city Nineveh, were descendants of Ham; and surely they are not spoken of in the Bible disrespectively. In 1 Chron. iv. 4 it is written, "and they found fat pasture and good; and the land was wide, and quiet, and peaceable; for they of Ham had dwelt there of old." This, I think, is very important testimony to the peaceable, quiet, industrious character of "them of Ham." A "wide," well tilled land, having "fat pasture and good," speaks well of their energy, industry, skill, and success, as agriculturists, as well as of their wealth. They had an ancient, honourable name—"they had dwelt there of old;" and that "they had dwelt there of old" seemed to be abundant reason, in the opinion of the sacred writer, for the respectability of the country, and its prosperous, wealthy appearance. The "quietness and peaceableness" of the country—the reason given for which was, that "they of Ham had dwelt there of old"—is sufficient testimony to the high character of that people; and it agrees exactly with what all know, who know anything, of the race: they are aware that Negroes exhibit most prominently those characteristics which accord with quietness and peaceableness. I set a very high value upon this piece of sacred testimony, and am very grateful that it is in the Bible. "Cursed be Canaan" did not hinder this!

I am not at all forgetful of the wickedness of the ancient Negroes. In this, as in other things, they showed their likeness to, their oneness with, the human race generally. They committed just such sins as did other people, and the impartial Jehovah treated them accordingly. Hence the overthrow of Egypt and the destruction of Assyria.

To come down to New Testament times, we find (Acts xiii. 1) among the teachers, Simeon, who "was called *Niger*"—I presume, because he was black. Dr. Patten thinks it was because of his black hair: there is nothing to designate that the adjective 'niger' relates to hair. But it is put in the masculine gender, while 'coma,' hair, is feminine; and it is so put as to indicate a surname, which in those days was significant of some such peculiarity as the term naturally implies. Queen Candace is spoken of in no mean terms, nor is her minister—Prime Minister, I believe—to whose chariot Philip had especial directions from heaven to "join himself."

I will not again allude to the great theologians of early days, of whom I have frequently spoken; but it is perhaps admissible to step aside to profane history for a few passages of testimony concerning the ancient Negro. Diodorus Siculus says nothing discreditable of the Negro of his times. Carthage was not the meanest of countries, though Hannibal, like his subjects, was black. No doubt there was a good deal going on in Carthage, while Hannibal was besieging Rome, which one could not but be reminded of last winter; but that was not (*so the Crimean campaign shows*) peculiar to blacks. But I will fortify this part of the subject by a single quotation, and that quotation shall come from an American, a distinguished American, the Honourable Alexander H. Everett. Speaking on this point, he says—"Trace this very civilization, of which we are so proud, to its origin, and where do you find it? We received it from our European ancestry; they from the Greeks and the Romans; those from the Jews; but whence did the Jews receive it? From Egypt and Ethiopia—in one word, from Africa? He then adverts to the fact, that "Moses, the great Jewish legislator, was a graduate of an Egyptian college." Speaking of their progress and great proficiency in some of the most useful arts, Mr. Everett holds the following language: —"The ruins of Egypt will be, what they are now, the wonder and the admiration of the civilized world, when St. Peter's and St. Paul's, the present pride of London and of Rome, shall have crumbled into dust." I do not agree with Mr. Everett, touching the "crumbling of St. Peter's and St. Paul's"; but the reader will recollect that Macaulay holds like opinions, combated by Lord John Russell. It is not strange, then, that Mr. Everett should hold them. The belief is very common, that nations "ripe and rot," and go away into a decline, of necessity. Mr. Everett maintains that belief: I do not. But his idea is, that Egyptian architecture and masonry will, as ruins, remain permanent when those of London and Rome shall be sought for in vain. Such is this learned gentleman's idea of the superiority of the former.

In the same speech Mr. Everett says, when alluding to the superior learning of ancient Africans, "Those stirring spirits, Homer, Pythagoras, and others, travelled among those Africans, as did the sons of the wealthy Greeks and Romans, to acquire the completion of their education, and to give the finishing touch to their verses, just as our sons and poets now travel in Germany and Italy for a like purpose."

Knowing that his countrymen are exceedingly unwilling to believe that anything good or great ever emanated from one wearing a black skin, and knowing that those who cannot dispute the honourable history of ancient Africans frequently deny that they were blacks, Mr. Everett remarks—"Sir, some persons say that, although the Egyptians and Ethiopians were Africans, they were not black. Herodotus, the father of history, travelled among them, and he tells you they were black men, with crisped wooly hair;

and I cannot bring myself to believe that Herodotus could not distinguish black from white, when he saw it. Moreover, the same testimony is borne by Greeks and Romans of undoubted veracity, who knew them as well as we know our Canadian neighbours." Mr. Everett was a citizen of Massachusetts, and he made the speech with which I have made so free before the Massachusetts Colonization Society, in 1839. This gentlemen was American Minister Plenipotentiary to China, during the presidency of Mr. Tyler. Another of the Everett family, the Honourable Edward Everett (who, during the administration of the same President, was Minister to the Court of St. James), bears like testimony concerning the Negro, before the American Colonization Society, at a later date. I regret having no copy of that speech at hand.

I hope I have in the several parts of this book shown that the modern Negro is worthy of his ancient paternity. He has endured oppression the deepest and most degrading—oppression that has fewer redeeming features than any other beneath the sun. John Wesley called it "the sum of all villanies—the vilest system of oppression upon which the sun of God ever shone." That the modern Negro has endured this, speaks much of his fortitude, and more of God's favour toward him. But in the midst of oppression, the Negro has shown both capacity and desire for improvement; which are not only commendable, but which entitle him to a place among the most progressive of the human race. Curran, Emmett, O'Connell, O'Brien, and Barrington, are names of which Ireland may justly be proud. To attempt to mention like names, among either the living or the dead, of England and Scotland, were to far exceed the limits of this humble volume. Among the peers of this good realm, how many are there not, who "rose from the ranks," as military men say—rose by the force of their learning, their industry, their talent! Are not the British bar and the British bench a sort of gateway and avenue to the highest distinctions of this kind? Across the ocean, and in the colonies, you see almost the entire population self-made men. They are justly honoured of all who know them. Everybody agrees that they are entitled to the greater credit, for having overcome mighty obstacles, in the shape of poverty and its thousand-and-one discouraging attendants; but not one of them was obliged to start from such a position as that in which slavery *keeps* its victim, or in which it *leaves* him when he becomes free, either by law or by flight. Those had honour, fame, emolument, to beckon them on; they had glorious precedents before them; the path of competition was as open to them as to any others; the road to distinction was as free for them to travel as for men of any grade or birth. These had no precedents, no encouragements, no lights by the wayside. They were discouraged on every hand. Schools were closed against them; colleges denied them their classic privileges —honours were not for blacks. Fame—fame for a Negro? The very idea was out of the question! He may fight his country's battles, as did many in the war of the Revolution; but after that, he must sink down to the condition of a mere Negro, deprived of the common civilities of social life, denied his rights, and trampled upon by all classes.

In the last war between Great Britain and the United States, blacks were twice called out to fight their country's battles. General Jackson said to them, in his second proclamation, "Soldiers! when I called upon you on a previous occasion, upon the banks of the Sabine, I knew that you possessed an enthusiasm capable of the performance of noble things; but your deeds of valour upon the field of battle far transcended my most sanguine expectations." They came again, at their general's call: they were no inefficient aid in the gaining of the celebrated "victory of New Orleans," 8th January, 1815: but all who were slaves before they entered the army were returned to their masters, when the battle was over! They were denied the least share in the liberties for which they had fought and bled.

The Negro has few or none of the stimulants and encouragements which urge and allure other men to great attainments. The Irish lad, whose father was a labourer, knows that if he can find a few friends to aid him, he may enter the university. Acquiring a good education, he may have the same opportunity to distinguish himself that any other Irishman enjoys. He may be, in his way, an Emmett or a Curran. He knows what made them what they were, and the same opportunities are his. The English boy whose father may be a mechanic or an artisan, and who aspires to something higher than the paternal condition, has but to nerve himself for the conflict with obstacles, and his good character, a little patronage, hard study, and persevering diligence, will do for him what it has done for some of those who now stand in the highest places in the land. No discouragement frowns upon him but such as some one before him has overcome. The path is a trodden one; the goal is before him; the prize glitters in his sight; facilities increase as difficulties are overcome. The race may be toilsome, long, requiring great effort; but there are abundant encouragements to run it. The Scotch lad, who desires learning and a place for usefulness, perhaps finds the readiest aids of all others. His master is both willing and able to instruct him. A Scottish clergyman takes a paternal interest in almost every child in his parish. If any evince talent, the minister is one of the first to find it out; he is the most anxious to develope it. Educational institutions abound in his country; they are within the reach of persons who are far from being rich. If he be poor, his neighbours will contribute to nothing more freely than to aid him in the acquisition of learning. He looks about him; he sees that many of the most able and the most useful men, in all the learned profession, the ministry included, were once poor lads like himself. Turning his eyes southward, he sees the same remark applies, in a very great measure, to England. He easily learns that in Wales and in Ireland this is true to a proverb. And as for obstacles, what Scotchman ever turned his back upon *them?* What are hindrances made for, but to be overcome? and what are Scotchmen made for, but to overcome them?

The Welsh boy has a history, the history of an unconquered people, to stir up his manhood. The Pole recollects the days of former Polish greatness and glory. The Slavonian eloquently recounts the wrongs of an injured nationality, until he sends a thrill through the hearts of countless sympathizers. The Greek knows no reason why modern Greece may not, at some time, establish other than mere historical relations to great Greece of old. Why may not he, and others of his generation, do somewhat towards this work? The Jew, proud of his unbroken relations to the patriarchs and the people most honoured of God, hopes for the restoration of Israel, and sees in the growing public favour of his cause, and the increasing wealth of his people, abundant reason to hope for their possession of long withheld rights in Gentile communities, and the dawning of the day when the sons of Abraham shall be gathered and blest. All of these have enough to cheer, encourage, and stimulate them. That under such auspices, they should produce men of power and renown, is not to be wondered at. It is, most appropriately, a subject of universal admiration.

But the Negro, especially the American Negro, has no encouragement of the sort. His sky is sunless, starless; deep, black clouds, admitting no ray of light, envelope his horizon. What is there for him in past history? Slavery. What is the condition of the majority of his class? Slavery. What are the signs of the times, so far as the disposition of their oppressors is concerned? Continual slavery. If educated, what position may he acquire? That of a menial. What are the opportunities for education? Such only as may be inferred from the rejection of Negroes from most of the halls of learning in the land. What encouragements has he from friends, from the feelings of the mass of the people, from the institutions of his native country? None, absolutely none. James McCune Smith was rejected from Geneva College, New York, because of the African blood in his veins. His schoolmate, Isaiah G. De Grasse, was received, because he was not known to be a coloured man. When the fact that he was coloured became known, he was treated coolly, made to feel uncomfortable, by those who always before gave him their friendship. Daniel Laing was driven from Haward College, where he was seeking a medical education, because of his colour; so was Martin R. Delaney. Alexander Crummell was denied, as was De Grasse, admittance into the New York Episcopal Theological Seminary (as *men*, they might be admitted as *semi-slaves*), when wishing to prepare for the ministry of that denomination. Their bishop gave them plainly to understand that they could never take seats in the Convention of his diocese. If a white man be rector of a Church of blacks, *he* is excluded from the Convention! William Douglass is the best reader of the Church Service in Philadelphia: he has no more seat in the Episcopal Convention of that State, than if he were a dog.*

If, then, we have among us men who have come up from slavery and made for themselves a name—a few of whom I have taken the liberty freely to refer to—they have done so in spite of discouragements, without aid, in the absence of cheering, stimulating, inviting prospects; indeed, without hopes. This short sentence embodies the history of the struggles of all the learned and useful black men we have in the United States.

I beg to add another fact. The educated Negro in America is a greater sufferer than the uneducated; the more his feelings are refined, the more keenly he feels the sting of the serpent prejudice. That is natural; but it is aggravated by the fact—one of great discredit to Americans—that an educated Negro, as a rule, is treated no better than one uneducated. But that is not all: he is made the object of peculiarly offensive treatment, because of his superior attainments; he is said to be "out of his place"; he is thought to be "assuming the place of a white man." Were he only a menial, of an ordinary labourer, then he would not

---

* This applies both to New York and Pennsylvania. In neither is a black Episcopal minister admitted to the Convention. The Hon. William Jay, and his son John Jay, Esq., have laboured to have the rule altered in New York, but to no purpose.

be treated so well as white men in the same position, but then he would be more "in his place." Any one can imagine how acutely an educated man must feel this. I am not an educated man; but I have seen those, who are, writhe under this worse than brutal treatment, until my heart has ached for them. May I be pardoned for saying, that the educated among us deserve the credit, at least, of a place and a name among the respectable of the world? Others mitigate their sufferings and multiply their means of enjoyment, by learning: but with us, this does not increase the latter (I mean in an ordinary sense), while it multiplies the former; and any attempt at education, both in itself and in its consequences, is "the pursuit of knowledge under difficulties," with a witness!

In this country it is difficult to understand how little difference is made in the treatment of black men, in respect to their position. Englishmen do not expect servants to ride in first-class carriages; but a person of wealth or position, of whatever colour, has, in this respect, just what he pays for. In New York, however, the Rev. Dr. Pennington can no more ride in an omnibus than any other black person, however inferior to him. The richest coloured man in Philadelphia cannot purchase a first-class railway ticket for New York; neither could he obtain for his son the opportunity of being educated in any college of the many in either New York or Philadelphia. What progress we have made has been under the frown of these obstacles. May it not be hoped that, having combated so much, we may overcome more? In that worst of all countries, the United States, the Negro not only exhibits the fact that

All is not lost,

but he shows a tendency for improvement; he gives evidence of having cultivated this tendency; he displays success in this endeavour. I beg to claim, that if other people have entitled themselves to lasting honour from mankind, for what they have done, for the brilliant specimens of manhood they have presented to the world's admiring gaze—specimens of self-made men, in unfavourable circumstances—my people, having done something like it in circumstances a thousandfold more forbidding, should not be altogether struck from the roll of, at least, *the respectable among mankind.*

I am quite free to confess that, in this regard, the American is more worthy than the British Negro. The time was, when slavery reigned triumphant in our colonies. Then, if a coloured man distinguished himself as did the Honourable Mr. Jordan, of Kingston, and others, they did so in the midst of the almost universal enslavement of their own race. Still they were free, and, as freemen, equal in law to all others. Prejudice did exist, as a matter of social caste; but it did not destroy legal rights, as it does in America.*

When the laws of Jamaica made distinctions as to colour, I doubt if black Jamaica made such attainments and progress as our people in the States. They acquired more property, but they excelled in nothing else. In these respects they resemble the present free blacks of the Southern States.

Now, if we of the British dominions do not advance rapidly, we shall have no excuse; and, what is worse, we shall burden our cause with reproach. I was at one time most anxious about this matter; but think now, we shall be able "to report progress," as they say in the legislature, and to do our share in the great work of redeeming and disenthralling the long-outraged race of Ham.†

I know not what is to be our future, but think these are very significant facts—that fourteen millions of us should be on the American continent: that slavery should have ceased in one half

* Since writing the above, I learn, from the excellent work of Mr. Phillippo, that in very early days blacks were disfranchised and otherwise oppressed in Jamaica. My remark above would apply to a much later period. I wish every Englishman would read "Jamaica in its Past and Present State" (Snow, 35, Paternoster Row).

† The improvement of the blacks in Canada may be inferred from Part II. As to those of Jamaica, *see* Davey and Phillippo.

of the American States, at so early a day: that in the Slave States the Negroes who are bondsmen are being rapidly improved, by the two following processes, viz.; 1, The constant admixture of the more intelligent slaves, from the more Northern Slave States, among those less intelligent, in the far South—a fact which grows out of the raising of slaves in the former, to sell in the latter. 2, The increasing admixture of Anglo-Saxon blood with that of the Negro. If slavery does not work its own ruin by those abominations, there is no truth in philosophy.

To return: Great Britain has freed all her slaves; France has freed hers; other European powers are earnestly discussing measures of a similar kind; the freed men of all countries are improving rapidly; Brazil has abandoned the slave trade; commerce with Africa is increasing; friendly feeling towards the Negro is in the ascendant everywhere, except in America, and it is increasing even there. It does seem as if God were preserving and educating the Negro for some great purposes, yet undeveloped; and as if the Anglo-Saxon were in some way to be connected with, first, his oppression, then his emancipation; and perhaps, finally, the two are to be associated in some important future service to the family of man.

Doubtless, all who think on this subject agree in desiring that whatever may be done shall be done in harmony with the divine will, as written in the great law of our common brotherhood.

CHAPTER IV

British Abolitionism

I was honoured, both in 1853 and in 1854, by invitations to address the British and Foreign Anti-Slavery Society; in fact, the honour of a similar invitation was conferred upon me this year, but I was unable to attend. Added to the pleasure of labouring, however, feebly, in the anti-slavery cause, was the fact that, upon the occasion first named, the Earl of Shaftesbury presided. To sustain any relation to that prince of noblemen, even for so short a time, was an honour any man might covet. Besides, among the gentlemen on the Committee of that Society are some of my dearest personal friends, to serve whom I would do anything. At that meeting, in 1853, I became acquainted with Lord Shaftesbury. No one had introduced me to him, and I was feeling all the awkwardness of being a stranger to the noble Lord whom, as chairman of the meeting, I was soon to address; but as the speaker next before myself was near concluding, his Lordship leaned towards me and said, "I believe *you* are to speak next, Mr. Ward." Thus the nobleman's affability removed my embarrassment, consequent upon the neglect of commoners. Thus I became acquainted with the head of the great house of Ashley: and there commenced a series of kind actions on the part of his Lordship which lay me under unceasing obligations.

It is sometimes said, that in Great Britain there is no need of discussing the question of slavery. Two very strong objections are made against it—one is, that there are no slaves in the British empire now, there is nothing for the British people to do on the subject; the other is, that as the discussion of slavery is necessarily, now, the discussion of a subject affecting other nations and governments than our own, such discussion will be regarded by those concerned as an interference with their affairs. This remark is made with especial reference to America and the Americans, who are, of all people in the world, the most sensitive on this particular point. That I was obliged to meet these objections, at different points of my travels, I hardly need say. To answer them formed no small part of my work in England. I hope I shall be pardoned for introducing here what little I have to say on this matter.

1. It is quite true, I am but too thankful to say, that the British flag does not float anywhere over slaves. Now, in the colonies as at home, the words of Whittier apply to every man, woman, and child—

> *Freedom, hand in hand with labour,*
> *Walketh, strong and brave;*
> *While, on the brow of his neighbour,*
> *No man writeth—Slave!*

The British people, to their infinite credit, responded to the clarion voices of their Brougham, Knibb, Buxton, Clarkson, Wilberforce, Macaulay, Allen, Cropper, and Rathbone, and shattered every stone of the accursed old Bastille of British slavery. Yet it is not to be forgotten, that long ere that was done, British hands had become red with the innocent blood of millions of slaves. The old slave trade, with its horrors (Liverpool being its chief mart); the horrible plantation scenes of Jamaica and other West India islands, the barbarisms of the Mauritius, the atrocities of the Cape —oh, these darkest, most guilty pages of British history, are not to be easily forgotten! While we were guilty of these abominations, and their attendant crimes, the whole weight of British influence was given to the furtherance of slavery in other countries; what they did, we did. They may have surpassed us in cruelty,* but still we were connected with the same atrocious system. The guilt of our colonies was endorsed at home; nay, the owners of colonial slaves were dwellers at the West End of London, our senators and our peers. Commoners who were planters, in London, Liverpool, and Glasgow, rolled in untold wealth, the fruit of the Negro's unpaid toil. They were regarded with a sort of deference, such as is paid to the American slaveholder at Boston, New York, and Philadelphia. A baronetcy or a peerage was scarcely more desirable or more honourable, than to be known as a *great West India planter*, the owner of so many hundred slaves! Sometimes, indeed, baronet or peer and planter, were associated titles of the same distinguished individual. These brought all the influence of wealth, name, position, patronage, and senatorial place, to bear upon the Government, which but too easily winked at the wickedness and obeyed the demands of the then British slave power. Thank God, I am writing *past* history; but history it is!

Having done so much for slavery, as a nation and as individuals, it is not to be denied that the British people have contracted no small share of blame for encouraging the slavery of other peoples, by their evil example. It can scarcely be said that the abolition of the slave trade, the procuring of some few treaties against it in conjunction with other nations, and the abolition of colonial slavery, at a very late day, wiped out *all* our guilt.

In May, 1772, a decision procured by the persevering diligence of the immortal Granville Sharpe, was rendered by Lord Chief Justice Mansfield, to the effect that the arrival of a slave upon British soil made him a freeman. In 1814 a number of Negroes escaped from North Carolina to the ships composing the British fleet, commanded by Admiral Sir George Cockburn.† Upon their being claimed by the American authorities, in behalf of their masters, Sir George refused to deliver them, in virtue of

* That is scarcely possible, however.
† See *Jay's View of the Action of the Federal Government in behalf of Slavery.*

that decision, declaring the law of the soil to be the law of the ship to which the Negroes had fled. In 1825 the American Government desired the British Government to deliver to them slaves who had escaped to Canada. This was refused, in accordance with Lord Mansfield's decision. But while, by virtue of that decision, we freed the slaves of foreigners, when they touched our soil, we, in spite of that decision, held slaves ourselves! Nay, more. Several American slave ships, with slave cargoes on board, were driven upon our West India Islands. Touching those islands, the slaves were made freemen. Still, we held hundreds of thousands of slaves on those islands—we made our soil free to other people's slaves, while upon the same soil *we* held slaves!

What a glaring contradiction was here! "British soil is free soil to the slaves of other countries; it is slave soil to our own subjects." That was substantially our saying. If the highest court in the empire made British air free to foreign lungs, why did it not make that air equally free to British lungs? in a word, why did not the poor slave of the colonial plantations receive the benefits of this decision? I beg to say, I cannot admit that

The why is plain as way to parish church.

Is it not true, that we held half a million of slaves in our colonies, in as open contradiction to the law as laid down by Lord Chief Justice Mansfield on the 5th of May, 1772, as do our American brethren at this day hold three millions in contradiction to their Declaration of Independence as laid down by Jefferson, *four years two months and twenty-two days* thereafter? and from the date of the former, until 1832, were we one whit better than our neighbours? We gave them the most practical encouragement. We began our hypocrisy more than *four years* before they began theirs. And it is a singular fact, that each nation, at the time to which I refer, robbed about half a million of slaves of rights which, according to public and solemn declarations of both, belonged to the subjects, to *all* the subjects, of each: indeed, ours was the greatest inconsistency, as we violated a judicial decision, while they simply trampled upon an abstract declaration of political sentiments. They incorporated the same sentiments in their Constitution, but this was not until 1789. We had been stultifying ourselves, then, for seventeen years! I submit whether such sinners, though penitent, "bring forth fruits meet for repentance" without seeking, if possible, to counteract the effects of their own evil example, by something more than merely emancipating their own slaves.

But there is, if possible, a still darker shade in this picture. On the sailing of Sir George Cockburn's fleet to the West Indies, the American authorities followed it, and renewed their demand for the slaves. Sir George, true to his British principles, repeated and persisted in his refusal to deliver them. The Negroes, of course, remained free. But the American Government, always persevering in such cases, made their demand for gold in payment for them, through their Minister at London. It was refused. A long correspondence then commenced, which did not terminate until 1836, twenty-two years after. And how did it terminate? By our Government paying, in gold, the sum of £40,000, by way of compensation for the Negroes; and after paying this, twenty-two years' interest was demanded, and we paid that! Some six or seven cases are on record, of our complicity in American slavery, by paying for the cargoes of slave ships wrecked on our islands: indeed, we almost always paid money in such cases, until after the passing of the Emancipation Act.

To say nothing of the perfect impunity with which we allow Spain to violate a treaty against the slave trade, for compliance with which we paid her £400,000, nearly forty years ago, and not to speak of the shamefully loose provisions of our treaty with the United States* for the same purpose, let us look at one more

---

* I refer to Mr. Jay again on this point, and ask attention to what that learned American jurist, the son of the great John Jay, says on the subject. I give the substance only of Judge Jay's remarks. It seems that the United States Government proposed to the British Government a convention against the slave trade. The British Government readily complied. After waiting a reasonable time, the latter gently re-

fact which shows that we are far from being innocent of *present* complicity in the crime of slaveholding.

In the Slave States it is law, that a free Negro from abroad or from the Northern States shall, upon landing on their shores, be imprisoned until his ship sails. When she sails, the captain must pay the charges of his arrest and imprisonment, or he is to be sold, to pay them, *into slavery for life!* For thirty years *this has been done to British subjects, to the knowledge of the British Government!* The Honourable Arthur F. Kinnaird has twice, within the past two years, brought this subject before the Government, but the answers to his questions have been most unsatisfactory. They reveal the fact, that but little care is felt about this matter in Downing Street. In the winter of 1854–55, one or two of the Atlantic Slave States so modified their law that a British Negro, arriving there, shall be forbidden to land, and the captain is put under heavy bonds, which are to be forfeited if the Negro goes on shore. This odious law is made for the security of slavery, by preventing free Negroes from associating with the slaves and teaching them the way to a free country. Conniving at it, our Government, certainly in a degree, shares its guilt. The rights of a British

---

minded the former that nothing had been done in the case. Another pause ensued. Then the British Government prepared a treaty, and sent it to Washington for sanction. That treaty provided that, if subjects of either Government were found engaged in the slave trade, on the coast of Africa, America, or the West Indies, they should be subjected, on conviction thereof, to certain specified penalties. The American Senate struck out the word "America"; thus exempting their own coast, for obvious reasons, from the operations of the treaty.

The treaty also provided that, should subjects of either Government be convicted of being engaged in the slave trade, in vessels owned *or chartered* by the parties so convicted, they should be punished, &c. The United States Senate purged the treaty of the words "*or chartered.*" Hence an American, or any one else desirous to engage in this abominable traffic, had only to charter—not to put himself to the expense of purchasing or building—a vessel, and proof of its being such exempted him from the punishment threatened in that treaty.

Again: the treaty, as it left Britain, provided that punishment should be inflicted upon subjects of either Government engaged in the slave trade, under the British or the American flag, upon conviction. The Senate of America struck out "or the American"; so that trading in slaves on the American coast, under the American flag or in a chartered vessel, is no violation of the treaty, as it now stands! I call this treaty "shamefully loose." Is it not so?

subject, of whatever colour, ought not to be suffered thus to be jeopardized for the accommodation of our trade in slave-grown cotton.

Considering the depth of our past guilt, and our share in planting, encouraging, and perpetuating slavery in America and elsewhere, I do not think we ought to close our lips until all whom we have for centuries aided in this sin shall be brought to repentance for it. Upon the high grounds of our common humanity and our holy religion, I am sure I need not say one word, except it be to deplore that mere business considerations, the arguments of Lombard Street and the Exchange, should so chill the hearts and dry up "the milk of human kindness" in Englishmen's bosoms as to put aside the claims of our suffering brethren.

2. As to its being considered offensive to American or other slaveholders that Englishmen condemn slavery and labour for its overthrow, it is well enough to observe, that part of what we discuss is our own guilty complicity. Surely this cannot be intermeddling with other people's affairs. The slave being our brother, and the slaveholder being our brother too, we may claim the right of obeying the command, "Thou shalt not suffer sin upon thy neighbour, thou shalt in anywise rebuke him." Besides, the great methods of a practical character by which British abolitionists seek to destroy slavery are made upon our own soil: they are, *the elevation of the British Negro, and supplying the British markets with staples from the British tropics*—thus rebuking slavery by the former; and competing with it, driving it out of the market, by the latter. Is it objectionable to elevate and make good subjects of our own Negroes? Is it objectionable to till our own soil, and sell the produce thereof in our own markets? Would our American neighbours listen one moment to any objections Englishmen might make to their doing things of like character?

It is said, however, by some persons who object most strongly to British abolitionism, that Great Britain entailed slavery upon the Americans. This I think is very doubtful. If it were true, however, it would not only *justify,* but it would *authorize,* the very thing that is complained of. Let us see. I do not believe the charge of the entailment of slavery upon America by the British. I admit, of course, that much guilt and great responsibility, such as I have already referred to, rest upon the people of Britain; but as to entailing slavery upon Americans, how can that be true, when they threw overboard *the tea* at Boston harbour, and threw off the British rule? Could they not have disposed of slavery quite as easily? If not as easily, had they not the same power over it? Had the British people or Government any power over them *after* they became independent? If they retained slavery *after that,* was it not because *they chose to do so?* They answer these questions by saying, as they do every day, that they found it impossible to agree upon a constitution without agreeing either to let slavery alone, or to secure it! They claim pay for their slaves, and they claim immunity from rebuke, on the ground that slavery is constitutional. If so, who made it so? If so, what becomes of the charge of its *entailment* upon them by Britain?

On the other hand, if it be true that British people *did* entail slavery upon Americans, *they* of all people are the ones to seek the *undoing* of what they have *done.*

The good example set to other nations by the British Government in this matter, and the sustenance given the Government by the British people, entitle them to be heard on the subject. They have sinned, and they have repented. They have a right to *"tell* their experience." The Negro in America looks to the Englishman as his friend. It is with his especial consent that the Englishman speaks in his behalf. The Englishman's friendly regard for the Negro is well known to the latter. The poor slave, even, cannot be kept ignorant of this. Some Englishmen, I am proud to know, are quite willing to be looked upon as guardians, protectors, and defenders, of the poor and needy Negro.

It was with the greatest delight that I found, in every part of England, Ireland, Scotland, and Wales, that abolitionism is not a mere abstract idea, but a practical question of grave importance. It is not because, to a certain extent, anti-slavery sentiments are fashionable and natural, that these persons approve them, but because of their intrinsic character. Generally, the children of the abolitionists of early days are proud of their anti-slavery inheritance. Some few, I regret to say, do not walk in their parents' footsteps: it may be because their pursuits are somewhat different. There is great occasion for rejoicing in the fact, that the leading abolitionists of Britain are among the most exalted of the land. I have mentioned the names of some of them. At their residences, where I had the pleasure of calling upon them, they impressed me most deeply with the fact. The Earl of Shaftesbury bade me call upon him as often as I pleased, to consult him upon matters relating to my mission. Upon one occasion his Lordship shook me by the hand, saying "God bless you, my good friend! Call again, when you can." On another occasion he gently rebuked me for not having called more frequently.* Lord Harrowby conversed freely and with deep interest on the subject, expressing his desire that Mr. Jordan, a coloured gentleman who was candidate for the mayoralty of Kingston, Jamaica, should be elected. Lord Calthorpe asked me kindly concerning the distinctions between blacks and whites in America, and remarked that, in the judgment day, no such distinctions would appear. The same nobleman most kindly took the chair at my meeting at Birmingham. I may as well say, briefly, that the nobility generally whom I had the honour of meeting treated both me and my cause with the kindest consideration; none more so than her Grace the Duchess of Sutherland, her Grace the Duchess of Argyll, and his Grace the Duke of Argyll. I am under great obligations to Lord Robert Grosvenor, Lord Haddo, Lord Ebrington, Lord Waldegrave, the Honourable Arthur F. Kinnaird, Sir Edward North Buxton, Sir Thomas D. Acland, Ernest Bunsen, Esq., Samuel Gurney, Esq., and many

* At that time his Lordship did me the honour to accept my miniature. The note acknowledging its receipt I keep as a priceless inheritance for my children.

others, too numerous to mention, but not too numerous both to deserve and to receive my warmest humblest thanks.

Besides the nobility, the English abolitionists are among the most devotedly pious of the laymen, and the most eminent divines of all sections of the Christian Church. The Rev. Dr. Campbell, of London, the Rev. Dr. Raffles, of Liverpool, the Rev. Dr. Halley, of Manchester, the Rev. John Angell James, of Birmingham, the Rev. James Parsons, of York, the Rev. Dr. Alexander, of Edinburgh, the Rev. Dr. Robson, of Glasgow, the Rev. Dr. A. Moreton Brown, of Cheltenham, George Hitchcock, Esq., Samuel Morley, Esq., John Crossley, Esq., William P. Paton, Esq., John Smith, Esq., William Crossfield, Esq., Edward Baines, Esq., George Leeman, Esq., are instances and illustrations of this fact. To know that the anti-slavery cause is in such hands in England and Scotland, and to know that the honoured names now mentioned are but representatives of a class embracing the best and the purest of the earth, is reason enough why one should feel quite certain of the final success of our holy cause.

It is a little remarkable to notice the likeness of English to American abolitionists, in character and status. In both countries this precious cause has for its advocates and standard-bearers the very "salt of the earth." It is as if God calls into the service of defending the poor and the needy those whom by his grace he has made most like himself. What abundant evidence there is, in this fact, that the cause is his!

CHAPTER V

Incidents, Etc.

When I arrived in England, I found Miss Greenfield, known in America by the *soubriquet* of "Black Swan," had arrived here. I had the pleasure of hearing her sing at Stafford House, at a concert attended by some of the most distinguished of the British nobility. It was a concert given on purpose to introduce Miss Greenfield at that house which is nearest in position to the royal palace, and whose mistress is nearest in rank to royalty. What a sight for my poor eyes! Stafford House, British nobility, and a Negress! I saw the perfect respect with which Miss G. was treated by all. The Prussian Ambassador was in raptures at her versatility of voice. Sir David Brewster said to me, "she has two throats"—alluding to the perfect ease with which she passed from the highest to the lowest notes. It was plainly enough to be seen that the concert had very significant connections with the anti-slavery cause. Mrs. Stowe and her brother were there. The Rev. James Sherman was among the guests. Lord Shaftesbury was among the most conspicuous of them. Then, to remove all doubt as to the great object of the concert, Lord Shaftesbury said to me, "We call this house Aunt Harriet's cabin (the Duchess's name being Harriet) ; and I tell her, that it honours her house to have it used for such a cause and such a purpose." This, said in the warm, earnest manner peculiar to his Lordship, made him appear to me more noble than ever. After music had ceased, the guests were invited to go over the house. Lord Blantyre* kindly showed us the magnificent pictures in the gallery, and treated us all as most welcome guests, which doubtless we were.

The day following, I was invited by Lady Dover to see from her drawing-room window a review of the troops, it being the Queen's birthday. Soon after, I attended a concert of Miss Greenfield's at Hanover Square Rooms. There I had the honour of being introduced to the Earl of Carlisle, at his Lordship's request, by the Rev. C. Beecher. Mentioning the object of my visit to his Lordship, he readily replied, "Nothing can be more interesting."

During a trip down the Thames, I had the honour of an introduction to the Honourable A. F. Kinnaird and his amiable lady; and, by Mr. Kinnaird, to Lord Haddo. The kind interest taken in the coloured people by these distinguished personages, being to me an entirely new thing, kept me in a state of most excited delight. Attending a meeting at Willis's Rooms, in June of that year, I was introduced by Lord Shaftesbury to Viscount Ebrington. Calling upon the latter at his residence, the next day, he was pleased to bring Jamaica prominently before me, and to express his deep interest in the people of that island. Stephen Bourne, Esq., had suggested it before. When the time came† that I was at liberty to consider the subject more definitely, I took the liberty of writing him on the subject, whereupon his Lordship honoured me with an invitation to dine with Lady Ebrington and a party. There I was introduced to the Earl of Harrowby, the Honourable John Fortescue, Sir James Weir Hogg, Governor Wodehouse, of British Guiana, and several other persons of distinction, all of whom gave me the highest assurances of their lively regard for the best weal of the Negro.

At another time,‡ I had the very great pleasure of being a fel-

---

* Son-in-law to the Duke of Sutherland.
† In February, 1854.
‡ 24th November, 1853.

low traveller with the Duke of Argyll and the Earl of Elgin, from London to Manchester. The interest these two representatives of the great houses of Campbell and Bruce took in the anti-slavery cause was far more than I was prepared for; but the intimate acquaintanceship with all the windings and intricacies of the American slave power, possessed by the great descendant of Robert Bruce, quite astonished me. In his place as Governor-General of Canada, Lord Elgin, with his clear comprehension of things has been seeing what was going on in the adjoining States so plainly, as to understand American politics and American politicians as well as if he had been born in that country. But what pleased me most was the perfect knowledge his Lordship showed of the anti-slavery question. Charles Sumner, the anti-slavery senator from Massachusetts, is an intimate friend of Lord Elgin. The career of Mr. Sumner in the Senate he understands perfectly; and with it, his Lordship understands all the minutiæ of the anti-slavery struggle, and its issues. Unlike too many Englishmen, the noble Earl does not keep his anti-slavery sentiments secret, when on the other side of the Atlantic. Participating in none of the Yankee feelings against Negroes, he does not act like them towards coloured men. Being guided by his own conscientious sense of right, he does not inquire what is popular, but treads the path which duty makes plain. Making no pretensions to philanthropy (though one of the most liberal of all our nobility), his Lordship, both in his administrations as Governor, and in his intercourse with others as a gentleman, commingles the strictly just with the charmingly affable. Like Lord Carlisle, Lord Elgin has a fulness and a minuteness of knowledge concerning everything around him which makes him a most ready instructor, as well as a most agreeable companion to men of good breeding, of whatever rank.

What I saw of Lord Elgin, that day, left me no reason to wonder that such a Governor-General should carry all hearts with him in Canada and in Jamaica, where his Lordship had been vice-regent. I saw just the man to reject the Larwill petition against the Elgin Settlement; and was abundantly prepared, from what I had the great privilege of observing that day, for the two following anecdotes of Lord Elgin:—When Governor of Jamaica, the noble Lord, like Lord Sligo, carried out his own convictions as to the rights and equality of Negroes. On one occasion a black man* proposed to bring his child to the font for baptism. The arrangement with the clergyman was completed; but shortly after, the minister learned that the Governor was about to bring his child on that Sunday, whereupon the Negro was advised to postpone the baptism of his child until another time. His Excellency, hearing this, expressed his entire willingness to have the black child brought to the font at the same time with his own; and when the time came, the Governor and the Negro stood, side by side, each for his own child, upon terms of perfect equality, before the altar of God. If any one say that was no more than right, I beg to remind him, that in those days, in an island where the Negro had been most shamefully oppressed, and despised alike by free coloured people and whites—at a time, too, when the status of the then recently freed man was much below what it is now, and when there was a universal ill feeling towards the Negroes, on account of what was called the "misfortunes" growing out of emancipation—at such a time, for a Governor-General, high and illustrious in rank, a nobleman, descended from the First of Scots, to make such a demonstration of his practical belief in the equality and the oneness of our human nature, and the common level upon which we all stand before the Almighty Father, was what we blacks may justly be proud of and grateful for. It was right, simply right; but in those days *right in that direction* was of rare occurrence, and therefore the more valuable.

The other anecdote of his Lordship I received indirectly, but in a most authentic form. Lord Elgin was at Washington in 1854,

---

* I do not know whether this occurred at Kingston or Spanish Town.

as Her Majesty's special ambassador to make what is called the Reciprocity Treaty between the United States and Canada. It was quite natural that a member of the British House of Peers should go into Congress occasionally, during a short residence at the American capital: Lord Elgin did so. He was there about the time of the closing scenes of the Congress of 1854 (the 3rd of March). The Honourable Gerrit Smith, from whom I receive the facts, in giving a most graphic account of this scene, especially the drunkenness of honourable members, says, "but what greatly increased my mortification was, that Lord Elgin, the Governor-General of Canada, sat by my side, and witnessed the intemperance of which I complain. I apologized to his Lordship for it, and he remarked that he had seen disorder and confusion in the House of Commons, in former days." Now, what is there in this remark of Mr. Smith? It is evidence that Lord Elgin, when in America, when in Washington, and in Congress, took a seat beside an abolitionist—being neither ashamed, as a peer nor as a representative of the Crown, in a twofold sense, to be found, in the presence of slaveholders and Northern slaveocrats, in such company, though knowing perfectly well how unpopular abolitionism is in that capital; nor disdaining to take his place in Congress beside the most radical, most decided abolitionist in the legislature. The reader must know two facts before he can understand how highly I appreciate these two anecdotes, especially the last. 1. He must know what it is to see and feel how strongly the current of public opinion sets, in that great country, against every phase and semblance of abolition. 2. He must know also, how few Englishmen there are who, visiting America, maintain their British principles on this subject while there. Throughout his entire career as Governor of Jamaica and as Governor-General of Canada, Lord Elgin always honoured his principles.

I said his Lordship makes no pretensions to philanthropy: I mean, he is a man above all pretensions—a man of practical realities. What he *is*, he *seems;* what he *seems*, he *is*. I mean, also, that Lord Elgin is not one of those who claim any especial favours for the coloured man, or who expect any especial worship *from* him. This is about the sum of some people's philanthropy, touching the Negro. Lord Elgin, however, does just what the British Negro needs at the hands of a British Governor or a British gentleman—treats him as he would any other man in like circumstances. For that I thank him on behalf of my people. For that reason I was most grateful for the Providence which gave me the honour of a journey of seven hours with so illustrious a fellow passenger. I write the more freely because Lord Elgin is a public man, because I write in behalf of a grateful people, and because I scarcely believe that this humble volume can travel so far northward as Dunfermline* before its humble author shall be quite forgotten.

The Duke of Argyll was also in the carriage at the time to which I allude. I had first seen his Grace at Stafford House. He did me the honour to say to Mrs. Stowe, he should like to see me. When I waited upon him, I was treated like a friend. I knew no other term suitably conveying my impression of the easy manner in which his Grace was pleased to receive and to converse with me. Afterwards, upon all occasions, that noblest of the Campbells laid me under obligations for like affability. As a Minister of Her Majesty this young nobleman has already distinguished himself, having been in two successive Cabinets charged with the war with Russia. At the head of one of Scotland's most noble houses, she may justly be proud of him. Early called to the peerage, at an early age entering the Cabinet, and frequently having to speak in the House of Lords, in debate with some of the most skilful tacticians of the Opposition, always sustaining himself by the exhibition of wisdom beyond his years, and giving promise of great future usefulness, England may reasonably rejoice that she has the services of one so able *now,* so hopeful for the future. Earnest

* Lord Elgin's residence.

and devoted in religion, the friends of Christian benevolence always find him ready with his purse, his pen, and his influence, to promote their objects and encourage their labours. That the British Negro has such a friend is both a cause of congratulation and a sign of future blessing. That the down-trodden slave of my native country may know of one so exalted, whose bosom is so full of benevolent feeling for him, is a matter for great thankfulness. Yes; we may all thank God for the gift of such a nobleman in our imperial senate, and we may all pray that God may long spare his useful life.

The Duchess of Argyll, eldest daughter of the Duke of Sutherland, is one of the most devotedly benevolent persons in England. She seems to have been especially blest with her mother's spirit, and to be thoroughly imbued with her principles. It seems to cost her Grace nothing to be kind, because it is so natural. She has, as well, a most kind manner of showing kindness. There is a great deal in *that*. Some persons are so rough or so cold, so distant, so haughty, in doing or rather attempting kindness, as really to spoil it; but the Duchess of Argyll makes her kindness double by her sweet, smiling, winning way of showing it. I do not wonder that she is a friend of the slave. Her mother, and her noble maternal ancestry for generations, have been so; and it would be difficult for such a heart not to feel for the woes of others, and condemn the wrongs inflicted upon them. In having made the acquaintance of the Duke of Argyll and her Grace the Duchess—in having seen the kind Christian manner in which they devote themselves to works of love, and educate their children to the same—I feel that I have enjoyed an honour and a pleasure which fall to the lot of but few colonists, and appreciate it accordingly.

Wishing to see all that I could while in England, and having a strong desire to go to the Houses of Parliament, I communicated my desire to the Honourable Arthur Kinnaird, M.P., and to the Earl of Shaftesbury. Mr. Kinnaird kindly gave me an order for the House of Commons, and Lord Shaftesbury procured for me

admission to the House of Lords. In the former there were no
questions of interest under discussion, and but few members were
in attendance. It was a morning session. Subsequently, Edward
Ball, Esq., member for Cambridgeshire, kindly showed me to the
visitors' gallery, where I had the pleasure of hearing Lord Palmerston and Mr. Frederick Peel. The veneration I had from my
childhood felt for Viscount Palmerston, as his name and that of
Lord John Russell had always been associated in my mind with
the greatest of past or present British statesmen, gave me a peculiar pleasure in hearing him. It was a peculiar time. The good ship
of the State had been but recently committed to his care. There
had just been a sort of mutiny, at least a desertion, of some of the
officers. There had been great dissatisfaction; alas, there had
been great cause for it! The public mind had been brought, by the
suffering of the army, the seeming want of vigour in the former
Cabinet, the apparent need of greater energy in the Crimea, and
the exceedingly severe comments of the press, to a state of great
excitement. Questions were poured in upon the Ministry, like a
torrent. The Premier was holden responsible not only for *what*
he said, but *how* he said it, and for honourable members *laughing*
or *crying* at what he said. It was indeed a most difficult time. A
firm, strong, steady hand at helm was needed. Reform must be
brought about, the war must be carried on, negotiations must be
conducted, despondency must be driven from some minds, the
doubtful must be assured—in short, all classes made all manner
of demands, and the Opposition took all manner of advantage of
the crisis. It was most interesting, on the 23rd of March, 1855, to
see Lord Palmerston, a man of seventy, with the appearance of a
man of fifty, at midnight, as if it were but noon, keep his place,
meet the Opposition, endure the public grumbling, maintain a
cheerful face, and, by his indefatigable industry and unwearied
attention to public business, conduct the nation through storms
and perils in the midst of which, while many found fault and
loudly complained, few dared, none could, take his place and do

his work. I know not of a more interesting occasion to see Lord Palmerston and hear him speak, than that. One seldom has an opportunity of seeing such a Prime Minister in such circumstances. I shall always remember that night. And, now that Sebastopol is captured, the English press lauds Lord Palmerston. St. Clare said, he judged of Aunt Dinah's cooking "as men judge of generals—by their successes." So is Lord Palmerston now judged by those who, at the time I saw him, could condemn and distrust the Premier, but could neither govern the country nor remedy defects.

It was in June, 1853, that I was in the House of Peers. If I was fortunate in the other House, two years after, I was more fortunate at the time I mention. It was during "the season," and before the war—so that many Lords were in attendance, and local matters of legislation occupied their attention. Lord Shaftesbury, with his natural kindness, met me at the door of one of the passages, and conducted me to the standing place (none but Peers, not even Ambassadors, *sit* in the House of Lords), and pointed out to me the several Peers and Bishops. The Earl Waldegrave left his seat, to come and shake my hand. The Duke of Argyll gave me his recognition. I was so fortunate as to hear the Lord Chancellor, the Lord Chief Justice, the Duke of Argyll, the Earl of Harrowby, the Earl of Aberdeen, Lord Grey, Lord Kinnaird, Lord Brougham, Lord Lyndhurst, the Earl of Clarendon, and the Earl of Shaftesbury. Such a display of senatorial talent one seldom has the good fortune to witness. But illustrious as were the names of those I heard, eloquent as were their speeches—and mortal men never spoke more eloquently than Lord Grey and Lord Brougham—the subject of these speeches, and the conclusion to which their Lordships came, interested me far more. After the disposal of some petitions, and other matters of routine, Lord Lyndhurst asked a question of Lord Clarendon concerning the position and intentions of Russia, in the Danubian Principalities. The noble Secretary answered the question to the satisfaction of the great

Ex-Lord Chancellor, and then came on the business of the day. Lord Redesdale took the chair, as the House went into Committee, and his Lordship is Chairman of Committee. The order of the day was Lord Shaftesbury's Juvenile Mendicant Bill. The Lord Chancellor made a speech against it; the Lord Chief Justice did the same. Lord Shaftesbury calmly sat in his place while these attacks were made. Soon after, the Bill was defended by the noble Premier (Lord Aberdeen) and the Duke of Argyll. Lord Grey made a most eloquent speech in its favour. Lord Harrowby brought to its defence the weight of his great name. Then uprose the Earl of Shaftesbury in defence of his Bill, meeting the objections of the Lard Chancellor and the Lord Chief Justice, utterly refusing to withdraw the Bill, from a sense of duty to his God and to his fellow men, and declaring that, "from the opposition it had received from the two legal Lords, he had made up his mind that its fate was sealed; but the responsibility of its being lost must rest upon their Lordships, and not upon him."

The earnestness, the eloquence, with which this speech was delivered, commanded universal attention. It showed that the great prince of British beneficence was a statesman as well as a philanthropist: it showed that a honest manly sense of Christian responsibility controlled him in the senate as well as in the Ragged School: it was quite consistent with the reputation he had earned when a member of the House of Commons, devoting himself like a Howard to the welfare of the neglected, and to the removal of the abuses which crushed them: and it gave me, who had learned to venerate him, the unspeakable satisfaction of seeing the most decided abolitionist in the House of Lords one of its most influential members; for, after he sat down, in less than twenty minutes the Lord Chief Justice and the Lord Chancellor gave in their adhesion to the Bill, Lord Brougham spoke in its favour, and it passed unanimously. I could not help congratulating Lord Shaftesbury upon his success, and he accepted the compliment kindly.

Now, what was that Bill? for *that* it was which impressed me with inexpressible admiration of the British peerage. The title of the Bill indicates the class to whom it relates. Its objects, briefly, were, to arrest the mendicant children of London, whose parents compel them to beg for a living. These parents neither support, nor educate, nor in any other way care for their children, but compel them to obtain money by begging or stealing. The consequence is, that these children are what Lord Shaftesbury called "a seedpot of crime"; for, in the great majority of cases, they become the worst description of criminals. The Bill provided for the arrest of these children, and placing them under the care of proper persons, to educate and teach them some honest way of earning a livelihood. I think it also provided some punishment or fine upon the parents. The debate, therefore, which engaged the most learned and the most eloquent, as well as those highest in rank, in the House of Peers, both in the Ministry and out of it, was upon the question, What shall be done with the mendicant children of the British Metropolis? On both sides, the most tender pity and the most anxious solicitude for these poor children was constantly expressed. The greatest point of difficulty was, to settle how far the legislature could interfere, consistently with the rights of the parties concerned. In the course of the debate a noble Marquis asked—"My Lords, who is to be the judge as to whether these parents perform their duty, or not? and if not, who is to assume their place, and act in their stead?" In his peculiarly graceful and easy manner, the Lord Chief Justice arose and replied, "I beg to answer the noble Lord by reminding him that the constitution puts the Lord Chancellor *in loco parentis* to the neglected and deserted children of England."

The subject of the discussion, and the result of it—the personages engaged in it, and the spirit in which they addressed themselves to it—filled me with such a sense of admiration for that senate, as I cannot express. The House of Lords, discussing their duties towards the lowest classes of Her Majesty's subjects! The rights of those classes, though criminals, as adults, and though mendicants, as children, seemed, to me, most delicately handled! The Lord Chief Justice, speaking both as a peer and a judge, saying that his fellow peer, the Lord Chancellor, is the guardian, the constitutional guardian, of these children of poverty and crime! The yielding of that noble House to the eloquent suasion of one of humanity's great British ornaments, the poor man's great model friend, the Earl of Shaftesbury! All these ideas crowded so upon my bewildered brain, that I was excited almost beyond endurance. It gave me such ideas of the British legislature and the British constitution, that I felt more than ever grateful to God that it is my lot, and the lot of my children, to be and remain subjects of the British Crown.

How different was all this from what was true of my unhappy native country! There, the poorest of the poor are sold in the shambles. There, honourable senators are but anxious to avoid legislating in their behalf: there, alas! legislation is chiefly devoted to rivetting the chains that bind them. More of American legislation is devoted to the promotion of slavery, directly and indirectly, than to any other interest whatever! *Rights of the poorest, in America!* why, one half of the time of American senators is spent in declaring what are the rights of all men, and the other half in depriving the poorest, the most outraged, those needing the most protection from the legislature, of all rights!

Besides, I should not dare visit the capital of my native country. It is in slaveholding territory; and there I could be legally arrested either as a runaway slave, or, if it were after ten at night, as a Negro at large without permission. In the latter case, I must pay £2 fine, or be severely flogged the next morning; in the former, I should be advertised. If no one came forward to prove me a free-man, or claim me as a slave, I should be sold to pay jail fees. But I had been in the British senate at the invitation of one of its most influential members; I had received from him marked attention; and I had seen him triumphantly carry what was to him a favourite measure, a measure having for its object the suppression and prevention of crime, and benefiting and blessing the poor. Who can blame a Negro for loving Great Britain? Who wonders that we are among the most loyal of Her Majesty's subjects?

In June, 1853, the Rev. T. Binney honoured me with an invitation to be present at the annual examination and dinner, at the Grammar School at Mill Hill,* and took me in his carriage. Charles Hindley, Esq., M.P., gave the toast upon civil and religious liberty, and in a kind and complimentary speech introduced me, as having been appointed to respond to it.

In June 1854 I was honoured with an invitation, through the kindness of James Spicer, Esq.,† to dine with the Company of Fishmongers. It there also fell to my lot to respond to the toast on civil and religious liberty.

My excellent friend Charles Makins, Esq., has on several occasions made me his guest at dinner parties, and I had to reply to the complimentary toasts to Canada, speaking in behalf of my North American fellow subjects; or to respond to the toast on the royal family, thus setting forth our Canadian loyalty.

Having intended and hoped to leave England in the latter part of the last year, the Chairman of the Congregational Union of England and Wales, the Rev. A. Morton Brown, LL.D, kindly and publicly took leave of me, in behalf of the body, in a speech full of the generous feeling wherewith his great heart abounds— such as he has always shown me at his house, in his pulpit, on the platform, and wherever it has been my good fortune to meet him.

But I cannot give one in a hundred of the incidents which made impressions of the most lasting kind upon me, during my sojourn in England. One chapter I thought must be devoted to them, and

---

* Rev. James Sherman showed me a like kindness on the 29th of June, by driving me in his carriage to Cheshunt College, where I had the honour of speaking at the anniversary dinner, my Lord Mayor Challis in the chair.

† A gentleman to whom I am under many great obligations.

that chapter must soon close. Those I have mentioned, I am sure, serve to demonstrate my most grateful sense of obligation to the many kind persons to whom I am indebted. I am equally sure that omissions will not be set down to a want of courtesy. But why write this chapter at all? For the purpose of stating, in connection with it, some two or three things by way of inference, and for the purpose of saying one word for myself.

1. For myself I only wish to say, that wherever I went, I always recollected that I was the representative of my people, and received in that light all the tokens of respect which were kindly given me. Not that I was ungrateful, but that I very well knew none of these kind feelings were expressed on my own account, stranger as I was, but on account of those whose cause I bear in my person and advocate in my public labours.

2. I mention these incidents as so many proofs that the abolitionism of England is not confined to any one class. It is an individual as well as a national matter. When the Duchess of Sutherland told me she had received abusive letters from American slaveholders, I could but see that English abolitionists, of whatever rank, suffer for the slave as well as feel for him a kind sympathy. When her Grace honoured me with an introduction to her daughter, Lady Kildare, who is, like her mother, an abolitionist, and when I saw the Duchess of Argyll evince so much of deep feeling for the slave, I said to myself, "the Duchess of Sutherland suffers abuse for us, but that does not induce her to abandon the cause: so far from it, she brings up her daughters to labour and suffer for it, thus giving it the influence of illustrious rank and exalted position." So, when I knew that Samuel Morley, Eusebius Smith, Ernest Bunsen, Charles Makins, Wilson Armestead, George Hitchcock, James Spicer, and Samuel Horman-Fisher, Esqs., were abolitionists, in spite of opposition, and at large expense to their pocket, I hailed with delight the fact that their principles were personal matters, deeply felt, fully considered, intelligently chosen, and, of course, firmly held. This is not the

sort of Englishmen who become pro-slavery men upon going to America. Such degeneracy is only true of those whose abolition-ism is mere sentimentality at home, and therefore good for noth-ing abroad. They only *drifted* with the current, here, in one direction; and they *drift* with it, there, in the opposite direction: it is *drifting*, and nothing more, in either case. Contending against the stream, in either country, is no work of theirs. But those whom I have named above, and all like them, were just the persons to free the British slave, when that was to be done—to feel, labour, and pray for the American slave, now, and to prove themselves true practical friends to the British Negro at all times.

3. I wish to follow in the footsteps of Mrs. Stowe, in recording my humble testimony to an important fact, in contradiction to an oft-repeated observation in America, concerning the British nobility in particular, and British abolitionists generally. The assertion is, that while these persons are earnest and untiring in their advocacy of the cause of the Negro, they pay no attention to, but actually trample upon, the poor of their own country, who are close to their doors. That is the American *assertion;* the *fact* is just contrary to it. Mrs. Stowe wrote her *Sunny Mem-ories* on purpose to dissipate this false though prevalent opinion in America, and I honour her for it. Her book has been severely criticized, and it is open to criticism; perhaps I have indulged in criticism as freely (though not with hostility) as any one: but the motive with which it was written was most honourable. I write this chapter with a like motive. The Earl of Shaftesbury and the Duchess of Sutherland are most widely known as the most prom-inent anti-slavery personages among the nobility. They, of all their rank, do most to ameliorate the condition of England's poor. Her Grace has educated her daughters in the activities to which she has devoted so much of her own time: those daughters are among the most active and devoted aristocratic patronesses of the charities of England which seek the elevation and relieve the wants of many of the poorest, at home.

The same remark applies to Joseph Payne, Esq., and all others amongst the middle classes who *work* in the anti-slavery cause in England: they are those who *work* most in the great plans of local benevolence which abound in this country. No colonist has spent so much time among these persons, at their work, as myself; and I have enjoyed opportunities of testifying to the truth touching the matter, to which many are strangers. I take the great pleasure in doing what in me lies to disabuse honest persons who have been misled. Those who choose to make a false assertion for the sake of disparaging Englishmen, do not care to be informed: indeed, they would rather cling to their error. Such, of course, I cannot hope to convince.

4. The anti-slavery men of England are among the most prominent of her great Dissenting Protestants. The mention of such names as I have had the honour of recording, names of men whose praises are in all the Churches, is abundant proof of this. I regard it as an evidence of God's great favour to our cause, as I have said before; and take very great pleasure in assuring these beloved brethren that the great mass of American abolitionists, and those of Canada, are of "like precious faith." They rely upon the gospel, as the great effective means of success. Those who think and act otherwise are a very small and diminishing number. They are not the men who either have or deserve the confidence or the co-operation of Christian abolitionists on either side of the Atlantic. I may perhaps, however, be allowed to say, that there is, in my humble judgment, great danger that pro-slavery professors of religion from America will receive too much countenance from British abolitionists. I think the co-operation with and indorsement of the American Board of Commissioners for Foreign Missions is a most undesirable step, in that direction. In that Board there is not a man, I believe, who has ever opened his mouth for the slave. As a Board, they have ignored the anti-slavery question, or allowed slaveholders to be appointed missionaries (as in the case of Rev. Mr. Wilson), or

provided for and winked at the admission of slaveholders into their Mission Churches, as in the case of the Cherokees and the Choctaws. Slaveholders, from one end of the country to the other, are members and officers of it; and the most decided pro-slavery men of the North are its chief promoters. That it should find indorsement in England, among Christian abolitionists, is especially to be deplored. Let but pro-slavery men, and slavery-sanctioning organizations, in America, be recognized and treated in this country *according to their character at home,* and they would soon feel compelled to alter their course. While they can obtain the approval of men in this country whose opinions they very well know how to value, they are encouraged to continue in their present attitude. Is this desirable on the part of British anti-slavery men? Can they better aid the cause of the slave than by sustaining its friends in America, and rebuking its enemies by their mighty moral power?

———————

CHAPTER VI

Scotland

Many of the most prominent members of the Anti-Slavery Society of Canada are natives of Scotland. Knowing the very active part some of the very best of their countrymen took in the emancipation struggle, and knowing as well how warmly the Scottish heart beats for liberty, especially upon its native soil, they kindly gave me letters of introduction to many persons of great eminence there. After I arrived in England, the Committee of the Glasgow New Abolition Society very cordially invited me to visit the North. What I knew of Scotchmen whom I had met, what I had read, and the natural desire to see such a country and such a people, made me but too happy to accept their kind invitation. Accordingly, in October, 1853, I paid my first visit to the land of Bruce and Burns, of Campbell, Gordon, and Scott. I was invited to attend a bazaar, and to speak. Though very ill, I made the attempt. The Rev. Dr. Lorimer was in the chair, sustained by some of the most learned of the Glasgow clergy, and gentlemen of high standing in other professions.

The kind and, I am sure, too partial manner, in which the excellent Dr. Roberton, of Manchester, had written and spoken of me, made me the welcome guest of Captain Hamilton,* of Rutherglen—a fit representative of the Scottish laird and the British officer. William P. Paton, Esq., and Hugh Brown, Esq.,

* Captain Hamilton did me the honour to introduce me to Rev. Mr. Monro, of Rutherglen, whose kind people contributed most liberally to our cause.

laid me under obligations by kindly receiving me at their homes, and by introducing me to some of the most eminent Scottish ministers. It was at the house of the former that I first had the gratification of meeting the Rev. Dr. Urwick, of Dublin, and the Rev. Noble Shepherd, of Sligo. At the house of Mr. Brown I had the pleasure of meeting the Rev. Dr. Arnot. At the hospitable board of the Rev. Dr. Lorimer I was honoured by an introduction to the Rev. Dr. Robson. Through the kindness of another friend, John Bain, Esq., I had the privilege of becoming acquainted with the Rev. Dr. Roxburgh.* John Smith, Esq., treated me like a brother, and Mrs. Smith sustained him in it. David Smith, Esq., the elder brother of Mr. John Smith, conferred upon me one of the highest favours a Scotchman could confer or a Negro could appreciate—*he gave me a copy of Burns' poems*, from his own library. That was almost equal to proffering me the freedom of Glasgow, or making me a Scotchman! Well did I use that volume, while sojourning in the country which gave birth to it and its immortal author! O that I liked *oaten cakes, haggis, cockie-leekie, or* BAGPIPES, as much as Burns! May my Scotch brethren forgive me for being so incorrigible a creature as to cling to old-fashioned likes and dislikes, acquired before I went to Scotland!

I have been speaking of my first visit to Scotland, in 1853. I was there again in May, 1855, and have therefore seen Scotland in winter and in May. The former taught me, almost as well as a Canadian winter, what Thomson meant when he said,

In Winter, awful Thou!

It was a cold, damp, foggy winter—a winter of such "darkness as may be felt." I had before heard that "a Scotch mist will wet an Irishman to the skin." A Scotch fog went *through* my skin, and gave me a worse congestion of the lungs than I had before suffered

---

* Dr. Roxburgh invited me to preach for him, and kindly allowed me to plead the cause of the Canadian Anti-Slavery Society in his pulpit. The collection was the largest I ever received, £50. 1s. 4d.

from in twenty years. So severe was it, as to compel me to suspend labour, and return to England. I went to the coast of Kent, to recover; and while there, received an invitation from my honoured friend, William Crossfield, Esq., to spend some time at his very pleasant residence, near Liverpool. In the course of a month I was able to resume my labours. Thanks to my kind hostess, Miss Jurdison, of Ramsgate; to the very amiable family of Mr. Crossfield, and other numerous friends in Liverpool, including Rev. Dr. Raffles, J. Cropper, Esq., E. Cropper, Esq., Rev. Chas. Birrell, G. Wright, Esq., the Misses Wraith, and others! Their great kindness did more than medicine towards my restoration.

I saw a good deal of Scotland, however, that winter, and became acquainted with some of the very best classes of Scotch gentry. I met, and worshipped with, and preached for, some of the best congregations—as Rev. Mr. Munro's, of Rutherglen; Rev. Dr. Wardlaw's, Rev. Dr. Roxburgh and others, in Glasgow; Rev. Mr. Campbell's and Rev. Dr. Alexander's, in Edinburgh; Rev. Mr. Gilfillan's, Rev. Mr. Lang's, and Rev. Mr. Borwick's, of Dundee; Rev. Dr. Brown's, of Dalkeith; &c.

I was in Scotland, alas! too late to see the Rev. Dr. Wardlaw. I had received from him kind, loving messages of sympathy, fraternity, and encouragement. They came like the words of one just entering the world of love—were destitute of stiff formality, and fragrant with the spirit of heaven. On an appointed day, a party of us went to his residence, to see him. The carriage which conveyed me arrived just as others were leaving, and the fatigue of the interview could neither be prolonged nor repeated. Thus I lost the opportunity of seeing on earth one of the men to meet whom will be one of the attractions of heaven. I had been equally unsuccessful in seeing Dr. Collyer, the first day I preached in his chapel. Before I was there again, he and the sainted Wardlaw were with Jesus.

I had the melancholy pleasure of mingling my tears with the

many who heard Rev. Dr. Alexander preach Dr. Wardlaw's funeral session. I never before heard such a discourse. It was a noble tribute to the learning, piety, attainments and character, of the deceased, by one who intimately knew him and dearly loved him. The oration spoke wonders both for the dead and the living. It showed that the living speaker knew how to appreciate the great and shining qualities of the deceased. The sermon was delivered in the earnest impressive style of Scotch divines, tempered and chastened by the superior refinement of the respected preacher, who is, I think, one of the most finished—if not, indeed, *the* most finished—pulpit orator I heard in Scotland.

The deep sensation felt all through the commercial metropolis of Scotland upon the death of Dr. Wardlaw, the words of praise which every lip gave him, the reverence with which his name was spoken, testified plainly, to the most casual observer, how deep and firm a hold he had upon all hearts while living. The same feeling pervaded all classes in the provinces. In his case was verified the scriptural expression, "The memory of the just is blessed."

Society in Scotland differs from that in England, as does the society of Boston and Massachusetts generally from that of Vermont, New Hampshire, and Maine. I was struck with this while travelling northwards. The northern people are more familiar, more democratic. A Scotchman does not feel under the particular necessity of sitting next to you all day in a railway carriage *without saying a word,* as an Englishman does. Betwixt different classes there is more familiarity, less distance, in Scotland, than in England. The different orders of society seem to approach more nearly to each other, without either losing or forgetting its place. There is less of the feeling, so prevalent in small towns in the South, that merchants and professional men must by all means avoid contact with shopkeepers. The chief order of nobility is the clergy, and all join to pay deference to them; but the general spread of religion, and the very upright and pious habits of the population—the familiarity of the ministers with people, join to produce a brotherly feeling of oneness, which is abundantly apparent in the national character and in the state of society.

Besides, I do not think that mere ceremony is half so much studied by the Scotch. They are great believers in realities; they are a substantial people; and what is merely formal, unless it be formal after the Scottish mode, is not commendable to them, and it costs them but little to say, "I canna be fashed wi sic clishma-claver." Hence, you get at a Scotchman's heart at once. He will not profess to be what he is not. When you go to his house, and he extends his hand and says "Come away," you may know you are welcome. I like this straightforward way of doing things: it is far more expressive of true generosity than the set courtly phrases of mere conventionalism.

A sort of independence of character is far more prevalent and observable in the Scotch peasantry than in either the English, the Irish, or the Welsh. Everybody expects to find it so; if not he will find himself much mistaken. Several anecdotes have been given me illustrative of this; but as I am not at home in telling Scotch tales, I dare not insert any of them. The fact, however, is most palpable. Doubtless the universal diffusion of education has much to do with it.

How readily, and how generously, did the Scottish people respond to the claims of the anti-slavery cause! Dr. Pennington found it so, when he was there; so did Mr. Garnett; so did Frederick Douglass. There is far more of active, organized, anti-slavery vitality, among the three millions of Scottish population, than among the seventeen millions of English people. There are classes in England which the anti-slavery cause never reaches—the classes who compose the multitude. It is not so in Scotland, because the whole population, high and low, attend divine service, and they naturally enough acquire the habit of attending the kirk on any subject for which it is open. In England, millions of the working classes (not to mention others) do not attend any place of worship, and therefore never hear, know, or care, about the moral movements of the age. The same result is seen in Ireland. There are multitudes there, to be seen in the streets, who never enter any other than a Roman Catholic place of worship, and who accordingly know literally nothing of what is going on in the great moral field. In Wales, on the other hand, religion is as universal as education is in Scotland. Hence the Welsh, like the Scotch, go *en masse* to the meetings for religious and benevolent purposes.

As I travelled about Scotland, both in 1853 and 1855, I found the anti-slavery feeling prevalent, deep, earnest, and intelligent. It is incorporated in the feelings, habits, and characteristics of the people. They are abolitionists from intelligent conviction, human sympathy, and religious principle. Anti-slavery principle will live in Scotland while religion has an abiding place in the hearts of her people. I attended meetings in Glasgow, Edinburgh, Dalkeith, Dunfermline, Dundee, Hamilton, Stewartown, Cumnock, Kirkaldy, Falkirk, Stirling, Montrose, Rutherglen, Greenock, Rothsay, Campbelltown, &c. To the kind friends in those towns whose humble guest I had the pleasure of being (in one case, when suffering from an affection of the chest and an inflammation in my feet; in another, when on crutches from a severe lameness—circumstances which made a kindness the more needed and the more acceptable), I beg hereby to tender my most hearty thanks. May the blessings of those ready to perish ever be upon them!

In Glasgow there are two Anti-Slavery Committees. My immediate connection was with the new one; but Mrs. George Smith, one of the old Committee, with whom I had the pleasure of breakfasting, is most catholic in her anti-slavery views and feelings. To the slave and his cause she is true, however she may differ from some of her coadjutors. I did not happen to meet any other person in Glasgow whom I knew as belonging to the old Society. It was not my business to inquire into the differences of abolitionists, but I presume they are about the same as those between anti-slavery people in the United States. Would that the time were come, when all Christians and all Christian reformers were prepared to say, "Let there be no strife, I pray thee, between thee and me, and between my herdmen and thy herdmen, for we be brethren." How much do we all need to study the lesson taught us by our Lord, in his reply to the disciples, when they informed him that they had forbidden some one to cast out devils, because he did not follow with them!

In other towns, I believe, this division happily does not exist. There is a very active society in Edinburgh, whose Secretary, Mrs. Wigham, treated me most kindly, inviting and introducing me to a meeting of the Ladies' Committee.* That Society, as such, allowed me to be the bearer of a very generous donation to those who sent me hither. They also gave me a token of kind wishes to myself personally. In Dundee is an earnest, energetic Society, whose Secretary, Mrs. Borwick, is indefatigable in its promotion. That Society also gave me tangible expressions of personal regard, and of sympathy with my cause, on both occasions of my visiting Dundee. In Greenock a Committee was formed while I was there, from which great good may be expected, because at its head is a lady† of such untiring energy, that her efforts will effect a great deal. With her are associated so many of the truly pious and benevolent of that beautiful town, that there will be no lack of service to the general cause from that very efficient Committee.

The Glasgow Society is the leading one, from its position, and the commanding influence of most of its members. Glasgow is the chief place of business north of the Tweed. Its commerce is constantly increasing; and its "merchant princes" and "factory lords" are augmenting their wealth, and that of their town, to an

* Mrs. Wigham sent her carriage to my hotel, to fetch me to breakfast with her family. There I had the pleasure of making Mr. Wigham's acquaintance.

† Mrs. Hepburn.

almost incredible degree. Hence, whatever is done in Glasgow is done for the whole of Scotland. The influence of Glasgow merchants and Glasgow ministers is considerable, owing to the greatness of this Queen of the West, and to the personal character and great learning which those ministers possess. These two facts, with the additional one that both merchants and ministers are members of the Glasgow Society, make it to all practical purposes a Society for all Scotland, as it might not improperly be called. Then, the very fraternal co-operation with it which the Anti-Slavery Societies and the ministers and Churches of the whole country show, certainly makes it a national more than a local organization. It *is* national, in fact, but it is the nationality of sympathy and co-operation, which is far better than that of mere name.

There is much in Scotland, especially in Glasgow, for the anti-slavery cause to contend against. There is a great deal of trade between Glasgow merchants and American traders. The former do not like to run the risk of damaging their business, by offending good customers—which they fear would be the result of their taking active, open, anti-slavery ground. This is less commendable, as some of the most prosperous, most successful firms, are anti-slavery men—a fact which certainly ought to assure the timid. But timidity is not all. They are not only "fearful," but "unbelieving." They are *not*, in heart, *with* the anti-slavery cause; but they *are*, in heart, *against* it. I could mention the names of more than one Lord Provost who refused, when in office, to show the least favour to our cause, because they did not approve of it. They are merchants, and look at things as Mr. Cunard does, "in a business light;" but why it should injure them more than it does Messrs. Campbells, G. Smith and Sons, McKeand and Co., Playfair and Bryce, Messrs. Smith, or Mr. W. P. Paton, all of whom are abolitionists, and merchants too, *I dinna ken.*

Some few of the clergymen, too, it is not to be denied, seem destitute of all interest in the cause of the slave. Then there are some who were formerly slaveholders in the colonies, and whose being obliged to release their Negroes did not at all change their hearts. But what in this world could have made a pro-slavery man of Mr. Baxter, M.P. for Montrose, I cannot imagine. His father was among the most ready to forward the cause which first took me to Dundee. His venerable grandfather, one of the princely patriarchs of Scotland, took me kindly by the hand, and made the largest contribution, save one, that I received in Scotland to the cause. I bowed with him at the altar of prayer; we united our supplications together: it was eight-and-forty hours after the demise of Dr. Wardlaw, whom the venerable William Baxter soon joined, in heaven. I have his autograph. It is doubly dear to me since his decease. Loving him as I did, I could but feel the deepest regret that a cause to which he was so ardently attached should be wounded by one in those veins flowed the blood of William Baxter!

In Edinburgh I found a warm coadjutor in the person of the excellent Rev. J. R. Campbell, M.A.* The Rev. Dr. Candlish put himself to some inconvenience to attend my meeting there. Mr. Joseph Watson, John Wigham, Esq., Mr. Thomas Russell, and the Rev. Geo. Cullen of Leith, gave me very substantial proofs of their friendly regard for the cause of my poor people. J. B. Tod, Esq., and his amiable family, made their house my home, and a most delightful home it was. Mr. Tod is one of the earliest abolitionists of Scotland. He was warm and devoted in the cause, in days when some were opposing, others doubting and hesitating. Mr. John Dunlop, of Burntisland, was an anti-slavery man in those days too. He sacrificed a small fortune in the cause, rather than retain the ownership of human beings. A more cordial friend the anti-slavery cause has not in Scotland, than John Dunlop, Esq.

Much excitement prevailed throughout Scotland in May, 1855,

* Now of Bradford, Yorkshire.

owing to the fact that the missionaries of the United Presbyterian Church had admitted slaveholders to the communion and membership of the body, at Old Calabar, in Africa. The arguments *pro* and *con* showed that the question of the religious character of slaveholders, and of their fitness for fellowship in a Christian Church, was one in which the denomination took a deep interest. Members of other bodies as well shared in the interest excited by this discussion. Without professing to understand the matter in its length and breadth, I feel quite sure that the honest disposition of all is, to arrive at the truth and to practise it. This is an earnest, not only of present right-mindedness, but of future success in grappling with the difficulties of the case, and overcoming them: as they must be, if the body be kept pure. The same honoured denomination is doing very much to evangelize Jamaica. No doubt their interest in the cause of the Negro will continue, while they are engaged in doing so much for his very best weal. It is to that body that my eloquent cousin, Rev. H. H. Garnett, of Westmoreland, county of Cornwall, Jamaica, belongs.

While I was in Edinburgh, I gladly accepted the kind offer of Mrs. Tod and her accomplished daughter, to accompany me to Holyrood House. I had read so much of that palace, and had made myself so familiar with the history of Mary, Queen of Scots, and her unhappy husbands (to accommodate oneself to a term not strictly correct), that I was anxious to visit it. Mrs. Tod is an Irish lady—whether of the old school or not, I cannot say; but of the school of kind politeness, refined manners, well stored intellect, and extraordinary conversational powers, with an abundance to converse about of that which is far above mere commonplace parlance. Her daughter, though born in Scotland, of a Scottish father, is to all appearance and to all purposes an Irish girl, in all that is good, accomplished, ladylike, and simple-hearted, which that term includes. With such companions, and a succession of servants to show us over the different apartments, we took our *tour* of Holyrood House—for it is no small journey—

and were first shown into the room in which King James is *said* to have been born. Our guide (as, unfortunately, is not very uncommon with such officials, in that country) was in a state that would pass among ordinary judges for drunk. He made some stupid blunder about the lock of the door, so that he could not unfasten it to let us out. There we were—Mrs. Tod, Miss Tod, our guide, and myself—locked in the room in which, he said, James the Sixth of Scotland and First of England was born! After the far less than sober guide had exercised his skill upon the door, the lock, and the key, sufficiently to convince us that he could never release us, I took an old battle-axe, affirmed to be 600 years old (everything is ancient in such places, according to the chronology of guides and servants), and broke the door open, effecting deliverance from durance for myself and party.

We were shown Queen Mary's bed, some tapestry of her own working, and a thousand and one curiosities connected with that unhappy woman, which every visitor of Holyrood has had pointed out to him, in her apartments. The fabulous blood of Rizzio was shown us, of course; what was it kept there for, but to be shown? But the most amusing thing was pointing out the stone, on the floor of the ruined abbey, where Queen Mary stood when *she was married to Bothwell!* That was a little "more than I had bargained for"; I therefore said to the person who showed it—"Will you be kind enough, first to tell me *when* she was married to Bothwell, or, whether she was married to him or not? We will see the stone they *stood upon when married, afterwards.*"

"There is, I confess, some doubt about it, in some minds, sir," he remarked apologetically.

"And I am one of the most sceptical," said I. The ladies laughed, and the guide kept better "within the record" after that.

Going over the apartments recently occupied by the royal family, I was delighted to see the simplicity and plainness of the furniture in the bedrooms. The bedsteads of the princes were just such as Masters Anybody in the kingdom would sleep on. In the royal apartments, which the person showed them told us were not exhibited to *all* visitors (hinting both that we were privileged and that we ought to pay for it), I saw two elegant chairs, which were brought from Montreal to the Exhibition of 1851. I was charged with being so delighted with these productions of my own colony, as to almost forget everything else I saw; and the charge, I must acknowledge, is more than half true. It was no small gratification, to know that one's own colony was well and honourably represented in that Exhibition, and to know that the royal family honoured that colony either by the purchase or the acceptance of those articles, and caused them to be placed in the ancient palace of Holyrood.

When at Stirling and Perth, I was so lame as to be unable either to walk about or ride on horseback; and was therefore obliged to leave both palaces without seeing their great beauties, and their points of almost classic interest. This was to me, a matter of deep regret; but, indulging the hope of visiting Scotland at some future day, with my family, I contented myself with the promise of then seeing the lakes, the highlands, the midsummer twilight of the far North, the city of Aberdeen, and the beautiful scenery surrounding Stirling and Perth. I was equally disappointed at Hamilton, Greenock, and Rothsay; but fortunate enough to receive the kind sympathy, active and hearty co-operation, and personal kindness, of the good friends of the cause in those towns.

I forgot to say, that the Glasgow New Abolition Society has a Committee of Ladies as well as one of gentlemen. These two, while somewhat independent, yet act together. It was my privilege to be employed by them for twenty days; and I shall not soon forget either their trueness and devotion to the cause, or their kindness to myself personally. There are a great many disagreeables connected with an agency, especially a travelling agency; that was the last I accepted, and I hope never to accept another: but all the unpleasant things naturally and necessarily appertain-

ing to an agency are very greatly modified, if not entirely overcome, by such kindness as that shown me by this society and
John Smith, Esq., its respected Secretary.

I think I can say of Scottish abolitionists generally, that they
are as laborious and self-sacrificing as any band of anti-slavery
people I ever saw. I have already said that it partakes of their
very intelligent religious character. But this is not all. It is formed
of the traits which make up the whole of Scottish character: the
elements of the latter enter into and comprise the former. It
follows, that whatever of sterling integrity, deep earnestness,
unfaltering perseverance, enlightened and large-hearted humanity, and high-toned religious sentiment, are peculiar to the Scot,
both by nature and by education, mark and distinguish his abolitionism. Hence, the announcement of a meeting or a contribution
brings the true Scot to the place of assemblage, and brings, with
him, his donation and his prayer. It may rain, his funds may be
low,* there may be other obstacles: but what of these? He is a
Scotchman. This is duty; its performance, with him, is not to
depend upon whether it be convenient or not. Hence, also, when
Scotchmen have gone to the colonies, they have made those distant countries feel the impress of their character in general matters, producing the best fruits of energy and intelligence; but
when they have so drifted with the stream, in slave-holding countries, as to become partakers of the evil deeds of their neighbours,
they have not been restrained from the lowest depths of wickedness to which many of other nations have sunk.

Scotchmen, in the West Indies, became slave-holders. They
were severely exacting and oppressive. It was just like them to
demand, and, if possible, to receive, the last *"baubee,"* from the
unpaid toil of their slaves. They required the exhibition of Scottish energy from their bondmen; if they did not receive it, they
were prepared to exhibit Scotch energy in forcing it out of them.

* *A man may tak his neebur's part*
Yet hae no cash to spare.

Instances of this sort are to be remembered of many Scotch slave-holders (and, alas! by many Negroes, who were their slaves) to this day. The record of them, and the names of their perpetrators, would be the largest, blackest roll and record of infamy that ever disgraced the Scottish name or blighted Scottish character. It is therefore most fit that there should be in their native country a fearless, persevering band, who are redeeming the name and character of the nation, disgraced by such recreants. It is true, also, that among the thousand and one voices into which no inconsiderable number of our fellow subjects from the North fell, when slaveholders, was that which violated the seventh commandment. Like others, they treated their children of African blood as half-castes, and denied them social equality with whites —raising them *above* the condition of their mothers, depressing them *beneath* that of their fathers—making them a silly, supercilious, unmanly, half-race, unfit for any social position, alike uncomfortable among whites or blacks. But it is true that, in these matters, Scotchmen showed themselves but human beings, it is also true that, unlike Yankee slaveholders, they did not, as a rule, *trade* in the persons of their own children! They would not disown them; they would and did educate them, and settle property upon them. This is, I believe, commonly true of Scotch slaveholders in America—more commonly than of any others. A Yankee will sell his own child quite as readily as one of his black neighbour's; and with as little remorse or concern. He can do that and belong to Church, and remain "in good and regular standing." A Scotchman, as a rule, says practically, "I canna do *that*"!

I must do Scotchmen the justice to add, too, that in America they do not forget, so soon as other men from these islands, the fact that they were born in a land of freedom and equality as to races and colours. They do not so easily learn to trample upon a free Negro, and to tread his rights in the dust. I do not deny that there are most lamentable cases of this description, but I do affirm that they are not nearly so frequent and so numerous as is true of other British nationalities. Perhaps I shall be excused for stating a case of some prominence, which illustrates my idea.

There is in America a total abstinence organization called the "Sons of Temperance." It is, in some respects, a secret society. It has done a great deal to promote the cause of total abstinence in that country, where such labours are greatly needed; but, like other benevolent societies in America, this order passes the black man by, and accommodates the prejudices of its members and the community by treating coloured persons after the ordinary way of treating them—refusing them membership upon equal terms with others. This is done by the Churches to which these gentlemen belong: and why should not a Temperance Society take the Church for its model? They also refuse to grant black persons charters empowering them to form Lodges of blacks. In a word, they seem to prefer the gratification of their ill will to the Negro, to allowing him to receive the benefits of their Order. I grieve to say, that they have not changed in the least, in this disposition. They still seem to say, "we prefer the continued drunkenness of the Negro, with all its attendant horrors, to admitting him to our fraternity. If some one will save him, well; but as for *us* and *our Order*, we prefer his going to perdition as he is, to the relaxation of our rule."

In the early history of the Order there was no rule on the subject. Accordingly, in some divisions (as the Lodges are called) remote from New York, blacks were admitted. Several were received in New England; many are in Canada. I was admitted in Cortland; but the dissatisfaction arising out of my case was so great, that the New York Division sent a deputy* to order my expulsion. In 1851, the National Division passed a rule declaring it "is illegal and inexpedient to admit coloured persons"; they have since that time confirmed this vote, by refusing to amend or alter it. In my own case, we threw our charter into their teeth, and dis-

* Captain Cady.

solved the Division. The presiding officer was a member of my Church; the next in rank was the clerk of the Church; another member was a deacon, whom I had ordained; many more were attendants upon my ministry. Could they submit to a demand to expel their chosen pastor, on account of his colour? Could they consent to belong to a fraternity demanding it? No; they honoured themselves, their principles, and their minister, by indignantly washing their hands of all participation in such an organization. It follows, that black persons are not legal members; of course, to such, charters are not to be granted. Besides, if blacks might form constituent Divisions, they would be entitled to be represented in Grand Divisions: that would never answer. It may be, that in another world, whether of bliss or woe, blacks and whites are in close association, or even in close contact; but on earth—*i.e., American earth,* and among *the Sons of Temperance* —such a thing is out of the question.

But what has this to do with Scotchmen? I will show. In the face of this general universal Negro-hate, several Scottish temperance men in the city of New York withdrew from the Order, formed the Caledonian Division, admitted black members, and granted them charters to form black Divisions on terms of the most perfect equality with themselves. The same, I am sorry to say, is not true of any other British nationality; but Englishmen, Irishmen, Welshmen, and Canadians, belong to the Negro-hating Divisions, and help to enforce and sustain the anti-Negro rule. I will take the liberty of saying here, that were all Scotchmen and other British people, upon going to America, to act as did this Caledonian Division, the whole current of pro-slavery opinion in America would be turned. So numerous—and so powerful, after a very short residence—are those who once were subjects of Britain, in that country, that they could have long since revolutionized public sentiment on this matter, had they chosen to do so. Let me state a case. The Rev. Mr. McClure says, that in one of the Methodist Churches in a large town in New Jersey, there were several English, and also several coloured, communicants. The rule was (a

rule almost invariable among American Methodists and others),
that the black members should not commune until the whites had
been served. These Englishmen, in a body, remained until the
coloured people were called, and then came and received the em-
blems with them—thus identifying themselves, as Jesus did, with
the poor. The consequence was, that the rule was broken down;
and now, whites and blacks are treated alike, as they should be.
Mr. McClure observes, that were the same thing, in like circumstances, done by Englishmen generally, in America, they are
numerous enough to carry their point in almost every community. I know that the same would be true of Irishmen and Scotchmen, had they the manliness to try it.

Emigrants from England, therefore, when going to America
and becoming Americanized on this subject, not only do great evil
to the Negro, but fail, guiltily fail, to do him the good which lies
in their power. I could not write so freely as I have concerning
American guilt, and be silent touching the like turpitude of former British subjects. In contrast with what is too common there,
I take great pleasure in bearing testimony to the noble stand of
the Caledonian Division; and beg to add, that one of the aims of
the Scottish Anti-Slavery Societies, and those in all other parts of
the three kingdoms, should be, in my humble judgment, the maintenance of a high-toned Christian anti-slavery sentiment in every
part of Britain, for the purpose of warning emigrants against the
guilt and danger to which they will be exposed in this matter,
when settled in the United States; and, in the event of their falling
into such practice, rebuking them for lapsing from principles
which it was their pride to avow when at home. While in Scotland,
I spoke freely upon this point; and am proud to be able to say,
that I did so with the fullest concurrence of the ladies and gentlemen of the Anti-Slavery Societies.

I never saw, before or elsewhere, such cultivation of the soil, as
in Scotland. I have travelled from Maine to Wisconsin, and over
the finest portions of New York, Pennsylvania, New Jersey, and
Ohio; but never saw farming so perfect as it is everywhere in the

Scotch lowlands. Ayrshire, the Lothians, the valleys of the Clyde and the Tay, the land surrounding Edinburgh, and the valley of the Tweed, exceed not only in fertility, but in highly finished and scientific culture, anything I ever saw. Give Canada such farming, and she will stand among the first agricultural countries of the north temperate zone—if not, indeed, becoming *the* first of them.*
Had Australia such farming, her inexhaustible gold mines would be but a subordinate source of wealth. If poor Jamaica were but advanced to an equal pitch of agricultural industry, she would become a source of illimitable wealth, and exceed in the future the palmiest days of her past history.

Perhaps I did not form so high an estimate of the religious character of the Scottish people as some travellers do; but what I saw of it was quite sufficient to make me thankful that it is what it is, and that it is doing so much to elevate the character of the colonies, to which its possessors are swarming in such vast numbers every year. My only criticism upon it is, an expression of the fear that it may possibly be more educational than spiritual, more intelligent than feeling, more doctrinal than practical—more refined, metaphysical, and casuistic, than reformatory. I utter this apprehension with extreme deference, hoping that the remark will be received as coming from a grateful, loving heart, not censuring, but simply criticizing, with the full recollection of my extreme incompetency to judge in such matters.

Nor do I agree with the great majority of travellers as to the alleged intemperance of the Scotch: indeed, I heard more about this from Scotchmen than from any others. The Scotch clergy do more in the cause of temperance than the clergy of any other country, save America or Canada. There is more legislation on the subject in Scotland than anywhere else in Europe. The subject is therefore more frequently spoken of, more thoroughly examined, and its statistics are more prominently brought out, than in the South. It is true that custom demands and sanctions,

---

* Except Scotland, of course.

in good society, drinking more whiskey than is used by the same amount of population in England; but that drunkenness is more common among the lower classes, or that the use of whiskey in the North furnishes occasion for saying anything more of the middle classes there than the use of wine here affords, is certainly neither according to my observation, nor to any comparison of the two countries on the subject which I was able to make, either from sight or reading.

That the temperance cause has yet very much to do in both countries, is most lamentably evident; that religious men are called upon to look this question directly in the face, and grapple with it, is equally evident: and it is most gratifying to say, that the good already done and now doing by total abstinence men is also as evident. Everybody is remarking upon the diminution of wine-drinking, and the almost entire absence of inebriation, in the middling and higher classes. Had the lower orders learned and practised like moderation for the past thirty years, how different would have been their state! how changed their present condition! What different prospects would both English and Scotch working classes present, as well to their temporal and present as their future and eternal welfare!

I spoke of "moderation," and know how that term is hated by some temperance men; but beg to say, that it is neither an unscriptural nor an unphilosophical term. However, in the case of a man to whom alcoholic beverages present to strong a temptation to allow of any use of such drinks without intoxication, his only course is immediate, lifelong, total abstinence.* May the demon of drunkenness soon be banished from this otherwise happy island!

* That some should abstain, for the sake of example to others, is most praiseworthy self-denial: all I claim is, that so to do is not, as I once believed, the demand of the Bible, in the case of all persons. I do not feel at liberty to write as if I were a total abstainer, now that I am not; yet would not on any account withhold my humble tribute of praise from those who are, nor say a word to injure the temperance cause.

CHAPTER VII

Ireland

I must beg the generous reader to indulge me in saying but
little concerning the Emerald Isle. It is a country so full of interest, making such rapid strides of improvement, capable of such
vast development, so rich in material and intellectual resources,
so deficient in moral and spiritual cultivation, that it would be
most unjustifiable presumption, in one who has spent but twenty
days there, ten of which were at Killarney, to attempt to speak of
it intelligently. If God spare me, I shall know more of that island
at some future day; *then* it will be time enough to speak of it at
length.

I was in Ireland a few days in September 1854, and in June
1855. The first time, I simply crossed from Holyhead to Kingston, spent a day or two there and at Dublin, and passed rapidly,
by rail, from thence to Cork, where I spent a night, and hastened
the next day, through Mallow, to Killarney. There, like others, I
did, as nearly as possible, nothing: in fact, went there for that
very purpose. We rode, walked, sailed, ate, drank, and slept,
daily, with some degree of regularity and perseverance, each ac-
complishing his task to his own satisfaction. The rich romantic
scenery, the beauty of the lakes, the fine old ruins of Mucruss
Abbey and Ross Castle, the beautiful grounds of Mr. Herbert, the
affability of the company we met, all gave us a variety of most
pleasing sights and sounds; and, being favoured with extraordi-
narily fine weather, we could but be gratified with our short sojourn in that picturesque locality.

I must not forget, that Mr. Schiell, the gentlemanly master of the Killarney Junction Railway Hotel, understood as well as any man in that business ever did, the art and science of making his guests comfortable. I went there to rest—another name for being lazy. So did others. We accomplished what we went for. Now, please excuse my giving descriptions of what I saw, for I have no descriptive power or talent whatever. I can only say, that after having lived four-and-thirty years in America, I was not so well prepared to appreciate Irish lake or mountain scenery as those visitors who had never been out of this kingdom. I appreciated the falls on Mr. Herbert's place, on account of his very great kindness in suffering visitors to witness them; but to one who lives within three hours' sail of Niagara Falls, they certainly did not appear *very wonderful*. As to lakes, I live on Lake Ontario, and have frequently sailed upon Lake Erie and Lake Michigan. When I tell the reader that one of these is 160 and another 180 miles long, he will not wonder that I was not beyond measure astonished at Killarney lakes. Then, as to small and beautiful lakes, I beg to say, with great deference, but most certainly with truth, that Skaneateles Lake, Geneva Lake, Seneca Lake, and Crooked Lake, in New York State, are neither excelled nor equalled by anything it has been my good fortune to see on this side of the Atlantic. Still I was pleased, greatly pleased, with the scenery of Killarney; and the above is introduced less by way of boasting, than apology for not being more perfectly captivated, charmed, delighted, overwhelmed, and "all that sort of thing," which some persons thought "as in duty bound" I ought to have been.

I met at Cork some friends and relations of my good neighbour, P. P. Hayes, Esq., of Toronto. Not having time to call upon Father Mathew, as I had promised, if I ever visited Cork, and having learned that he was about to proceed to Florence for his health, I had the melancholy pleasure of sending him my card, and an expression of best wishes for the speedy recovery of his wonted strength. I had met the venerable priest at Cleveland, Ohio, in 1851. He was in my native country, pursuing a most laudable work. Differences in religion were of no moment to me, as compared with the great work of philanthropy. I was but too happy, therefore, to receive the invitation of Father Mathew to visit him; and, had circumstances favoured it, should have been delighted to do so.

I had not the good fortune to hear the Rev. Dr. Urwick on the Sunday I was in Dublin; but, at Kingston, had the great pleasure of hearing that most indefatigable and most successful pastor, the Rev. Joseph Denham Smith, whom I had before met in England, and from whom I received the kindest attention. Mr. Smith is one of the English ministers who have gone to Ireland to do good, and have become most enthusiastically fond of Ireland and the Irish. I saw this in all whom it was my pleasure to meet, during both visits to that country. The singular devotion which the Independent ministers show to the people among whom they live, and their great admiration for the land of their labours, tend in no small degree to the almost incredible efficiency and success of their labours. Disconnected from the State, receiving not one penny of State pay, they make manifest to all the disinterestedness of their work; and show as well, that great good can be accomplished now, as in the days of the apostles, by voluntary, persevering, religious effort. In no country is this more manifest than in Ireland, where the class of ministers to which Mr. Smith and his co-labourers belong are obliged to compete with State Churchism in so many forms. This remark is not made offensively. I am giving utterance to my own religious opinions, without disguise; and repeat, that their correctness, in practical working, never struck me so forcibly as during my last visit to Ireland: nor can I bring myself to believe that any honest, honourable Christian, of whatever denomination, will find fault with my refusing so far to play the neutral, as to write as if I had no opinions or were too unmanly to express them.

My second visit to Ireland was on a short anti-slavery tour. Leaving Glasgow on June 1st, I took a steamer at Greenock, at

7 P.M., for Belfast. A most pleasant trip down the Clyde, on a moonlight night, and across the placid waters betwixt the Scotch and the Irish coasts, brought us into Belfast at five the next morning. Breakfasting at the Imperial Hotel, and taking the first morning train, I started on my way, having to be in Sligo the next day. I travelled by railway only to Armagh; the remainder of the journey, seventy or eighty miles—Irish miles, in that brief period —had to be made in such conveyances as I could find. At Armagh I found in the coach a most ladylike fellow passenger, in the person of Mrs. Caldwell, of Clogher. By this kind lady I was introduced to Mrs. Maxwell,* the Secretary of Clogher Anti-Slavery Society. I seemed to Mrs. M. no stranger, as she had been corresponding with my good friend Mr. Armistead, of Leeds, concerning me. Professor Allen was to speak there the following Tuesday, and both Mrs. Caldwell and Mrs. Maxwell kindly and politely invited me to attend with him. It was with deep regret that I found myself unable to do so.

I went on to Enniskillen, arriving at about 5 P.M. I there learned, to my dismay, that there was no public conveyance thence to Sligo, until the next morning. I had no other way than to post on twenty-one miles, to Manor Hamilton, which I reached at eleven o'clock that night. On Sunday morning I drove eleven miles into Sligo, in time to preach for the Rev. Noble Shepherd, as per appointment. The next day (Monday, 4th) a very large meeting was convened in Mr. Shepherd's beautiful church, to hear me speak on slavery. The Right Honourable John Wynne, at Mr. Shepherd's request, favoured the meeting and the cause by taking the chair. He did so in a manner that showed his interest in the anti-slavery question to be of no recent origin. Mr. Wynne being connected with the first families of the Irish aristocracy, both by birth and by marriage, and having been Secretary to Her Majesty's Representative in Ireland, I may be justly proud of

---

* A relative of Lord Cavan, I believe.

that gentleman's services and favour on that occasion. In that meeting I saw a feature of Irish Protestanism which one does not see in England. The Rev. the Rector attended this meeting, and took a lively interest in it. The place was completely filled, in every part, with a generous auditory, no small proportion of them being Episcopalians. A rector would not have attended a meeting in an Independent chapel in England; there it would have been considered necessary to hold the meeting on "neutral ground"—in a hall, or school-house, or some such place. Except in the case of the Rev. J. McConnel Hussey, of Kennington, who took the chair on the 17th of October, 1854, at a meeting held to promote education in a Dissenting community,* I do not recollect ever to have seen an Episcopal clergyman in England so favouring the objects, and so countenancing the movements, and so recognizing the brotherhood, of Independents. It is a beautiful feature, I repeat, of Irish Protestantism—of true catholicity.

On the 5th, I journeyed a long, long way, sixty-six miles, from Sligo to Mullingar, in a coach. Coaches, in these railway days, are "slow" enough. Sixty-six Irish miles are equal to eighty-four English. Packed, four of us, in a coach of no very ample dimensions, was, if comfortable, what we were not quite aware of. At a certain stage of our journey, I asked the guard (a most perfect specimen of an Irishman, "a broth of a boy")—"How far is it to Mullingar, guard?"

"Two-and-twinty miles, yer honor."

"Irish miles are longer than English miles, are they not?"

"Yes, yer honor, and *quite as wide*."

We travelled over *both dimensions* till we reached Mullingar, heartily tired of our day's jolting, and heartily glad to be once more in sight of a railway; at least, that was my feeling, and my fellow passengers acted as if they felt so too. After a very pleasant passage from Mullingar to Dublin, some forty miles, I was glad to secure rest at the Hibernian Hotel, my Dublin home.

* Rev. William Leask's school.

Early on the morning of the 6th I took the railway to Limerick, being met there by Rev. Wm. Tarbotton, and a gentleman whose "Irish jaunting car" and large Irish heart were ready to welcome me. It's meself that's to blame for niver remimbering the gintleman's name, at all at all; and what is worse, I cannot remember the name of his *kind lady,* nor the name of *his brother,* nor his *brother's lady.* Being almost cured of my lameness, I was able, in the excellent company of Mr. Tarbotton, to walk over most of Limerick, which is a fine thrifty town, one of which the people of that county may well be proud. Some of its warehouses are the most massive structures of the sort I ever saw. The elements of wealth in the trade and resources of the town, and the surrounding country, but more in the enterprise of its inhabitants, ensure for Limerick not only the continuance of its high place among the commercial towns of Ireland, but mark out for it a most brilliant future.

A very full meeting did me the honour to listen to me, in Mr. Tarbotton's church; William Cochrane, Esq., kindly taking the chair, in the absence of the gentleman who had generously consented to do so, but to whom an accident had occurred the day before, rendering him unable. The account given of the meeting, the speech and the speaker, and the interest shown in the cause, by the Limerick newspaper, were full and kind; and I was grateful to see in them tokens of the most genuine anti-slavery feeling, set off with real Irish warmth and cordiality.

Reluctantly leaving my kind Limerick friends, who seemed like old acquaintances, I took the railway on the 7th to Cork, where a most crowded and attentive meeting greeted me, presided over by the Worshipful the Mayor, Sir John Gordon. The Rev. M. A. Henderson had kindly arranged the meeting for me. It was convened in his church, the same in which Rev. John Burnet had preached when labouring in Cork. A most devoted anti-slavery family invited a number of the Profesors of the College to meet me, and these learned gentlemen kindly participated in the proceedings of the meeting, which was the most enthusiastic one I ever held, even in Ireland. Every one seemed as if he came to the meeting on purpose to be pleased, and was pleased accordingly. I am sure the feeling of the audience, on their own part, had much more to do with that enthusiasm than the speech; and if the speech were worth anything, it caught much of its inspiration from them. Perhaps the best way to state the matter is, that we had a good meeting altogether. To the Mayor, to Rev. Mr. Henderson, to the Professors of the University, and to our excellent friends the Jenningses, are especial thanks due, for the arrangements and good influences with which the meeting was appointed and held. It was my last meeting in Ireland.

Wishing to visit my beloved friends Dr. Collis Browne and his lady, at Queen's Town, and knowing the necessity of being in Dublin on the evening of the 8th, I rose early on the morning of that day, and took what I think is the most delightful little trip Ireland affords—from Cork down to the Cove of Cork, or Queenstown Harbour as it is now called. Returning in the afternoon, I bade the Doctor and Mrs. B. farewell, taking the 3 P.M. train to Dublin, hoping to see them again in a few days; but, alas! the time has not yet come, and it may be that we shall meet no more on earth. I reached Dublin at 10 P.M., and on the morning of the 9th set off for Wales and England. Being then able to walk without crutches, I gave mine to two servants at the Hibernian. May they never need them! That day I breakfasted in Dublin, dined at Holyhead, and supped at Preston. Thus far extends the account of my two short tours in Ireland.

I beg now to say a few words about what I saw while rapidly passing through that most interesting country.

1. I have already spoken of Rev. Joseph Denham Smith, of Kingstown, and his labours. I now add, that the Rev. Wm. Tarbotton, Rev. Noble Shepherd, and Rev. M. A. Henderson, occupy positions of like difficulty, influence, responsibility, and useful-

ness.* They are, in like manner, devoted most earnestly to the land in which, and the people among whom, their lot is cast. I saw the same in the excellent Presbyterian minister at Queenstown; and cannot help repeating my solemn conviction, that the Independent ministers, so far as I was able to judge, have specially the position which gives them, in spite of all opposition, the greatest advantages of all others in Ireland, in "contending for the faith once delivered to the saints." That position is one of real issue with Papal Catholicism. Their Church government, their independence of both the control and patronage of the State, and the success of their labours, are all-potent Protestant arguments in themselves. The standpoint from which one party sees things, and the ground occupied by another party, when exhibiting truth, are manifestly matters of great importance. The Roman Catholic population see Protestant truth from a standpoint whence they view all apparently coercive State machinery in religion, with the feeling of a persecuted party. Hence, in my humble judgment, the peculiarly happy adaptation of the Independent branch of the Christian Church to Ireland; for what denomination soever is there connected with the State, less or more, has, in that respect, an unfortunate standing-place for influence with our Roman Catholic fellow subjects: and surely the same remark applies to all other Papal countries.

That Ireland is hopeless, no one believes. The truth that prevailed in this and other countries will prevail there. Advancing light, increasing education, material improvement, the very increase of wealth, will aid partly in undermining and partly in openly assaulting, but at all events, finally, in the utter overthrow, of the Papal power in Ireland, as elsewhere. In no part of Europe, Protestant or Papal, is that system, either temporally or spiritually, what it was a hundred years ago. It can never regain its

---

* Doubtless the same is true of other ministers, but these are the only men in such circumstances I had the pleasure of meeting.

lost prestige, but it must certainly lose its hold, upon the minds of its own votaries. It has no elements adaptable to the middle of the nineteenth century. Its doom is sealed in Ireland, as elsewhere. It is menaced by the emigration of Irishmen, by the spread of education, by the elevation of tenants, by landlords, by Agricultural Societies, and by the onward, rolling tide of progress, which, having once set in upon Ireland, will never ebb, but sweep before it all systems and customs which accord not with itself. Yet it is right and dutiful to do what has to be done in the very best way: and one who loves Ireland as I do, cannot but grieve that among Protestants things should exist which weaken their power to do good; while one rejoices to know that other and better ideas prevail to some extent, and that, in spite of the defects hinted at, good is being done—the proclamation of the gospel is being blessed, and its truths will finally become triumphant—in that island gem.

2. The resources of Ireland must be immense. The mountains, from all appearance, are rich in coals and slate. The rivers are large, and capable of an indefinite increse of commercial advantage. Some of the harbours are equal to any in the three kingdoms. The situation of Ireland for commercial purposes is most fortunate and convenient, being nearer than any other part of Britain to America. Why Galway, for example, should not be the point of *entrée*, I cannot imagine. We sail along the coast of Ireland four-and-twenty hours before we reach Holyhead. Why should we not land on that coast? we should greatly shorten the voyage by so doing. But if it be objected, that another sea must be crossed before reaching England, let it be remembered, that those who wish to go to Ireland from England must cross that same sea, and so must all the goods from Ireland landed here; and, descendant of an Irishman though I be, I will not admit that it is any further from Ireland to England than it is from England to Ireland! Besides, there is to be a very great increase of agricultural produce and of manufactured commodities, especially in the

north of Ireland; and there are now six millions of population, which doubtless will be very greatly increased, in numbers and in wealth. These will give ample employment, at no very distant day, to a line of steamers devoted to Ireland and America, with one occasionally, or at regular periods, to the West Indies. Hence, whatever may be said about Ireland's being the point of arrival from and departure to America, surely Ireland need not always be tributary to this island in that respect, so far as her own commerce is concerned.

The soil of that island is most surprisingly rich. The moisture of the atmosphere, and the mildness of the climate, make it the most natural grazing soil in the world. With anything bordering upon Scotch cultivation, there could scarcely be any limits to the agricultural wealth of this country. It was indeed sad to leave Scotland one evening, and to arrive in Ireland the next morning, and witness the great, too great, contrast between the culture of the soil, in the two countries. Ireland never looks worse than when entered from Scotland. The neatly trimmed hedge, the smoothly turned furrow, the air of industry and thrift, with their abundant reward smiling on every hand, were left behind, on the other side. The neglected broken hedge, the slovenly-looking field, the air of neglect, and their legitimate consequences, frowned on every hand upon us and around us, with the rarest exceptions, from Belfast to Sligo, from Sligo to Mullingar, from Dublin to Cork.* Like frowns upon the face of beauty, these Irish farms gave abundant evidence that they were capable of presenting a very different aspect. They told us plainly enough, that what had made sterile Scotland what it is, would have done far more for Ireland. "The hand of the diligent maketh rich," indeed. One could not but be smitten with the unwelcome thought, that the neglect of such land, affording such opportunities for the most ample supply of all needs, is a species of sinfulness upon which

* The most perfectly Irish thing I saw in my tour was a field whose fences were completely destroyed; but it had *iron gates, every one of which was locked.*

our Heavenly Father looks with the deepest disapprobation. It is the neglect, the misuse, of a very valuable talent. It is most gratifying to know, however, that very important improvements are being introduced, and that a spirit of reform has entered the bosoms of landlords and tenants, from which the best consequences are to be expected. Having so practical a man as Viceroy in the Earl of Carlisle, it is quite certain that no suggestion will be withholden by his Excellency, and no aid sought refused, by which the improvement of Ireland, so greatly needed, and now happily begun, may be promoted.

In manufactories, Ireland must ere long be among the first of nations. There is every natural and artificial facility for manufacturing, in the north of Ireland, that there is in the north of England. Ulster might be another Yorkshire or Lancashire. Nor is this confined to the North. When speaking of these facilities, I was frequently told that want of capital is an obstacle. But English capitalists wish to make good investments, and would as readily invest in Ireland as in England, if they could only be "secure," if it would "pay." Belfast and its vicinity answer any query on those points; so does Limerick. In these material temporal matters, most brilliant is the future of Ireland.

3. Would that I could speak as hopefully of the Irish working classes as of the soil and resources of the country. Happily, the two are so connected, that the improvement of the one will develope the other. In America, where land is cheap, and in Canada, where corrupting influences are less common than in the United States, I have seen the material improvement of the Irish pauper elevate him above the depressions of mind and morals which were considered inseparable from his lot in Ireland. Then, the next generation almost seem to belong to another race—to have lost the degradations, and to have cultivated the upward tendencies, of the Celt, to a most commendable degree. That, doubtless, is the reason why they rise superior to the influence of their priests, in the colonies and in America. It is impossible to treat Patrick Thaddeus Mulligan, Esq., *now*, as you treated him when

he was nobody but poor, ignorant, ragged, barefoot, Pat Mulligan. What raises Pat to Mr. Patrick, in America, will do it, in spite of any naturally depressing system, in Ireland. I know a man in the county of Kerry, who is a Freemason. He has been to America, made a little fortune, and returned, able to live upon his property, although he gratifies his industrious inclination by actively pursuing business. When a poor man, no one was more subject to his priest than he; now Dr. Cullen the Primate, and all the priesthood together, are unable to drive him out of Masonry, or to hinder his forming a Lodge in the town of his residence. He told me this with his own lips. Of course I give here no expression of opinion as to Masonry; but mention this instance to illustrate my idea, that improvement in the temporal circumstances of our Irish fellow subjects will elevate them mentally and morally, and that in spite of any religious system. The best thing which the Papal system can do for itself is, to adapt itself, so far as it can, really or seemingly, to this inevitable and approaching state of things. If it does not this, it must submit, in Ireland as on the Continent, to be shorn of its power over that people whom it has so long enthralled; and when it wanes visibly, palpably, in Ireland, its power for evil in this world is gone for ever. I verily believe Ireland to be its last stronghold, the place where it is to receive its death-wound.

I am aware that this full expression of my candid and, it may be, mistaken opinion, will not be palatable to some who may cast a glance over these humble pages. I have, however, been so accustomed to *speak* plainly, that, to write at all, I must *write* plainly. I am aware of no reason for withholding my honest sentiments, being myself alone responsible for them; and if it is my duty to write, it is included in that duty to do more than seek to offer amusement for the passing hour, on so grave a subject. To offer a book to the public, under any circumstances, seems, in me, little less than presumption; but that I should impose upon my fellow men a book both brainless and heartless—shallow enough, at best, in thought, and destitute of soul—is more than I

can consent to attempt. Roman Catholics freely express their
opinions: why should not one of the humblest of Protestants? I am
conscious of doing so kindly, and should be sorry to speak otherwise. After all, I expect less fault-finding, with what is said on
this and a preceding page, from Romanists, than from squeamish,
timid Protestants. Be that as it may, "I have believed, therefore
have I spoken."

To return from this digression: I could but grieve, joyous as
is the prospect before the Irish peasant, that his present condition is so degraded. I belong to a degraded race. Of the one hundred and sixty-four million of my unfortunate race, one hundred
and fifty millions are heathens, eight millions are slaves! In
speaking, therefore, of the Celt's degradation, I do not forget
the Negro's, nor my own sad inheritance of and share in it. How
can I forget an ever-present fact? But I must be permitted to
say, as I said freely when in America, that in no part of that
country where Negroes are nominally free, much less where they
are really free (and I doubt if the same remark will not, with
some exceptions, apply to the enslaved class), did I ever see such
degradation as abounds not only in the towns, but in the rural
districts, of Ireland. In other countries, poverty is deepest in
towns—it recedes as you reach the farming districts; but in Ireland, the roadside cabin and its inhabitants are as dirty, as un-
thrifty, as scantily fed and clad, as those who swarm in the most
densely populated towns. I have seen Ann Street, the worst haunt
of the most debased coloured population of Boston—the Five
Points, the Aceldama of New York—the Moyamensing District,
the incomparable, unfathomable slough of Philadelphia's in-
deceny; but never saw so large a proportion of a population so
utterly degraded, as that in the neighbouring island.

I may be told, on the one hand, of Saxon rule as the prolific
parent of this terrible state of things; on the other hand, I am
told of Papal religion as the producing cause of it. I will not discuss either of these, but admit the force of both. Who can deny
the fact of Saxon rule? Who can deny the fact of Papal religion?

Who denies that the Irish peasantry have for generations been subject to both? Neither is perfect. All that is true. I will not stop to compare dates as to the priority of these; nor inquire what have been the tendencies of either, or both, in other countries. It is aside from my present purpose either to consult history or to express my opinion upon these points; for I maintain that degradation, idleness, filth, such as abound in Irish dwellings—and beggary, the abominable profession of a very great number of hale, strong, Irish men, women, and children—are self-chosen, self-imposed. Neither Saxon rulers nor Papal priests can hinder a peasant's cleanliness of person, nor his wife's use of the broom and the brush. It is not owing to the rule of the one or the religion of the other that a peasant's cabin is, by the peasant's election, a pigstye. Begging, instead of working, is the choice of the Irish beggar. A decent self-respect would make it impossible; but you cannot enter a town, nor stop at a country tavern, nor walk the streets, nor stroll on a country road, nor take your way to "the place of prayer and praise," but at every yard or two you are beset and besieged with persons sound in health and strong of limb, with rags and reeking with filth, begging, and doing nothing else, that you can see, for a living. Kingstown swarms with them; in Dublin they dog your footsteps at every turn. The same is true of them in Cork, in Sligo, everywhere. *That* you will not find among my unfortunate people, in any part of America or elsewhere.

"They are poor:" so are the Welsh. "They are taxed to support a religion in which they do not believe:" so are the Welsh. "Wages are low:" so they are in Wales. "Their cabins are small, and rudely constructed:" so are Welsh cabins. "The landlords do not encourage them:" nor do Welsh landlords. "They cannot purchase comforts:" but they purchase whiskey. "They are under other than Irish rule:" what were they before that? The Welsh are under other than Welsh rule. Why I compare these two nations shall appear in another chapter. I introduce it here for the purpose of remarking once more, that, in spite of all other causes, it must be admitted that the degradation of our Irish fellow subjects is a matter of their own choosing: so I say of the degradation of the Negro, who in many points is very like the Celt. After all that slavery, like original sin, has done to give us wrong tendencies, it is our business, with God's help, to bid defiance to those tendencies, by cultivating self-respect—at least, by imitating the good qualities of those around us. Can I say less of the condition and duty of the Irishman? The latter is, to rise above his present condition, and be a *man;* the former is of his own election, and therefore his own fault.

4. I now come to the most unwelcome part of my task. Ireland furnishes my native country with a larger proportion of immigrants than any other country in Europe—except, perhaps, Germany: I can only say "perhaps," not having statistics before me, and not recollecting the figures accurately. Of all Europeans, the Irish immigrant becomes, as a rule, the most ready dupe of the proslavery men. His low, vulgar habits at home—the general readiness of one low class of population to prey upon another—the example of the Americans, and the quickness of the immigrant to learn evil habits—most fully account for it, I know; and know as well, that human nature is such a poor, cowardly, knavish thing, that it will readily join in trampling into the dust him whom everybody treads upon: and I see nothing in the *low Irish* department of human nature to make it differ from the common type. It turns out, that the man who on his native bog is unwashed and unshaved, a fellow lodger with his pig in a cabin too filthy for most people's stables or styes, is, when arriving in America, the Negro's birthplace, the free country for which the Negro fought and bled, one of the first to ridicule and abuse the free Negro—the Negro, who has yet to learn how to sink into such depths of degradation as the Irishman has just escaped from! The bitterest, most heartless, most malignant enemy of the Negro, is the Irish immigrant.

Nevertheless, were the Irishman true to the sentiments I found prevalent in every part of his native country on this subject, he would with but little exertion turn the tide of persecution from the Negro, and, proving himself his friend, receive his gratitude; then the two would grow up as brethren. The wit, warmth, and enthusiasm—the capacity to imitate, to improve, and to endure— the cheerfulness, bravery, and love of religion—said to be peculiar to the Celt, are well-known natural characteristics of the Negro. They are in these points, when degraded and ignorant or when educated and refined, alike, in a most remarkable degree. The Negro, perhaps, has most of natural mildness of temper: indeed, if he had not, he would be a terror to the Irishman, as the Irishman is to him. How I wish that the immigrant from the Emerald Isle understood the doctrine of the brotherhood of man, and practised it towards his coloured fellow citizen! If he did, one of the most serious obstacles to the cause of the Negro would disappear, in America. I do hope that Irish abolitionists will be true to emigrants, exhorting them to save themselves from the abominations of proslaveryism, and rebuking those who ruthlessly trample upon the Negro—who found friends in O'Connell and Madden, and who now, for the best of reasons, blesses the names of Richard Webb, Mr. Jennings, the Marquis of Sligo, and the Right Honourable John Wynne.

If, however, the present hostility of the Irish towards the black continue, it may pass the bounds of even a Negro's endurance, and provoke such a reaction as all must regret. The increasing numbers, growing intelligence, and advancing progress, of the Negro in America, will one day make him no mean foe for the Celt to contend against. Before such disaster befall both races, and that a spirit of mutual good will may prevail,

> ——let us pray, that come it may,
> An' come it will for a' that;
> That man to man, the warld all o'er,
> Shall brithers be, an' a' that.

CHAPTER VIII

Wales

At the invitation of Richard Griffiths, Esq., I accompanied him into Wales in August, 1854. It was my first visit to the Principality. I was peculiarly fortunate in having as a fellow traveller a gentleman who knew the country thoroughly, and who could, when occasion required, speak for me the language, and translate it to me. We visited Bangor, Holyhead, Beaumaris, Caernarvon, Llanberris, Snowdon, Aberystwyth, Welshpool, and so forth. My stay was so short that I can say but little of Wales, but must say that little with very great pleasure; for no country, no people, ever pleased me so much—excepting black people, of course.

I spent a Sabbath at Bangor, preaching three times to audiences of whom some could not understand sufficient English to follow a discourse. They came, however, because they wished to encourage the cause I represented, and to show their interest in the gospel, though preached in a language of which they could understand but few words. In one instance, however, there was a sermon in Welsh from one of the native ministers. This gave those who could not understand me an opportunity to receive benefit in their own tongue.

I had a very large anti-slavery meeting in Bangor, and the kind feeling of the audience was peculiar to that most benevolent people. Fortunately, all the remarks made concerning the speech were in Welsh, whereof I understood not one syllable, and therefore remained in happy ignorance as to whether I was praised

or blamed, until they gave me kind, *tangible* tokens of their regard. *That* I understood; that was not Welsh, it was the language
of the heart. I do not say that Welsh is not: but only, that I
understand the one, and not the other. At Beaumaris I spoke on
temperance, part of the evening, and the other part, on anti-
slavery; the same at Holyhead and Caernarvon. On one of the
days of our sojourn at Bangor we visited the Penryn slate
quarries, belonging to the Honourable Colonel Tennant. It is a
most gigantic work: the number of men employed would make
quite a town, in Canada. The good order, steady industry, and
regular habits, of the workmen, were quite evident. The village
near the castle, composed of the labourers' cottages, and the
schoolhouse and gardens, are the most beautiful and the most
comfortable cottages in North Wales: indeed, I know of none
equal to them anywhere. Lady Louisa, Colonel Tennant's wife,
had them erected according to models of her own drawing. The
school, I believe, is at her expense. Neglected as the labourers of
Wales generally are, it was most gratifying to see this specimen of
kind carefulness.

Beaumaris is quite a fashionable watering-place, and it is a
very quiet, neat little town. It has a most capital hotel, quite
equal to the great majority of English ones. The same may be
true of Bangor; but the kindness of Mr. Edwards, our host, would
not allow us to know. Caernarvon is, of course, rich in historic
interest: its castle is a fine ruin. I spent some two or three days
there very agreeably, being the guest of Mr. Hughes, a most
kind and hospitable gentleman. From his house we made up a
party to visit Snowdon—ascending it on foot, and returning in
the same way. A more fatiguing journey of five miles it was never
my fortune, good or ill, to make. What added to the discomfort
of it was, that on reaching the top, we saw nothing but a thick
Welsh mountain fog! but we had a most delightful view of the
neighbouring hills and dales, from a point about half way to
the summit. Being obliged to drive eight miles and speak that

night at Caernarvon—to travel ninety-seven miles the next day, in a stage coach—and to preach three times the third day—made no small affair of the exercise.

Reaching Aberystwyth late on Saturday night, I was glad to take the comfortable quarters offered to the weary in the Royal Hotel. It had rained all day; but, in spite of rain, it was most delightful to travel amid the beautifully diversified scenery betwixt Caernarvon and Aberystwyth. It is bolder than Irish scenery, and the cultivation is far better—though not so good, I thought, as the Scotch; but the farming of Wales is far from being indifferent. I spent some four or five days in Aberystwyth, making some acquaintances I shall ever remember: among them are the excellent pastors of the Churches, and the Rev. Mr. Davies and his excellent mother. I had the honour, too, of making the acquaintance of Mr. Lloyd, one of the leading gentry of the country, now Lord Lieutenant of Cardiganshire. Mr. L. took the chair at a meeting which I addressed; and was kind enough to say, one of his inducements to attend was, that the meeting was to be addressed by a gentleman from Canada. Having been in early life stationed there with his regiment, the gallant gentleman had acquired an interest in my adopted country which did not leave him upon his return to Wales.

From Aberystwyth I returned to England by Welshpool, where I spent an evening, and attended a temperance meeting. The drive through that part of Wales is one of the most beautiful in this island of beautiful scenery. It reminds one of the valleys of the Genessee, the Susquehannah, and some portions of the St. Lawrence Valley. I know not when or where I have enjoyed a drive more than those through North and South Wales. Anybody else would be able to describe the scenery: all I can say is, it was most beautiful. What with the waving, ripened corn, the youthful-looking greenness of the recently mown meadows, the sparkling streamlets, the clear sky, and the gorgeously brilliant August sunlight, I was charmed beyond expression. I am sorry I cannot tell it better: please kind reader, accept the best I can perform. Since then, I have passed through portions of Wales in very rapid flying tours, as when returning from Ireland, last autumn and last spring; but have not had the pleasure of making any stay there. I think, however, that I have seen enough of Wales and the Welsh to have formed some tolerably correct views of their character.

First, however, to record an incident of no small interest to me, which occurred during my sojourn at Aberystwyth. A gentleman named Williams, an agent for one of the wealthiest landlords in Wales, lives about a mile from Aberystwyth. I learned that a little boy, a son of Mr. Williams, who was ill, was anxious to see me, and that his parents wished me to call. The Rev. Mr. Davies kindly consented to accompany me, and we drove there. We found Mr. and Mrs. Williams most kind and affable persons; and upon being introduced to the chamber where their son lay, we were struck with his emaciated appearance; but in spite of this, his eyes beamed with intelligence, and about his lips a most cheerful smile played constantly. His mother told us he had been a great sufferer. His bones were but slightly covered with a wasted colourless skin. He could not stand or walk, from lameness; and I believe there was but one position in which he could lie. When we saw the helplessness of the child, we were glad that we had visited him. He had read *Uncle Tom's Cabin;* he felt interested in the slaves, and daily prayed for them; he had carefully laid by the little presents of money which had been given him, and had a donation to give me, for the cause of the slave. But what made the deepest impression upon us was, his mother's telling us that, in the midst of the very severe pains which tortured the little sufferer, he would cry out, but immediately check himself, saying "Mamma, I ought not to complain so. How much more did Jesus suffer, for me!"

We left that house feeling that we had been highly privileged. We had learned the lesson of patient suffering at the bedside of that dear child—had seen a babe, as it were, praising God. That the child could long live, seemed out of the question; but the wheat of the surrounding fields was no more ripe for the sickle, than was that child to be gathered unto God. Since that day, I never suffer pain, complainingly, without fancying I see the bright, beaming eye of little Williams rebuking me, as he hushes his own cries, in the midst of anguish, by the recollection of "how much more Jesus suffered for him." That child may, ere this, have been called to his rest; he may be with Him whose sufferings he learned so early to contemplate: but until I meet him in another world, I shall ever remember the lesson learned at his bedside. Since that time, some of the severest pangs I ever felt have been mine, both in body and mind; but their coming is accompanied by the remembrance of what that beloved child learned, in agony. And, blessed be God! the divine consolations which lulled his pains are abundant, infinite in efficacy!

Wales is the most moral and most religious country, and her peasantry the best peasantry, that I know. Doubtless, many will differ from me; but such is my very decided opinion, based on the following reasons:—

1. The courts in Wales have fewer cases of scandalous crimes and misdemeanors to deal with than the courts of any other part of the kingdom, of the same population. The difference betwixt Wales and Ireland, in this respect, is immense.

2. But go to a Welsh town (such as Bangor), and how quiet and moral is it, compared with any town of the like population you can name in England, Ireland, or Scotland! Not a woman walking the streets of lewd purposes, not a dunkard brawling in the highways, no rows or fights; quietness and order reign everywhere. Holyhead is a seaport; it is the same there, and so in every town I visited.

3. The temperance cause has done more for Wales than for any other part of the kingdom. A drunken peasant is, indeed, a rare sight in Wales. The miners, the farm servants, and the ordinary labourers, all agree, somehow or other, to be temperate. Not

that all are abstainers; but a more temperate peasantry, I am free to confess, there is not, even in Maine!

4. There is no begging in Wales. There are children who run after the carriages of tourists and cry, "ha'penny!" about the only English word they know; and this more for sport than halfpence. But there is little or no encouragement given to it by the inhabitants; and there is no such thing as a swarm of beggars at every corner, door, hotel, church-gate, and everywhere else, as in every part of Ireland.

5. The Welsh are poor as well as the Irish; and their landlords sufficiently neglect them, as to their dwellings: but the cleanliness of the peasantry is most striking. The contrast betwixt Holyhead and Kingstown, within four hours' sail of each other, is most remarkable. One can scarcely believe that he has not been to two opposite sides of the globe, instead of across a narrow channel. The reader will now see why I blame the Irish for their defects, in contrast with the Welsh.

6. The industry of the poorer classes in the Principality is most commendable. I know this has much to do with any people's moral and religious character. No one believes, as no one ought, in a very high-toned and exemplary morality, or a very devoted religion, conjoined with idleness. I do believe that the Welsh labouring classes are more correct in this than even the Highlanders in Scotland. Patient though not overpaid toil, mitigated by few comforts, is not only the lot, but to all appearance the choice, of the Welsh peasant. I have seen more idlers in one street, in Kingstown—in a circumference of 300 yards, in Glasgow—or in a small village, in Essex or Norfolk—than one can see in the whole of Wales.

7. The Welsh population not only attend divine service, but are religious: I say "the population," because it is not true, as in England, of a few persons only out of the many, but, like the Scotch, of the people generally. There are some curious and interesting facts in connection with this. In the first place, the Welsh are not Episcopalians: nine tenths of them dissent from the

Establishment. It is most ridiculous to tax them for its support, for they do not go near it. Still, they quietly go to their chapels, and as quietly pay for their support. In the next place, they are not mere nominal members of Churches. The majority belong to the Calvinistic Methodist denomination, whose rules are highly and properly rigid. No laxity in morals is allowed to pass un-rebuked. Besides, in travelling through Wales, it is seen that almost wherever there are a dozen houses, one of them is a chapel. The people feel their religious wants, and supply them. Moreover, the ministers of the denomination alluded to, and all others, take especial care and pains in looking after their flocks. Their preaching is deeply earnest, practical, scriptural, plain, and personal; also, most pathetic and affectionate. These combined influences are in constant operation, and are producing the very best effects upon a remarkably straightforward, simple-minded people.

Compare these sturdy, honest preachers, with the priests of Romanism! Compare their flocks with the Papal populations of, I care not what country! I cannot consent to argue the case: in the living history of present fact it stands out in bold relief. It speaks for itself, in language clear and intelligible; its truths are undeniable, unquestionable: and though our fellow subjects of the Principality are less wealthy and less learned than some more flattered inhabitants of other portions of these islands, they excel us all in some of the best, noblest, traits that ever adorned human character. Should they diffuse education more thoroughly, cling with less tenacity to their mother tongue, draw more largely from the "well of English undefiled," and mingle more with the other elements of British population, then that brave little Principality will one day be more often visited and considered: it will take rank as high in other matters, as in morals; and, in peculiar distinctive character, appear, to its present despisers, beautiful as its own valley scenery, elevated as Snowdon's loftiest summit!

I have spoken mostly of the labouring classes in Wales; and have only to add, that the better and higher classes are essentially Englishmen—with the exception, I must once more remark, of being very far behind Englishmen and Scotchmen (and, according to the papers of the day, behind Irishmen as well!) as landlords. They need to follow more closely the example set by the Honourable Colonel Tennant and the Lady Louisa, in caring for those who minister to their comforts and convenience. I am sure any one who visits the village referred to will join me in this remark.

I know what will be said, in other countries than Wales, in reply to what I say of the chastity of the Welsh female peasantry. Reference will be made to the stupid system of courtship called "bundling"—a practice for which there is no defence: most certainly, I have no word to utter in its behalf. That it has not been attended with far worse consequences, is to me a marvel. But I have the great happiness to know, that the pulpit, which is more powerful in Wales than in any Protestant country elsewhere, has turned its whole power and influence against this barbarous practice, so that not even it, to any extent, forms a drawback to the remarks I have made upon the morality of the Welsh peasantry. It is to be hoped that a custom which has nothing better than its antiquity for its apology, but is liable to the very gravest objections on the score of morality and decency, will soon be known merely as a matter of history. Surely, when a custom so pernicious shall once be put away, all will rejoice, and all will wonder that a people of such sterling sense should have suffered it to continue so long. It certainly has outlived the former bad taste of the people; and therefore, if for no higher reason, it ought to live no longer. Most earnestly is it to be hoped that this abominable relic of ancient British barbarism will soon be so completely banished, as no longer to mar the otherwise good and exemplary character of the honest youths and maidens of that delightful Principality.

CHAPTER IX

Grateful Reminiscences—Conclusion

Although I fear having written too much already, without contributing to the amusement or profit of the reader, I cannot conclude without speaking somewhat definitely of some things which are, to me, of more than ordinary interest.

It is true that I cannot feel an Englishman's interest in relics of antiquity. My life has been spent in a new country, and I cannot bring myself to admire old buildings and ruins. Rhyl is preferred, by me, before any other town in Wales, because of its new and fresh appearance; for the same reason, Cheltenham and Southampton suit me better than any other towns in England. However, I visited Westminster Abbey, heard the janitor's tale of who lies here and who lies there, and felt that my knowledge of English history, with its dates and figures, was refreshed and increased. But the statues of Pitt, Wilberforce, Buxton, and Clarkson, interested me more than all the ancient things put together: in them I saw, not simply the features of men eminent in days recently gone by, but of those who were dear to me and my people, on account of their devotion to the cause of freedom. I visited the place where their monuments are, as one would visit the tomb of his benefactors: they were my benefactors. I wished to convey back to my people the impressions I felt upon looking at the marble which represented, as well as it could, faces and forms once glowing with life and teeming with energy; both devoted to the cause of the Negro.

I went to see the Cathedral at Canterbury, and attended a service in the chapel; also visited, in company with the Rev. J. A. Miller, St. George's Cathedral at Windsor, and attended service in the Knights' Chapel. By invitation of the Earl of Shaftesbury, I attended a service for the charity children, in St. Paul's. The vastness of this great cathedral, the immense number of neatly dressed children, the beauty of the service, and the rich spiritual sermon of the Bishop of Chester, overwhelmed me with feelings and impressions I cannot describe.

The Rev. James Parsons, of York, with his usual kindness, requested Miss Parsons to accompany me to York Minster. We attended service, and heard the beautiful intonations in which cathedral services are usually performed. The beauty of that great Gothic pile impressed me most profoundly. I could but exclaim, "If this be Gothic, a great many buildings, *called* '*Gothic*,' are simply *Vandal!*"

Mrs. Finley, the niece of Captain Hamilton, kindly accompanied me to see the Cathedral of Glasgow. It is a fine old structure, full of historic interest, and must be a most charming sight for any one fond of old things; but I, poor backwoodsman! take far more delight in seeing a newly built, freshly painted building!

I confess, however, that there were two old buildings, near to Ulverstone, in Lancashire, which I visited with very peculiar interest, in company with the Rev. James Browne. They are historical buildings, and, to me, of great importance, because of their relation to an honoured branch of the Christian Church to which my people are very much indebted; those buildings are, the former residence and the chapel of George Fox.* I saw the house which he frequently visited when a bachelor, and in which he lived after his marriage: also, the window from which he first preached his principles to the people of the neighbourhood. The chapel is a low place, of small size, but neat and substantial; it

* Bunyan's Chapel, at Bedford—Baxter's, Oxendon Street, London—Doddridge's, Northampton—in each of which I have preached, were to me most interesting.

stands in a pretty, well kept enclosure, still used as a burying-
place. The meetings of the Friends, in that locality, are holden in
that venerable chapel. Here arose the "Society called Friends,
or Quakers." From this humble meeting-house began that sect
whose members are in all parts of England, some of them among
the most wealthy of living men. In America, how many of their
meeting-houses are very much larger than this, the birthplace of
Quakerism! indeed, I know of none there so small as this. Here
arose a sect despised, ridiculed, persecuted. They spread, however, all over Christendom; they preached the gospel of peace
to almost all the families and tribes of living man; they purged
their own sect of slave-holding; they have impressed their principles upon the generations among whom they have lived; they
have been, in all times, the friends and helpers of the poor and
the needy. No sect better than they deserves the distinct appella-
tion of *Friends*.

They may not now be increasing in numbers; the very reverse
of this true, in some, many, places. In America there have been
some sad divisions, and more lamentable heresies, among them;
some, indeed, have quite forsaken and forsworn the anti-slavery
principles of the sect. But the Society of Friends has accomplished
a very important mission; and it may be that, since their principles and distinctive ideas are so well understood, and so many
of the most useful and most catholic for these principles impressed
upon and promulgated by other sects, this pure and honoured
denomination can afford the diminution of its members. The
defections and heresies of which I have spoken seemed, to me,
to be gently rebuked by the old Bible of George Fox, which was
chained to a desk in the old meeting-house. It is a quaint old
volume, of the date of 1541, and reads after the style of that day.
It was the corner-stone of George Fox's faith, the armoury whence
he drew his weapons, the directory of his spotless life. Nothing of the antique, nothing of a past age, gave me deeper interest, than the residence, the chapel, and the Bible, of George Fox.

If not so antique as other places and things, it was the most ancient of Quaker things, the earliest of the interesting relics of that sect, which has done more for mankind than, perhaps, any other of like numbers, since the days of the apostles and the martyrs.

In connection with this part of the present chapter I beg to observe, that in the winter of 1853–54 I had the pleasure of holding a meeting in the Friends' meeting-house in Kendall. The chairman was the venerable Mr. Braithwaite. He had kindly invited several of the most distinguished personages, including his Worship the Mayor, to meet me. The next morning I met several members of the Braithwaite family, many of whom are married, at the old family mansion, at breakfast. Among the guests was a daughter of the Missionary Moffatt, from Africa. The Scriptures were read, according to the good old custom of the Friends; and then Mrs. Braithwaite, who has been a minister for many years, preached a short sermon. I never heard any discourse more pointed, more benevolent, more touching. She began upon the fact that there were in the room persons from different and distant countries, representatives of different races and climes, professing love towards and faith in a common Saviour, and worshipping the same Heavenly Father. She dwelt with delight upon that scene, as one somewhat similar to the gathering of the redeemed around a common board in heaven, at a future day. I do not pretend to give her words, but shall never forget the Christian kindness which was breathed in every one of them. Upon leaving, Mrs. Braithwaite warmly shook my hand, and bade me "farewell," giving me advice as to my health, and commending me to the gracious protection of God. We never shall meet again on earth; but to have met such a disciple of Jesus once, was a privilege worthy of more than ordinary appreciation.

John Morland, Esq., a member of the Society of Friends, did me the honour, upon hearing me at Croydon, in February last, of coming to me after the meeting, to make arrangements for a lecture in the Friends' School, in Croydon, that the pupils might have an opportunity of hearing me plead in the slave's behalf. The meeting was arranged and held. Mr. Morland kindly made me his guest, and took me in his carriage to introduce me to the venerable Peter Bedford, Esq., the coadjutor of Clarkson. After the meeting, the boys of the school presented me with a generous donation, and a most kind and affectionate written address, which I shall preserve as a memento of those most interesting young gentlemen. "May the angel who redeemed Jacob from all evil, bless the lads!"

To another member of the Society of Friends—John Candler, Esq., of Chelmsford—I am under peculiar obligations, and must state them, though without his permission. I had read of that benevolent gentleman, before coming to Europe—had known of his travels in Brazil, the West Indies, and America, in prosecution of his zealous anti-slavery labours. I knew that, like Forster —the venerable and self-sacrificing Forster—he was ready, if God pleased, to lay down his life in a foreign country, rather than be disobedient to the dictates of duty, as impressed upon him by the Spirit of God. But it was not my pleasure and privilege to meet Mr. Candler until last November: indeed, when I was first at Chelmsford, Mrs. Candler, whom I had the pleasure of meeting, informed me that he had not returned from America, whither, at an advanced age, he had accompanied Mr. Forster on his last errand of mercy to the slave.

In December last, by an arrangement which Messrs. Wells and Perry had kindly made for me, I spoke in Chelmsford. The Rev. Mr. Wilkinson kindly occupied the chair. A vote of thanks was to be proposed, according to arrangement, and Mr. Candler generously consented to perform this part. In speaking, as his abundant experience and extensive travels fully qualified him to do, he entirely confirmed my statements; and publicly said that, if in going to Jamaica I should visit the parish of St. George, where he owned a parcel of land, I should be most welcome to fifty acres of it. Since that time Mr. Candler has confirmed his gift, and given instructions accordingly to his solicitor, W. W. Anderson, Esq., of Jamaica. And, that I may do full justice to my benefactor, whose munificence commenced with me in a public meeting, on public grounds and for public purposes, I may venture to add, that Mr. Candler has sold me his entire interest in the tract referred to, at a price so nominal as to make it equivalent to a gift. He has also advised Mr. Anderson, who owns the remaining moiety, to treat me with like kindness. I have already arranged with Mr. Anderson for that moiety. Thus, if my family shall be relieved from a position of dependence, after my death—it will, under God, be owing more to Mr. John Candler, of Chelmsford, than to any other man. That I propose changing the name of the estate from Albany to Candler Park,* will not appear strange.

The duty of spending a portion of every year in Jamaica, until my son shall be old enough to attend to that property, is thus made clear to me. It may be, that our Heavenly Father will permit me to be of some service to my people in that island.

I now wish to say, more distinctly than heretofore, that I feel under peculiar obligations to the Rev. Dr. Raffles, for the very great kindness and sympathy he showed me, at the time I received the sad intelligence of my mother's demise. Handing Mr. Bolton's letter, containing the intelligence, to the Doctor, as I sat in his breakfast room, he most readily and most warmly entered into my feelings, and treated me with such kindness and consideration as I shall ever feel grateful for. I beg to add, that generous-hearted gentleman has, on all occasions upon which I have had the pleasure of being in his society, taught me by his amiable demeanour to look upon him as a friend, and, if I might say so much, a father.

Upon several occasions, magistrates of towns have honoured the cause which I came here to plead, by presiding at my meetings. I tender my hearty thanks to John Hope Shaw, Esq., and

* There is another estate called Albany, in the county of Cornwall. This is in the county of Surrey, on the Great Spanish River.

Mr. Wilson—each of whom, when Mayor of Leeds, conferred
upon me that favour. I am under like obligations to the late
Mayor of Bury St. Edmunds, the late Mayor of Bedford, the
present Mayor of Southampton (Samson Payne, Esq.), the
Provost of Dunfermline, the Provost of Dundee, the Provost of
Montrose, the Mayor of Cork (Sir John Gordon), and George
Leeman, Esq. (who, when Lord Mayor of York, not only presided, but gave me *other* most ample tokens of kind regard).
Other exalted personages, not magistrates, but of great influence
and status, have shown me like kindness. To the Right Honourable John Wynne, Samuel Gurney, Esq., the Right Honourable
the Earl of Shaftesbury, and the Right Honourable Lord Calthorpe, I beg hereby to express thanks, both for myself, and those
whose cause I humbly plead, and whom I feebly represent.

I owe thanks to James Spicer, Esq., for many acts of very great
personal kindness, at times and under circumstances of peculiar
trial. It is most gratifying to acknowledge the obligation in this
way, and through this medium. To the many kind friends (among
whom is Isaac Beeman, Esq.) who most generously contributed
to aid me in my own personal mission, I beg to say, the accounts
of those contributions are with Mr. Spicer; and that, while living,
I shall never cease to be grateful to him and to them, for their
repeated and, I may say, multiplied acts of generous regard.

I have reserved for myself until now, the pleasure of placing
on record the fact which has given me most pleasure of all others,
during my sojourn in the British isles. It is, the growing, abounding love of the simple gospel, among religious classes of all denominations. The great wealth, high rank, vast learning, and
unrivalled inexhaustible resources, of the British people, would,
one might naturally suppose, tempt them to a proud forgetfulness
of the great matters of the soul. As a stranger, I came here expect-
ing to find among Dissenters an earnestness and a spirituality
such as I had always been taught to believe they possess. I
imagined, however, that the prestige of the great names of their

fathers, and the worldwide fame of many of their living divines, would naturally have led them away from simplicity. In the Church of England, I took it for granted, State power, social status, and courtly fashion, had eaten up whatever of vitality had remained before Tractarianism arose; and that, since its rise and in its progress, the religion of that denomination had been swept away, or had degenerated into the merest formalism. The first sermon I heard, however, in London, was preached by the Archbishop of Canterbury. Hearing that sermon not only gave me the most exalted opinion of the venerable Primate, but it led me to conclude that, if the clergy or any considerable portion of them were preachers of that stamp, I had been most mistaken in my views concerning the religious state of the Established Church. When, afterwards, I had the pleasure of hearing the Bishop of Chester, the Rev. E. Hoare, the Rev. Mr. Marshall, the Rev. Mr. Goodheart, and a few others (Englishmen, Irishmen, Scotchmen, and Welshmen, gave me opportunities to hear *but few*), and when I had the pleasure of conversing upon religious subjects with some of the most pious laymen of that denomination, I felt most thankful to be disabused, and correctly informed, on this most important subject. Two facts always exhibited themselves in connection with this: one was, the deep, earnest, biblical piety, conjoined with most active benevolence, a readiness to every good word and work, and accompanied by the sweetest simplicity, which the pious class of Episcopalians exhibit; the other was, their entire catholicity of spirit. In every part of England, and among persons of all ranks, I had the unspeakable happiness to find this. Nor was it shown by studiously avoiding such points of difference as lie between themselves and other denominations; for in the frank, though kind, expression of them, they showed how capable they were of *differing* with brethren, and *loving* them *as* brethren, at the same time. I hardly need say, that towards myself, personally, this feeling was invariably exhibited.

I was most gratified to find that, among Dissenters as in the Establishment, simple faith in Christ's salvation is the great theme of the pulpit. Rev. J. Sherman I heard first; afterward, Rev. John Angell James, Rev. H. J. Bevis, Rev. Dr. Halley, Rev. Dr. Raffles, Rev. J. Baldwin Brown, Rev. Dr. Alexander, Rev. S. Bergne, the Hon. and Rev. Baptist Wriothesley Noel, Rev. Henry Allon, Rev. Samuel Martin, and Rev. C. H. Spurgeon. Varied in style, talent, learning, and other peculiarities, as are these gentlemen, and different as are the classes of their hearers, they all agree in preaching Jesus and his cross, for the redemption of a sinful world. Thus the Christian Churches in Great Britain are *one* in the maintenance and promulgation of that truth which saves; they are *one* in their love of the simple gospel, and in bringing forth the fruits of that gospel in their lives. Thus, for all practical purposes, the section of the Establishment to which I refer, and the Dissenting denominations, "walk together," because "agreed."

Coming from a distant colony, as I do, and knowing how powerful is the Christian Church of this great country in moulding the religious character of the colonies—knowing, too, how much the colonies have to do with the evangelization of the heathen* contiguous to them—it is impossible for me to express how deep and thorough was my gratification to find the religious state of Great Britain what it is, in this respect: indeed, there is no possibility of exaggerating the extent of holy influence which must, of necessity, flow from this all-important fact. The growth of wealth, increase of power, and widening political influence, of Britain, being considered, how thankful ought Britons to be to Britain's God, for the present religious condition of this mighty empire! As one of the most obscure of those whose privilege it is to live on British soil, I beg to express hereby my high and grate-

---

* I am among those who believe that the British colonies are both the agency by which, and the medium through which, the gospel can, ought, *must*, be given to the heathen world. The situation, origin, growth, progress, language, and relations, of those colonies, all seem, to me, to point in that direction.

ful appreciation of this, the most pleasing feature of British society, the most shining trait of British religious character.

If I am suspected of forgetting the very lamentable neglect of religion by too many, of all classes, in these islands, I have to say, that I do not forget, but recollect it vividly, as it stands forth in forms and illustrations most painfully abundant, everywhere. What I rejoice to know is, that God, in his infinite mercy, has been pleased to grant to his people here the power and the privilege of seeing the evils that are around them, and of holding and wielding the "spiritual weapons" which, being "mighty through God," fully enable them to "demolish the strongholds of Satan." I know not of a brighter, more hopeful, evidence of God's gracious favour to his modern Israel, than the earnest, simple love of the gospel—than its being sought for, preached, believed, felt, and honoured, by all departments and branches of the British Church. Long may this greatest of blessings be vouchsafed to them! Long may we of the colonies be blest with the benefits flowing from it! Widely may it extend, and may it yield fruits most abundant to the praise and glory of the Great Head of the Church!